AF166410

AutoUni – Schriftenreihe

Band 149

Reihe herausgegeben von/Edited by

Volkswagen Aktiengesellschaft
AutoUni

Die Volkswagen AutoUni bietet Wissenschaftlern und Promovierenden des Volkswagen Konzerns die Möglichkeit, ihre Forschungsergebnisse in Form von Monographien und Dissertationen im Rahmen der „AutoUni Schriftenreihe" kostenfrei zu veröffentlichen. Die AutoUni ist eine international tätige wissenschaftliche Einrichtung des Konzerns, die durch Forschung und Lehre aktuelles mobilitätsbezogenes Wissen auf Hochschulniveau erzeugt und vermittelt.

Die neun Institute der AutoUni decken das Fachwissen der unterschiedlichen Geschäftsbereiche ab, welches für den Erfolg des Volkswagen Konzerns unabdingbar ist. Im Fokus steht dabei die Schaffung und Verankerung von neuem Wissen und die Förderung des Wissensaustausches. Zusätzlich zu der fachlichen Weiterbildung und Vertiefung von Kompetenzen der Konzernangehörigen fördert und unterstützt die AutoUni als Partner die Doktorandinnen und Doktoranden von Volkswagen auf ihrem Weg zu einer erfolgreichen Promotion durch vielfältige Angebote – die Veröffentlichung der Dissertationen ist eines davon. Über die Veröffentlichung in der AutoUni Schriftenreihe werden die Resultate nicht nur für alle Konzernangehörigen, sondern auch für die Öffentlichkeit zugänglich.

The Volkswagen AutoUni offers scientists and PhD students of the Volkswagen Group the opportunity to publish their scientific results as monographs or doctor's theses within the "AutoUni Schriftenreihe" free of cost. The AutoUni is an international scientific educational institution of the Volkswagen Group Academy, which produces and disseminates current mobility-related knowledge through its research and tailor-made further education courses. The AutoUni's nine institutes cover the expertise of the different business units, which is indispensable for the success of the Volkswagen Group. The focus lies on the creation, anchorage and transfer of new knowledge.

In addition to the professional expert training and the development of specialized skills and knowledge of the Volkswagen Group members, the AutoUni supports and accompanies the PhD students on their way to successful graduation through a variety of offerings. The publication of the doctor's theses is one of such offers. The publication within the AutoUni Schriftenreihe makes the results accessible to all Volkswagen Group members as well as to the public.

Reihe herausgegeben von/Edited by
Volkswagen Aktiengesellschaft
AutoUni
Brieffach 1231
D-38436 Wolfsburg
http://www.autouni.de

Weitere Bände in der Reihe http://www.springer.com/series/15136

Jasmine Shahani

Limits and Opportunities of a Matrix Organization

A Study of Coordination Mechanisms within a Multiple Brand Organization

With a Foreword by Prof. Dr. Eric Davoine and
Dr. Martin Hofmann

 Springer

Jasmine Shahani
AutoUni
Wolfsburg, Germany

Dissertation, University of Fribourg, 2020
Any results, opinions and conclusions expressed in the AutoUni – Schriftenreihe are
solely those of the authors.

ISSN 1867-3635   ISSN 2512-1154   (electronic)
AutoUni – Schriftenreihe
ISBN 978-3-658-32260-1   ISBN 978-3-658-32261-8   (eBook)
https://doi.org/10.1007/978-3-658-32261-8

This Springer imprint is published by the registered company Springer Fachmedien Wiesbaden GmbH
part of Springer Nature.
The registered company address is: Abraham-Lincoln-Str. 46, 65189 Wiesbaden, Germany

To Cathy & Ravi

Foreword

The study of Jasmine Shahani investigates the coordination practices and mechanisms of the matrix organization in the contemporary multiple brand Multinational Company (MNC). The functioning of a matrix organization, especially in a multiple brand holding, is a topic that is highly relevant for contemporary MNCs but had not received a lot of attention in academic research in the last decades, though a few authors, in particular Wolf and Egelhoff (2017), call for more empirical studies. Matrix organizations have been criticized in the past for their increased amount of inter-organizational conflicts, for slow decision-making processes as well as for excessive administrative activities. Considering the complexity and the conflictual dimensions of the tasks and of the decisions that should occur by coordinating units and brands, especially on a global level, it is not surprising that complexity and conflicts are being observed in matrix organizations. On the contrary, following Wolf and Egelhoff, one should consider that conflicts and complexity are the "raison d'être" of the matrix organization. The study therefore aims to show empirically how a holding company matrix deals with complexity and conflicts, how coordination between subsidiaries and brands happen, and which facilitating factors may support the coordination activities of the holding functions within a matrix organization.

The study is based on an extensive PhD case study research within the TRATON Group, formerly Volkswagen Truck and Bus, a multiple brand organization coordinating several brands, including two major European competitors of the sector, Scania and MAN. The thesis of Jasmine Shahani was been carried out while she was working within the newly formed holding in an HR function of TRATON, supported by the Volkswagen *Doktorandenprogramm*. This explains the privileged access to the research field with corporate documents and the ability to approach interview partners across all brands and hierarchies. Despite the interviews, the empirical knowledge of the organizations through her own experience of participative observation in the different projects also explains her very practical and empirical insights into the topic, which makes the thesis relevant and interesting for all practitioners around the topic of matrix organizations.

She defines several fields of investigation at the beginning of her research journey, fields that are all relevant for managers as well as for management researchers. The research questions associated with the matrix organization concern the facilitation of knowledge sharing on a global level, the coordination of decision-making processes, the development of ambidexterity in innovation, the ways to solve conflicts between actors, and the ways to deal with cultural differences and to develop boundary spanning activities. The first chapter presents a literature review about the concept of matrix organizations and cultural dynamics within MNCs. This chapter defines the matrix organization as a form to coordinate the complex activity of MNCs and presents a theoretical framework of different dimensions to be explored in the empirical study: decision-making processes, power and conflicts, culture and identities, boundary spanning activities and skills. The review of the literature on matrix organizations is exhaustive and brings a good overview of relevant topics and issues from the literature on MNCs.

In the empirical part, key aspects of the matrix coordination have been studied through the analysis of cross brand projects. The study is based on a very rich set of empirical data with 42 interviews with managers and project members, an analysis of corporate documents and a deeper knowledge of the field company. Different aspects of the matrix coordination practice have been systematically investigated within two functions (HR and R&D) through the analysis of 5 projects in HR and 4 projects in R&D. Thus, this approach allows a multiple case study with nine cases and a synoptic analysis about commonalities and differences between the cases.

The study brings some original contributions to the field of MNC research, by shedding light on the coordination activities of holding functions in MNC cross brand projects, and by showing a matrix organization in action. The study shows how holding matrix functions could work and how they can promote lateral co-ordination and knowledge transfer between the subsidiaries. It brings a first contribution to the contingency approach of decision-making processes, developed by Wolf and Egelhoff (2017), considering two modes of decision making, balanced and rule-based, and their uses in matrix organizations. The study offers several illustrations of these decision-making processes and shows how matrix projects with balanced decision-making help to develop trust between the parties. Finally, the study therefore recommends to start with balanced decision-making processes before gradually moving towards a certain level of rule-based decision-making.

Another contribution to the MNC research field is to bring interesting insights into the dynamics of national, organizational and professional cultures, as well as in the role of culture and identities in the conflicts between units and brands. Looking at the 'micropolitics' between brands and units (e.g. Becker-Ritterspach, Blazejewski and Geppert, 2016) the study shows how cultures and identities are associated to power capabilities in the interactions and negotiations between actors and units. It also shows how projects can be used as a lever for socio-cultural integration, by using formal and informal transversal coordination mechanisms.

A major contribution of the study is on boundary spanning activities to deal with the conflicts of the cultural dynamics. Boundary spanners and boundary spanning activities have been exhaustively discussed by MNC researchers and identified as a major facilitating factor of socio-cultural integration within MNCs (e.g. Barmeyer and Davoine, 2019). This study focuses on boundary spanning skills needed and developed by a matrix organization, inspired by Arthur et al. (1999). It develops a classification for boundary spanning skills that can be very useful for HR decision makers, by developing a framework of three categories of skills: know-who (having a network within one's own organization and within the matrix), know-how (having technical and brand specific knowledge and information) and know-why (being aware of brand and group goal and being able to sell these goals within the project and towards top management).

From a company point of view, the study shows the importance of cross brand projects as a coordination tool and the crucial role of the holding. Furthermore, the study underlines the impact of the matrix organization in identifying the right people, the right balanced configuration of teams and the right skills to drive the collaboration. It demonstrates that active management is decisive in designing and steering projects as those projects will transform organizational culture and facilitate the cross-brand activities. The study confirms that successful results as an outcome of cross brand cooperation are dependent on the quality and the evolving maturity of the matrix set-up. With her research, Jasmine Shahani added practical insights to a more theory driven discussion. Looking into the future, the matrix organization could remain a core element of steering and managing cross brand set-ups and it will be beneficial to reflect on the findings and lessons learned provided in this book.

Prof. Dr. Eric Davoine, University of Fribourg (CH); Dr. Martin Hofmann, Volkswagen AG (DE)

Acknowledgements

First of all I would like to thank my two supervisors for this thesis, Professor Dr. Eric Davoine and Dr. Martin Hofmann for their support and guidance during my research. I could not have hoped for a better pair for this time, each offering their unique and balanced view. Eric Davoine offered insightful and patient guidance throughout the research period, helping me understand the academic requirements for this work. Martin Hofmann always challenged me, both with his thoughts and continued feedback as well as by inviting me to question my work and go the extra mile. I could not have done this without their continued support and encouragement.

I would also very much like to thank Professor Dr. Dirk Morschett for accepting to be my second supervisor and taking the time to read and correct my work, as well as Professor Rudolf Grünig who has accepted to preside the jury for the defense. It is very much appreciated.

Furthermore, I would like to thank Professor Dr. Joachim Wolf for taking the time to come and discuss the topic of matrix organizations and my research in the Braunschweig offices. It was an honor to be able to discuss with one of the most knowledgeable people in my field.

I would also like to thank the participants of the Atlas-AFMI seminar, especially Professor Dr. Philippe Very, Professor Dr. Hanane Beddi, Professor Dr. Jacques Jaussaud, Professor Dr. Dora Triki, Professor Dr. Ulrike Mayrhofer and Professor Dr. Eric Milliot for their expert opinion and feedback on my work during the doctoral seminar and the conference presentations.

On top of that, the doctoral students of the Chair of Human Resources and Organization have my gratitude for the exchange and support during the doctoral seminars in Fribourg. In the same way, I would like to thank the students within the Volkswagen Doktorandenkolleg and the MAN Doktorandenkolleg, for openly accepting me into their organizations and giving me opportunities to present my work along the way.

The heart of this work is the empirical analysis based on interviews. I would therefore like to thank all the colleagues who shared their knowledge, opinions and information, allowing me to bring this work to life. This work would not exist without their valuable input.

To my colleagues at Volkswagen Truck & Bus and TRATON, many thanks for putting up with me, encouraging me, as well as giving me ideas and sharing contacts. Overall, you created the environement which allowed me to finish this work. In particular, thank you to Maike Hecht for supporting me and helping me in the last six months of this thesis.

Finally I would like to extent a special thank you to my family and friends for the emotional support, the motivation and the celebration of all the small milestones along the way. It made all the difference.

Jasmine Shahani

Table of Contents

List of Figures

List of Tables

List of Abbreviations

CAD	Computer aided design
CEO	Chief Executive Officer
CHRO	Chief Human Resources Officer
CFO	Chief Finance Officer
CTO	Chief Technical Officer
CVPSK	Commercial Vehicle Product Strategy Committee (*Kreis in German*)
HQ	Headquarters
HR	Human Resources
HRM	Human Resource Management
HRMC	Human Resources Management Committee
IB	International Business
IHRM	International Human Resource Management
IT	Information Technology
KPI	Key Performance Indicator
M&A	Mergers and acquisitions
MAN T&B	MAN Truck & Bus
MNC	Multinational Company
MNE	Multinational Enterprise
R&D	Research and Development
TBTC	Truck & Bus Technical Committee
VW	Volkswagen
VWCO	Volkswagen Caminhões e Ônibus

Abstract

The present work investigates the functioning of contemporary matrix organizations based on a case study of the TRATON GROUP, a member of the Volkswagen Group. The research is based on data from over 40 interviews performed within the three brands of this group, MAN, Scania and Volkswagen Caminhões e Ônibus, as well as the TRATON Holding. The investigation creates understanding of the matrix organization through the analysis of matrix projects within two departments, namely Human Resources and Research and Development within these three brands and the holding. The literature on matrix organizations presents a challenge due to the fact that most of it is outdated and little current research can be found based on empirical evidence. This is due to a management fad which led to the matrix gaining popularity before losing consideration both in practice and academia. However, according to the few current researchers on this topic, the matrix organization should not be neglected, and is still very much in use in organizations today. This thesis creates a framework for research of the matrix, starting by building an understanding of the contemporary MNC and its challenges, applying these to the context of a matrix structure. It draws on the MNC literature, in particular the understanding of the shifting role of headquarters. Furthermore based on the existing research on matrix organizations, the topic of decision making and conflict in the matrix, as well as their typologies and antecedents are further identified. These topics are addressed largely in the classic matrix literature and have been developed here in the contemporary MNC. Additionally, this work contributes by adding the topic of culture and identities as key to creating a view of a matrix, something which has not been developed in an empirical way. This research takes a closer interest in the issue of organizational culture. Finally, another significant contribution of this thesis, through this framework, is the addition of boundary spanning as a lens for the study of matrix organizations. A particular contribution here are the findings on temporal boundary spanning, a new field of study in multinational companies. Using this framework, the empirical findings are analyzed in a systematic way using the template analysis method. The contributions of this thesis can be summarized in the following way. The first contribution would have to be the framework for analysis which has been developed as it would serve for a comprehensive tool for analysis of a matrix organization. Furthermore, this work serves to demonstrate empirically how a contemporary MNC can promote lateral coordination as well as deal with the control gap through the use of a matrix organization. On top of that, the most recent matrix literature has been added too, in particular through the analysis of the two modes of decision making, balanced and rule-based, and their uses in matrix organizations, contributing to the contingency theory developed by Wolf and Egelhoff (2017). In addition of that the causes and consequences of conflict and the associated power capabilities deployed within matrix work has been further understood and contributes to the micro-political understanding of matrix organizations. Beyond the classic matrix issues, thanks to the aforementioned analysis framework, this thesis has been able to add to the research on cultural and identity issues in the matrix organization. In particular, an understanding of the impact of organizational culture, as well as the identity issues (observed more strongly in the R&D department) offer interesting insights. Finally, the importance of boundary spanning as well as the boundary spanning skills needed and developed by a matrix organization have been identified. Thanks to this, a classification for boundary spanning skills has been developed. This is a significant finding as it is a concept which had yet to be applied to the context of matrix organizations. Overall, this thesis contributes to multiple streams of literature related to matrix organizations, adding significant empirical understanding to the issue thanks to a rich research field combined with a novel framework for analysis of matrix organization.

1 Introduction

This introduction will start by explaining the research framework which was created in order to understand this case, before going over the research questions identified as pertinent based on previous academic work. Then it will give an overview of the research field and the methods used to gather data and analyze it, before finally explaining the contributions and giving a brief outline of the thesis.

The present work aims to investigate and further understand matrix organizations in the contemporary MNC. The idea behind this research was to understand how a holding-matrix organization functions and what the facilitating factors contributing to its success are. This was an excellent opportunity to build on the current body of literature on matrix organizations in the contemporary MNC, generally led by J.R. Galbraith, J. Wolf and W. Egelhoff, who have spearheaded the research on this topic in the last 15 years. This research will incorporate several streams of literature relevant to the understanding of this case. To start with, matrix literature will obviously greatly contribute to the creation of the research framework. However, as will be further explained later, this research is generally outdated and lacks empirical evidence, therefore requiring us to also integrate further streams in order to build a compelling framework. Three streams of literature will mostly be used to supplement the matrix literature. The first is the literature on headquarter-subsidiary relationships. As this case is based on a holding matrix organization, this stream is particularly pertinent. Furthermore, this literature is vast and will allow this study to build a potential understanding that the sole matrix literature does not, especially since the idea of a holding matrix has only ever been mentioned by authors without being deeply empirically studied. Furthermore, this research will also pull from the mergers, acquisitions and international joint ventures literature. It is useful to this work, because the idea of integrating brands under the umbrella of one holding organization, even if they are not explicitly being acquired, can be comparable to the situation experienced in the context of a merger. Finally, the concept of boundary spanning will be added, which has yet to be taken into consideration in a matrix context within academic literature. This study shows that the actors within the matrix play an important boundary spanning role. Taking this view to explore how the matrix functions will both contribute to theory on matrix organizations and boundary spanning alike.

A matrix organization can be defined as an elementary structure with an additional dimension (Wolf & Egelhoff, 2017). Sayles (1976) stated that most organizations have some form of matrix organization and in 1978, Davis and Lawrence (1978) stated that matrix organizations were being used more and more and predicted that such structures would become the norm. In 2008, Galbraith reported a growing interest in matrix structures in many companies and Appelbaum et al. (2008) found that "matrix management has become a standard within certain industries". A recent Gallup survey found that eighty-four percent of their respondents (4000 workers in the United States) were at least "slightly matrixed", meaning they either worked on multiple teams on some days, worked on multiple teams every day while primarily reporting to the same manager, or worked on multiple teams every day while reporting to different managers (Bazigos and Harter, 2016). Galbraith (2008) found that "the corporate function – business unit matrix is standard practice in business today". Overall, evidence shows that many multinational corporations (MNCs) today are regularly using matrix organizations to implement their increasingly complex strategies (Appelbaum et al.; 2008, Galbraith, 2009; Bazigos and Harter, 2016; Egelhoff & Wolf, 2017). There is existing academic work on matrix organizations, but as it is rather dated it does seem logical that fifty years later these structures would have evolved

© Springer Fachmedien Wiesbaden GmbH, part of Springer Nature 2020
J. Shahani, *Limits and Opportunities of a Matrix Organization*, Auto
Uni – Schriftenreihe 149, https://doi.org/10.1007/978-3-658-32261-8_1

and therefore an already relatively undefined concept needs to be redefined (Wolf and Egelhoff, 2013). There is lack of significant recent empirical research on the topic and a large portion of quality sources date back to the 1970s and 1980s (Appelbaum et al., 2008, Gos, 2015, Egelhoff & Wolf, 2017). Overall, there has been "little reported academic research on matrix structures in large, complex organizations over the past 30 years" (Egelhoff and Wolf, 2017, p.5). However this lack of interest cannot be justified by the absence of need for study, lack of companies for research or significance of the topic, but rather from the fact that matrix organizations, and simultaneously their study, followed a clear management fad. They were hastily adopted and promptly abandoned (Galbraith, 2009) before coming back into use in the recent decades. One of the most cited reasons for matrix abandonment is the increased amount of inter-organizational conflict, as well as slow decision making which led to the creation of excessively administrative organizations and to a drop in the overall performance of the organization (Peters, 1979, Egelhoff & Wolf 2017). Today however, the accelerating rate of change and increasing global competition means that MNCs are attempting to implement increasingly complex strategies. In order to implement these strategies, similarly complex structures, such as matrix organizations are required (Egelhoff & Wolf, 2017). Indeed, not only are today's matrix organizations potentially different to those in the 1970s and 1980s, but the MNCs themselves have also changed, making the need for updated research on the topic clear. The concept of the contemporary MNC has evolved from the simple goal of global efficiency to a more complex and heterogeneous strategy of global efficiency, local responsiveness and cross border learning (Bartlett and Ghoshal, 1989). Linked to this the role of the subsidiaries and headquarters is changing, with subsidiaries influencing firms from the bottom up. Therefore it is interesting to study a holding company matrix, which effectively illustrates one way in which a matrix can be used to coordinate and gain value from subsidiaries. The main issues reported in the literature regarding the management of matrix organization are generally the issue of decision making and excessive conflict. The level of conflict coming from the confrontation of two or more dimensions of the organization is often cited as being one of the reasons matrix organizations were abandoned in the past. Furthermore, the issue of decision making and power in the matrix have also been studied, but there is still much to understand. Indeed, when looking at the past literature, the main consensus was that the matrix should aim to have a balanced form of decision making with shared power between the dimensions. Today however, it seems that a form of rule-based decision making (Wolf & Egelhoff, 2017), where one dimension is given the power over the other, may in some situations benefit the matrix rather than hinder it. Furthermore, the same authors have also found that the levels of conflict in a matrix are not necessarily higher than in an elementary structure. On top of that, the idea that this conflict could actually be the "raison d'etre" of the matrix, the place it draws its value from, is interesting to explore further in an empirical study.

Today, there is no question that organizational culture is an important factor for organizational success, and has been studied at length in IB literature. However, its impact in the context of a matrix organization has not been studied. The reason for this could be attributed to the history of research on matrix organizations. Indeed, the rise of research on the concept of organizational culture and its importance happened in the 1980s (Jung et al., 2009), therefore coinciding with the downturn of research on matrix organizations. In the context of a matrix organization, one can only assume that organizational culture will also play a major role, as the basic concept of the matrix is to confront different dimensions, and, one could assume, subsequently different cultures. It has been shown within the context of M&As and joint ventures for example, that this collision of different values, norms and assumptions can lead to issues. It is therefore relevant to consider culture, on multiple levels, as a factor for analysis when attempting to understand the contemporary matrix organization.

When looking into complex international organizations, such as matrix organization, one should consider the boundaries within this organization. Indeed, MNCs can be considered to be groups of units with different interest, goals and practices, which act in various local environments (Tushman & Scalan, 1981). This generates boundaries within the organization, where friction can happen and interactions between units can be harder (Barner-Rasmussen et al., 2014). Therefore studying the dimensions of the matrix by considering their boundaries could potentially further contribute to understanding the success factors of such a matrix. Indeed, looking into the necessary boundary spanning activities and the skills required by the actors in the matrix could contribute to furthering the understanding of the roles and skills of matrix actors.

Now that a brief overview of the research framework has been given, which will be used for this thesis, the research questions and rationale of the work will be derived. The general premise and idea of this thesis is quite simply to ask how a matrix organization works. Then based on the analysis of the literature on matrix organizations, and, based on the assumption that matrix organizations, also suffer and benefit from the same issues and facilitating factors, to a certain extent, as MNCs in general, the following research questions have been developed. The rationale and the literature gaps that these questions will attempt to contribute to will be developed in part one of this thesis.

1.   How can a contemporary holding company matrix facilitate knowledge sharing on a global level while allowing for subsidiary autonomy?
2.   How are decisions made in a holding matrix organization?
3.   How is ambidexterity facilitated by a flexible matrix structure?
4.   What role does conflict and the power capabilities deployed by the actors play?
5.   What is the impact of cultural differences within a matrix organization?
6.   How is the concept of boundary spanning deployed in a matrix organization?

A rich field of research came up in the form of an internal research position within the TRATON GROUP. This was a very promising field, as not only was the access unparalleled, the timing was very interesting as the matrix organization had just been set up, in the form of a holding coordinating its brands. This is particularly interesting as it not only allows for a study of a matrix organization up close, but also provides evidence of the changing role of headquarters in the contemporary MNC. This research is done from within, by an embedded researcher within the holding, allowing for deep insight and plentiful data on the workings of the matrix organization. The TRATON GROUP is owned by Volkswagen, which is currently the 18th largest public company in the world according to Forbes (2019). The TRATON GROUP is mainly composed of three brands, MAN, Scania and Volkswagen Caminhões e Ônibus, headquartered in Germany, Sweden and Brazil, respectively. The collaboration between these three brands is being coordinated by a central function, the TRATON holding, which is based partly in Germany for the administrative functions and in Sweden for the technical office. The two biggest brands, Scania and MAN are heritage brands with over 100 years of automobile and transportation industry experience, and Volkswagen Caminhões e Ônibus is much younger and smaller. The TRATON GROUP aims to become a global player and has a clear expansion strategy, because although the company has a strong presence in Europe and Brazil, it wishes to expand worldwide. From a group perspective it seems that there is not a desire for complete centralization or even formalization. Instead the TRATON GROUP was set up as a matrix organization, with cross-brand projects which are more or less centralized. When the idea of the TRATON GROUP was first implemented in 2015, then operating under the name of Volkswagen Truck & Bus, it came from a simple premise. The Volkswagen Group counted three powerful truck and bus brands which operated independently, namely Scania based in Sweden, MAN from Germany and Volkswagen Caminhões e Ônibus in Brazil. These brands were successful on their own and contributed individually to the Volkswagen Group, in the same way as all its passenger car brands, such as Audi, Seat and Porsche for example. However, there was clear opportunity for synergies which had yet to be tapped into. Indeed, where on the passenger car level, the Volkswagen Group was exploiting synergies to a great extent, this had yet to be the case on such a level between its truck and bus brands. Indeed Volkswagen is traditionally a passenger car manufacturer, and although it has counted truck brands within its group for a while, it was not its core business. Therefore a holding company, whose main focus was to foster collaboration between these three truck and bus brands by identifying and exploiting synergies to a much greater extent than had been the case previously, was set up in a matrix organization structure. This matrix organization structure sent a message, the goal was not to centrally steer all operations, but rather to act as a horizontal collaboration facilitator for these already successful brands, creating value without destroying the operational success of each individual entity. This case study is a rather unique one, as it was started in 2016, shortly after the holding was officially set up and during the ramp-up phase of the holding, both in terms of personnel, where the holding company grew exponentially in the first years, as well as in the cooperation capabilities of the brands, where cross-brand projects went from being mostly a new phenomenon, although there were already a couple of scattered cooperation projects existing, to a more usual and to a certain extent natural activity. The interviews which constitute the core of the empirical data for this research were done approximately over the course of a year, therefore not in longitudinal way. However, the understating of the matrix organization of the interviewees is particularly poignant, because of the fresh and new aspect of it, allowing for the understanding of the actual impact of this set-up.

> *"Our Group consists of strong unique brands, but TRATON makes us even stronger. Under one roof we are able to join forces and bundle our innovative power. TRATON connects the brands and fosters our collaboration"*
> *Henrik Henriksson, CEO Scania (VW press release, 2018)*

TRATON can be considered to be representative of many MNCs, as big groups with multiple brands attempting to find synergies is quite common, a good example simply being TRATON's mother company, Volkswagen. This is however also the case across other industries, such as the luxury sector, or the food and drink industry. This research is an in depth single case study, based on data from over 40 semi-structured qualitative interviews. The research focuses on the transnational projects from the Human Resources and R&D functions of the TRATON GROUP. This research is a unique opportunity to study the workings of a matrix organization from within. Furthermore, the fact that the matrix is new, could potentially allow interviewees to have a clearer picture of the impact of the matrix, as the comparison with their previously non-matrixed organization remains fresh in their minds. Overall, the access to this research field is most definitely an opportunity and the findings from this research will contribute to the research on matrix organizations.

This research will add to the literature on matrix organizations, by not only explaining how a matrix organization holding functions, but also describing and analyzing the decision making processes and the factors that influence them. Furthermore, it will identify the main sources of conflict in this organization and the factors which ensure either successful conflict resolution or minimize the negative effects of the conflict. On top of that the processes surrounding knowledge and learning will be looked into. Finally the impact of the multiple cultures and identities interacting within this project context will be analyzed as well as the role of boundary spanning. The expectation of this research is to contribute both to research and practice by identifying the facilitating factors for project success in relation to these matrix issues. In particular, this thesis will be able to contribute to multiple streams of research thanks to this study, while keeping the central focus on the functioning of contemporary matrix organizations. It will provide an example of how such an organization works and how it supports knowledge sharing between subsidiaries and from the subsidiaries to HQ, as well as showing how a matrix can be used to deal with the control gap of very autonomous subsidiaries. Furthermore, the study provides empirical evidence of the two types of matrix decision making, as described by Egelhoff and Wolf (2017), as well as offering more insight into decision making within a contemporary matrix organization and the stakes at play, overall contributing to the literature on decision making in matrix organizations. Furthermore, the challenges for ambidexterity within the matrix organization and the potential facilitating factors and challenges regarding knowledge sharing in such an organization will be observed. Through this, the key role played by boundary spanning activities and the importance of building trust to facilitate knowledge sharing, and subsequently innovation will be identified. On top of that, this thesis will also add to the current understanding regarding conflict in matrix organizations, and more particularly their causes and the factors which influence them. This topic has, as of yet, not been researched deeply in an empirical fashion, with studies usually concentrating on comparing the quantity of conflict in a matrix compared to the levels found in an elementary structure. An original contribution to the literature on matrix organizations will also be made through our study of the impact of cultural differences and identity issues on matrix work. This work will also identify facilitating factors for dealing within these issues, looked into through the theoretical lens of boundary spanning. Indeed, another contribution of this thesis is the combination of the theoretical field of boundary spanning and matrix organizations. Indeed, this is an interesting and value adding lens to use to further understand the facilitating factors or matrix organizations and particularly the role and skills played and required by the actors involved in the matrix work. Furthermore, this research will offer new insights into the boundary spanning skills required for matrix organization work, as well as further the understanding as to how they are developed. It also offers further empirical evidence of a new form of boundary spanning in research, namely temporal boundary spanning.

The structure of this thesis will now be presented. This dissertation is divided into four major parts. The first part is the literature review. For this thesis a rather broad range of themes has been reviewed. To start with the research on MNCs and in particular the contemporary MNC and the role of headquarters is reviewed. Then the literature on matrix organizations is reviewed. Following that, the topics of culture and conflicts, negotiations, and power capabilities are reviewed, as they relate directly to the main issues in a matrix organization, as will be explained in the review. Then the role of boundary spanning in the MNC, and in a matrix organization in particular is explained. Finally the research questions are explained in detail, based on this review of the literature. The second part is the research design for this study. For this part, first the methodology for this research, a case study, is presented as well as the research paradigm, ontology and epistemology. The choice of a case study is justified and the seals of quality for such a methodology are presented and applied to this case. Furthermore the ethical practices necessary and the measures taken are explained. Then the case study is described, the TRATON

GROUP and the companies that are part of it, namely Scania, MAN and Volkswagen Caminhões e Ônibus. The interviewee sample is also explained as well as the method for analysis. Finally the projects which are studied within this case are described. The third part of this thesis, analysis and discussion, presents the empirical results of the study, starting with the presentation of the HR results and then the R&D results. This will be done using the framework developed from the findings of the literature review and the gaps identified. For each of the main projects observed within these departments, the matrix issues and facilitating factors are reviewed and summarized to create an overall picture of the functioning of this holding company matrix organization. Finally the fourth part presents the contributions and conclusions of this research, starting by summarizing the empirical results and then discussing the key findings. Then the contributions in relation to the literature review as well as the limitations of the study and outlook for further research are discussed.

Note: Please note that the "we" form in the text is for style purposes only and refers to the author, myself.

2 The Contemporary Matrix Organization & Concepts

Matrix organizations have been implemented and studied within large organizations, MNCs, who play an essential role in the global economy, because of their economic power. Indeed, looking into the available figures on MNCs, in 2009 there were 82,000 TNCs worldwide, with 810,000 foreign affiliates (UNCTAD, 2009). As globalization has increased, multinationals have become more and more important, and they in fact play a significant role in international economic coordination (Whitley, 2001).

MNCs can be defined as corporations with regular cross-border operations (Morschett et al., 2010) or quite simply as an organization with entities in two or more countries. In the same vein, Heidenreich (2012, p. 549) defines MNCs as "companies that coordinate and control subsidiaries across national boundaries and […] operate in different national contexts."

Today's multinationals are among the most complex and sophisticated firms in the world, and according to Galbraith (2014), one of the most important success factors for MNCs is an appropriate, well-implemented and smoothly operated organizational structure. Because MNCs tend to be so complex, their context allows for an understanding of the issues and challenges associated with matrix organizations (Egelhoff & Wolf, 2017). That is why this section of the study will start by reviewing the literature on MNCs in order to understand their context. After this review, this section will go on to provide an overview of the current state of knowledge on matrix organizations. Due to the turbulent history of these structures, matrix organizations in the contemporary MNC remain relatively misunderstood. Then the most common issues of these structures will be elaborated upon, namely conflict and decision making in the matrix. Then, based on the previously mentioned premise that the complex context of MNCs brings matrix organizational issues to life, additional potential matrix issues based on the currently researched issues in the MNC will be studied. To start with, simply looking at the most popular alternative to the classically organized MNC, the network organization and the rising popularity of informal forms of coordination in the MNC, one can posit that boundary spanning will have an important role to play in the contemporary matrix organization too. Furthermore, the question of culture in MNCs obviously comes to mind, as the basic premise of the MNC, namely that it has operations in multiple countries, leads to cultural issues being brought to life. As the matrix organization forces dimensions of the organization together, it is safe to assume that it could potentially be interesting to look into the issue of culture within a matrix organization.

2.1 Towards the Contemporary MNC

MNCs had to change their goal from just "global efficiency" to global efficiency, local responsiveness and cross border learning (Bartlett and Ghoshal, 1989, Wolf & Egelhoff, 2012), As a result, in order to reflect this, MNCs had to introduce more complexity and heterogeneity into their strategies and organizational designs. Matrix structures and network organizations, create this internal complexity (Wolf & Egelhoff, 2012).

Morgan et al (2001) identify three major topics which are addressed in the literature on multinationals. The first concerns how firms make decisions on how to expand abroad. In this case, these companies are seen as "rational actors balancing costs and benefits of different forms of serving foreign markets" (Morgan et al., 2001, p3). Second, the stages or sequences of the internationalization process are addressed within this stream of literature. This topic includes

© Springer Fachmedien Wiesbaden GmbH, part of Springer Nature 2020
J. Shahani, *Limits and Opportunities of a Matrix Organization*, Auto
Uni – Schriftenreihe 149, https://doi.org/10.1007/978-3-658-32261-8_2

the question of whether these stages are fixed, the concept of psychic distance (distance between home market and foreign market cultures) and the premise that firms internationalize as a network, where risk taking firms will "drag" their suppliers or distributors into new foreign markets. The third approach, and the one most relevant to this project, concerns the managerial issues associated with this process. This stream of research posits that managers need to understand the environment and create an organizational structure and management system that "fits" to these conditions. Egelhoff (1982) described the structure-strategy fit concept using an information processing approach: "there is a good fit between structure and strategy when the information-processing requirements of a firm's strategy are satisfied by the information-processing capacities of its structure" (Egelhoff, 1982, p436). He later also developed this concept for the matrix organization. In fact the matrix organization was the basis for a certain amount of research within this field, where the issue of global integration versus local responsiveness (Prahalad & Doz, 1987) or global integration versus national differentiation (Bartlett and Ghoshal, 1989) was described as a key issue facing MNCs. Depending on the sector and product, a firm can commercialize a product or service globally or needs to adapt it to local needs. Based on this, in their oft cited work, "Managing across borders: the transnational solution", Bartlett and Ghoshal (1989) describe a typology of four types of organizations. The first, multinationals, are described as decentralized, sensitive to local environments but with weak ties to subsidiaries both across national and divisional boundaries. Global companies are highly centralized entities, with little sensitivity to local contexts. The international company is defined by centrally generated core competencies which are transferred and adapted within subsidiaries based on local conditions. Finally transnational companies are described as "dispersed, independent and specialized with differentiated contributions by national units to integrated worldwide operations and knowledge developed jointly and shared worldwide" (Bartlett & Ghoshal, 1989, p65). Nohria and Ghoshal (1997) further developed this concept and named it "differentiated network". Following this, two further streams of research have been developed. The first concerns itself with the functioning of subsidiaries and how their operations are linked back to headquarters' strategic goals and the second deals with the issue of organizational learning within these differentiated multinational networks (Morgan et al, 2001).

Overall in these streams of research, assumptions are made, taking an economic, rational and efficient view of the world and MNCs. MNCs are seen as "cohesive, goal-directed rational actors" (Morgan et al., 2001, p1). However, this does not take into account the "social determinants of organizational structures, the political nature of decision making, the irrationality of organizations, and the social construction of markets" (Morgan et al, 2001, p9). Taking into account the social embeddedness of rationality, a multinational organization can be seen as a "structured set of relations between a range of actors with their own powers and interests. Decision processes are characterized by political bargaining and negotiation" (Morgan et al., 2001, pp 9-10). In this view, MNCs can be considered as a "transnational social space" within which many different activities take place. This does not mean that the economic stakes are no longer considered; this view just also incorporates interactions that happen in parallel and influence the change, conflict, cooperation and dynamism within the MNC.

Therefore taking into account the basic premise that complex strategies require complex structures and that MNCs are not only rational entities but are also political organizations which are influenced by the interests of the actors which compose it, this work will attempt to understand how these complex structures, such as matrix organizations can be used to successfully implement their equally complex strategies.

2.1.1   From a Hierarchical Coordination Perspective to a Network Perspective

In this section we will look into the history of the research on MNCs and show how it has evolved from a hierarchical perspective to a network perspective. This will help bring into context the contemporary matrix organization.

In the earlier research on the role of the headquarters, in the 1960s to the 1980s, the literature concentrated on the HQ-subsidiary relationship. Hierarchical coordination was considered to be the "primary mechanism for coordinating interdependency within an MNC" (Egelhoff & Wolf, 2017a, p72). Here, the HQ plays an active and dominant role, and within this literature, the HQ is seen to be the most important actor. In a top-down perspective, the focus is on how the HQ can influence and control subsidiary behavior.

The more recent literature on the role of HQ in the MNC, which dates from the 1990s to today, tends to focus more on the non-hierarchical and lateral coordination between the subsidiaries. Here the HQ is expected to play a more indirect and passive role. The HQ needs to create a culture which facilitates this non-hierarchical coordination and provide resources (Egelhoff & Wolf, 2017a). Within this literature there are four main streams of research which will be discussed below. The four streams are the following: the MNC as a heterarchy, the transnational organization and later the differentiated network, the MNC as a business network and finally the subsidiary development literature. Hedlund (1986, 1993) views the MNC as a heterarchy, meaning that the MNC should be less hierarchical and more heterarchical. The MNC is made up of unpredictable and constantly changing interdependencies which lead to uncertainty. Therefore there is a need for more lateral knowledge sharing, stronger shared vision and decision making based on consensus. This type of MNC is appropriate for knowledge creating, whereas a hierarchy better suits a knowledge exploiting MNC (Hedlund & Ridderstrale, 1997). Bartlett & Ghoshal (1989) developed the concept of the MNC as a transnational corporation. The transnational corporation requires a multidimensional strategy in order to globally obtain efficiency, and learning as well as local responsiveness. Because the traditional hierarchical MNC structure could not do this simultaneously, the transnational organizational design uses more informal means of coordination. The transnational corporation is more flexible, more specialized and symmetrical than a tradition hierarchy and because of this it is better suited to deal with changes in strategy organizational design and behavior. As mentioned above, Ghoshal and Noria (1997) further developed this view into the "differentiated network", where the MNC is viewed as a network of sub-units which is coordinated through shared vision and non-hierarchical mechanisms.

Another view is to consider the MNC as a business network. As already mentioned, MNCs had to change their goal from just "global efficiency" to global efficiency, local responsiveness and cross border learning (Bartlett and Ghoshal, 1989). Therefore, in order to reflect this, MNCs had to introduce more complexity and heterogeneity into their strategies and organizational designs, matrix structures and network organizations create this internal complexity (Wolf & Egelhoff, 2012). Network organizational designs have been said to be the answer to the heterogeneity of MNCs (Bartlett & Ghoshal, 1989). Yet Wolf and Egelhoff state that a matrix structure is a valid alternative to the network organization since the matrix structure is implemented in order to deal with such heterogeneity or dual focus (Sayles, 1976; Sy and d'Annuzio, 2005; Burton et al., 2009).

Finally, some authors focus on subsidiary development. This stream of research focuses on how subsidiaries influence firm-level strategy in the MNC; effectively a bottom-up view. It focuses more on the HQ-subsidiary relationship and the changing role of these subsidiaries towards a more prominent entrepreneurial role (e.g. Andersson, Forsgren, & Pedersen, 2001; Birkinshaw, 1996; Forsgren et al., 2005). Here the subsidiaries will use non-hierarchical networks to influence the organization. In this view, the HQ tends to have a weak role, being the referee between the subsidiaries or in some cases it simply has an undefined role (Birkinshaw, 2000; Birkinshaw & Hagstrom, 2000, Egelhoff & Wolf, 2017a).

Because the MNC is dependent to a certain extent on the resources of its subsidiaries, the management of knowledge flows in the MNC is supposedly one of the most important sources of competitive advantage for the organization (Bartlett et al. 2004; Doz et al. 2001; Gupta and Govindarajan 2000). Apparently, the more it is dependent on a subsidiary, the more it will attempt to control it (Ghoshal and Nohria 1989). Therefore the HQ-subsidiary relationship will vary based on the strategic importance of a subsidiary. Some have developed different typologies of subsidiaries in the MNC, generally based on resource dependency theory, which explains that organizations are dependent on others because they cannot generate all the resources they need by themselves (Aldrich 1976; Pfeffer and Salancik 1978). In this way, the power of a subsidiary resides in the influence it has over resource allocation, the importance of the resources it possesses for the organization as a whole and whether these resources can be replaced by alternatives (Taylor et al. 1996). For example, Gupta and Govindarajan (1991) developed a categorization of subsidiaries based on incoming and outgoing knowledge flows to and from the subsidiary, either between the HQ and the subsidiary or with the rest of the organization. They suggest four types of subsidiary. The first, the Global Innovator, is a source of knowledge for other subsidiaries. The second is the Integrated Player, who receives and transfers comparable amounts of knowledge throughout the organization. Then there are Implementers, who do not create knowledge but rather are dependent on knowledge inflows and finally local innovators who create knowledge locally but do not send or receive much knowledge. The first two types of subsidiaries are the ones where HQ will attempt to exert the most control. However, Global Innovators are the least dependent on HQ input and therefore have the most possibility to resist this control (Taylor et al. 1996). They also require autonomy in order to be able to preserve their local contacts and generate these valuable skills and knowledge (Harzing and Noorderhaven 2006). Therefore managing this balance of autonomy and control from HQ requires complex and subtle balance. Indeed, MNCs must find this balance between central control and local autonomy (Bartlett and Ghoshal, 1986). Prahalad and Doz (1981) however warn against the risk of granting too much autonomy to subsidiaries, which could lead to a "control gap", which could lead to the fact that MNCs do not obtain the full competitive advantage which comes from global integration.

This is particularly interesting for this thesis, as in the case of a matrix holding organization, the subsidiaries can, for the most part, be considered as Global Innovators, as they are independent companies, perfectly able to function autonomously. This research will therefore attempt to see how a matrix holding organization can attempt to achieve this subtle form of control, while not hindering the value of subsidiary autonomy.

It must be noted that the literature on headquarter – subsidiary relationships look into the power capabilities involved in the transfer of practices within MNCs in the case of a central authoritative HQ position dealing with foreign subsidiaries. This therefore excludes the consideration that subsidiaries can influence strategic issues from "below" (Andersson et al., 2007). Therefore, Andersson et al (2007), model the MNC as a federation, seeing the headquarters and subsidiaries as "dispersed structures of power", where knowledge and expertise rests in the national context of the subsidiary (Geppert & Dörrenbächer, 2011) which are involved in a constant bargaining process (Andersson et al, 2007, p01). Here, the headquarters have "little ability or interest to exert full control" (Geppert & Dörrenbächer, 2011, p23). Moreover, their model not only focuses on the headquarter – subsidiary relationship but also on the relationship between subsidiaries. This theory is more relevant in the case of a holding company matrix organization, and therefore for this research.

2.1.2   Mechanisms of Coordination and Control in the MNC

Management control can be described as "a process whereby management and other groups are able to initiate and regulate the conduct of activities so that their results accord with the goals and expectations held by those groups" (Child, 1984, p136). Martinez and Jarillo (1989) define mechanisms of coordination as "any administrative tool for achieving integration among different units within an organization". These mechanisms of control and coordination are not specific to MNCs; every organization has them, but the complexity found within the MNC is what makes these mechanisms particularly interesting (Martinez & Jarillo, 1989). Ferner (2000), when analyzing the dependency between power resources and management control mechanisms, distinguishes three types of management control. The first, "personal control", is the "direct close personal supervision of lower levels by higher". The second, "bureaucratic control", relies on the formalization of systems and processes as well as the creation of common rules and regulations. Finally, the third, "social" or "cultural" control, "depends on developing in managers an identification with and commitment to the values and objectives of the corporation" (Ferner, 2000, p. 522). Nobel and Birkinshaw (1998) make a similar distinction as the quote below describes:

> *"Centralization, in which decision-making power is retained at the headquarters; Formalization, in which decision-making is routinized through rules and procedures; and Socialization, whereby organization members develop common expectations and shared values that promote like-minded decision-making."* (Nobel & Birkinshaw, 1998, p. 483)

Martinez and Jarillo (1989), when studying these mechanisms of control, found a clear evolution in research from the formal mechanisms (personal and bureaucratic) towards the more subtle social mechanisms. They suggested that this evolution in research may be due to the fact that MNCs are, in practice, moving towards using these social mechanisms. Moreover they posit that these mechanisms are not replacing the "old" formal ones, but are rather cumulative and necessary to deal with the increasing complexity of organizations. Gassmann and Von Zedtwitz (1998), in their study of R&D organizations, illustrate a similar concept, as can be seen in the figure below. They explain that the hierarchical structures (the regional R&D centers and the hierarchical organizations) are supplemented by both a project structure and informal relations. They claim that the role of these informal structures is that they can help overcome the issues of the formal structures, notably allowing for a more flexible and dynamic company.

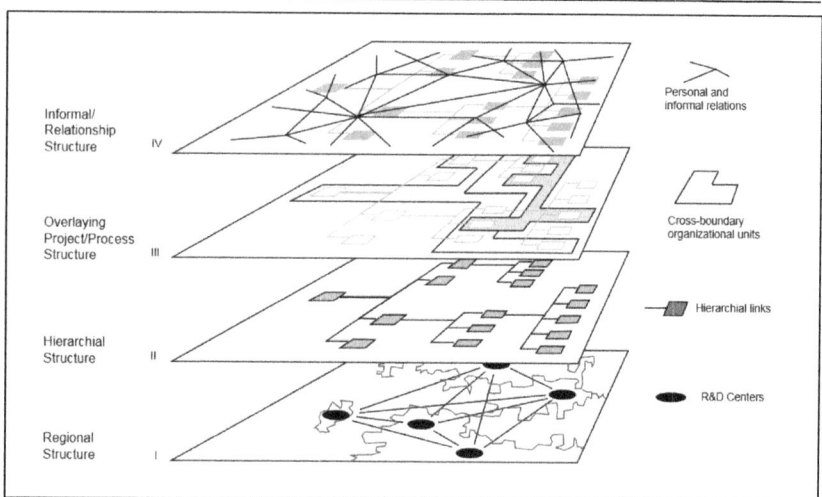

Figure 1: Four levels of structure in international organizations (Gassmann & Von Zedtwitz, 1998)

Ferner (2000) finds that the formal control mechanisms will not necessarily be adopted and implemented. For this to happen, the headquarters need to deploy power capabilities, which will act as a lever and support the implementation of the formal mechanisms. Klimkeit (2013), while also finding a similar relationship between formal and informal mechanisms, posits that the effectiveness of informal and formal mechanisms are contingent on two drivers of collaboration, interdependency and interest in the project's success. This thesis will attempt to further understand the power capabilities leveraged by the different dimensions of the matrix organization, and how this affects the control mechanisms deployed.

Today, as mentioned previously, there is an accelerated rate of change leading to a need for more coordination within MNCs. In particular, the communication and transport costs are decreasing and the trade barriers are weakening, leading to more global strategies and an increased interdependency between sub-units. Furthermore, there is more environmental uncertainty due to accelerating speed of change in technology and the environment. On top of that, global competition is intensifying, leading to MNCs needing to make global economies of scale and scope. These elements lead to future strategies being increasingly transnational (Egelhoff & Wolf, 2017a). Therefore, Egelhoff & Wolf (2017a), define the contemporary MNC as having high levels of environmental change and complexity, high interdependency among subsidiaries and where the important decisions are often made on a subsidiary level and there are high levels of network coordination between them. The changes in international environments and strategies, which lead to increased need for coordination results in a more complex role of HQ than ever before. As can be seen above, the two perspectives on the role of headquarters in the MNC are radically different and difficult to reconcile. However, the contemporary MNC needs to have the coordination capacities of both the hierarchical and network perspective (Egelhoff & Wolf, 2017a). Therefore today's challenge for MNCs is to reconcile the hierarchical view of the past with the more recent network perspective in order to deal with the challenges brought on by the environmental changes and increasing competition. This thesis will consider the matrix organization as a potential way of dealing with this issue.

2.1.3   Relevance and Associated Research Questions

Within this section an overview of the contemporary MNC is given, starting with the history of the MNC coming from the hierarchical perspective to the current trend in organizations, namely the network perspective. It has been shown how, in parallel with these changes in organizations, the role of the headquarters has changed from a command and control perspective, appropriate in a hierarchical perspective to a softer and more bottom-up approach, encouraging lateral forms of knowledge sharing coinciding with the contemporary forms of organization. This has led us to look into the coordination mechanisms of the MNC. Within the hierarchical perspective, the formal mechanisms were predominantly studied, whereas today there is more of a focus on social mechanisms. However, studying either the formal or the informal mechanisms is no longer sufficient. There is currently a debate and a need to further understand how MNCs today can combine their formal and informal coordination mechanisms. Therefore this thesis will attempt to understand how a contemporary holding company matrix can facilitate knowledge sharing on a global level while allowing for subsidiary autonomy. Indeed there has been an evolution both in our understanding and in practice on how organizations coordinate their activities, stemming from the changes in the environment that MNCs evolve in (Bartlett and Ghoshal, 1989, Wolf & Egelhoff, 2012). Indeed, there has been an evolution from the formal to the informal mechanisms of coordination. However, the state of literature still has gaps on how these formal and informal mechanisms work together in the contemporary MNC, and how the headquarters can contribute to creating the necessary framework to facilitate these mechanisms to coordinate their activities. (Egelhoff & Wolf, 2017a). There is a call for further understanding on how MNCs can leverage their informal coordination mechanisms and power resources in order to support their formal mechanisms in the coordination of their activities (Ferner, 2000). Through the lens of a holding matrix organization, this work will ask how are the mechanisms of control and coordination are deployed as well as attempt to understand how the holding influences the decision making through these mechanisms.

This thesis will address the issue of overlaying informal mechanisms on top of the formal hierarchical ones using the more recent literature stream on boundary spanning. The reason behind this is that the dimensions of a matrix and where these dimensions meet can be considered as boundaries. This allows for the study of the boundary spanning roles of the matrix actors and the skills required. The concept of boundary spanning will further be developed in the section dedicated to the review of the literature on boundary spanning. Furthermore, the growing importance of the role of subsidiaries had been noted, as well as their need for autonomy, to allow for knowledge creation within the subsidiaries, combined with the desire of control from HQ, in order to successfully integrate this knowledge. In order to achieve this, a subtle balance is required. This work posits that a potential way of obtaining this balance could be done using a holding company matrix. These questions are obviously very complex, and this thesis does not hope to fully answer them. However, the goal is to provide a potential avenue of response to the issue of central control and subsidiary autonomy in the contemporary MNC, in the form of a matrix organization.

2.2 Understanding the Matrix Organizational Form

It is often stated that the first written mention of matrix organizations was made by John Mee in 1964 (Appelbaum et al., 2008, Gos, 2015), where he described a matrix as "a web of relationships". Therefore, matrix organizations are clearly not a new phenomenon, yet they remain difficult to define. Back in 1992, Ford and Randolph (1992) stated that the matrix organization was still not fully defined even after 30 years of research on the topic and that matrix management tended to be redefined to fit the company or the study it was addressed in. Twenty-five years later this seems to still be the case, and in 2008, Appelbaum et al. (2008) found no global, clear definition of a matrix organization. Matrix structures are said to be an appropriate organizational form for complex international organizations, of which there seem to be an increasing number today (Galbraith, 2008; Qiu & Donaldson, 2012; Galbraith, 2013; Hall, 2013).

This field of research offers many opportunities for further exploration. Indeed, much of the quality literature dates back to the 1970s and 1980s, as Gos (2015) showed in his extensive quantitative review of the literature. Considering the accelerating rate of change in technology, and the socio-economic environment, it is very likely that this literature is already outdated. However, there is evidence that MNCs have continued to use matrix organizations, even though the academic interest in them waned (Egelhoff & Wolf, 2017). On top of that, the literature on the topic is very much contested with many disagreements. Therefore there is a clear knowledge gap on the topic today. This is why the upcoming section will review the existing literature on the topic in order to give an overview of the current state of knowledge, in order to build on it.

2.2.1   The Matrix Organization in the Field of Organization Theory

One of the reasons the matrix remains relatively undefined is that matrix has quite clearly followed a management trend. Galbraith (2008) is of the opinion that the concept of matrix organizations is already over a hundred years old. He states that Frederick Taylor had already mentioned the advantages of having multiple managers in the early 1900s although his idea was rejected due to the complexity of it. He then explains that matrix organizations also originated in Henry Fayol's line-and-staff model, which consists of each employee only having one boss but some employees having specialist roles and giving expert advice throughout the organization. Matrix organizations then first became popular after they were used in the aerospace industry in the 1950s (Egelhoff & Wolf, 2017). The dual strategic priorities in the United States for technology that was both state of the art, cost-effective and on-schedule led to the aerospace industry massively adopting a matrix structure in order to get a man on the moon by 1970, which was an objective set by Kennedy (Galbraith, 2008). These matrix structures consisted of a project management structure overlaid on top of a function division structure, driven by the need to manage several projects at the same time. After this, Research and Development divisions started to reorganize into matrix structures. Matrix organizations reached their peak of popularity in the 1970s in MNCs when this spread through the rest of the organization, beyond just R&D. Companies implemented matrix organizations on a broader scale, as opposed to the aerospace industry project management matrix structure (Goggin, 1974, Sayles 1976). It is at this time that books were written about this structure, such as "Matrix" by Davis and Lawrence (1977). Then in the late 1970s and 1980s, after reports of failed attempts of implementing a matrix (Kates & Erikson, 2008; Egelhoff & Wolf, 2017), most were then of the opinion that matrix management did not work. Galbraith (2008, p.323) attributes these implementation failures to the fact that matrix organizations were "wrongly adopted, hastily installed and inappropriately implemented". After that any publications on matrix were usually critics of the structure, such as the book "In Search of Excellence" by Peters and Waterman (1982), which claimed that no excellent company used a matrix (Galbraith, 2008). One can however balance this out with Galbraith's point that, in fact, companies such as Intel, Texas Instruments and Boeing all used matrix and Gobeli and Larson's (1986) findings that during this time the matrix still had a high frequency of use. The word "matrix" was out of favor and managers avoided it (Galbraith, 2008).

In the late 1990s the trend was reversed when managers started to see that some companies had a successful matrix organization and they recognized that there were some situations where matrix could be more valuable (Galbraith, 2008). Phenomenon such as globalization, the accelerating rate of change and increasing competition lead to an overall increasingly complex environment for MNCs to evolve in. This requires more complex strategies to be implemented, and, if one follows the strategy-structure fit logic, matching complex structures are to be expected (Wolf & Egelhoff, 2017). Indeed, there have been significant changes within today's macroeconomic environment; consumer markets are evolving much faster, new generations have entered the job market and the way we develop products is more efficient and effective (Vargas, 2013). Potentially, the advantages of a matrix could be more valuable today than they were in the past. Furthermore, it seems that company cultures and employees could be better adapted to working in a matrix situation (Derven, 2010; Gos, 2015).

These factors could potentially explain the increased interest in matrix organizations in practice. However, although there has been an upward trend in research on these organizations, it is still restricted to a few researchers, most prominently the late Galbraith, as well as Wolf and Egelhoff and their colleagues. This lack of interest could potentially be linked to the bad reputation of these structures, or to the current trend focused on network organizations. However, there are valid reasons for implementing a matrix organization structure today, as will be seen in the next section.

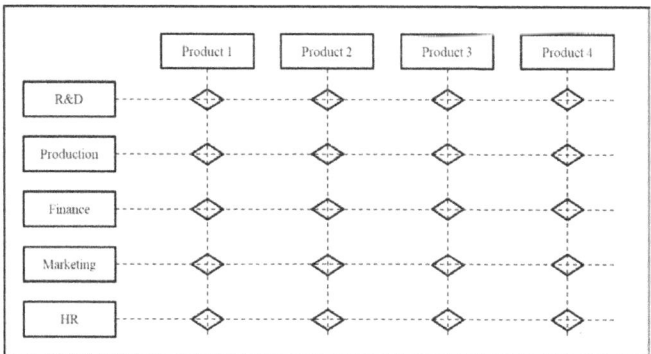

Figure 2: An example of a product / function matrix (own elaboration)

The reasons for implementing, or not implementing, a matrix have been discussed by academics and practitioners at length. As written by Sayles (1976), it is a common misconception that matrix structures are only useful in R&D. There are in fact many drivers to matrix implementation that can be used in all types of organization. Yet there are many who, especially in the 1980s to 1990s, were against implementing a matrix. For example, Bartlett and Ghoshal (1990) stated that using increasingly complex organizational structures was actually a trap which companies fell into, rather than a solution. Peters (1979), in his much cited work, "Beyond the Matrix Organization", also argues against the implementation of matrix, stating that the answer is no longer organizational restructuring. He explains that structural solutions are tempting because they seem simpler than changing management information systems, management styles, and informal communications network. These authors raise arguments just as compelling as the ones in favor of matrix implementation.

The easiest justification for implementing a matrix comes from the nature of the structure itself. Indeed, the main idea behind this structure is to combine two dimensions of an elementary structure to create a two-dimensional structure. It is this two-dimensionality, which leads to the ability to have a dual focus, and this ability to focus on two or more objectives (Sy & d'Annuzio, 2005) that is often cited as a root cause for matrix implementation. For example, Sayles (1976) sees matrix as the possibility for the coexistence of centralization and decentralization and that it can be used to balance the needs of specialization and the needs of coordination. Burton et al. (2009) see the matrix as an appropriate choice when both efficiency and effectiveness are needed, and state that this is necessary when the environment is unpredictable and complex in order to both be able to exploit current resources and capabilities as well as explore new things, the issue of exploration and exploitation. Brown and Agnew (1982) see matrix as a balancing of project performance and technical excellence, which they view as conflicting objectives. Many agree that a dual focus is a driver for matrix implementation (Davis & Lawrence, 1977, Sy & d'Annuzio, 2005, Kuprenas, 2001). Yet, as pointed out by Qiu and Donaldson (2012), although it is widely agreed that a matrix organization can be used to pursue dual strategies, which strategies in particular remains unclear. Using matrix as a response to an increasingly complex and uncertain environment is often mentioned in the literature (Sayles, 1976; Davis & Lawrence, 1977; Ford & Randolph, 1992; Burton et al. 2015). Sayles (1976, pp 95-96) describes uncertainty using the following criteria: "frequency of exceptional cases (requiring non standardized solutions), decisions require simultaneous accommodation to diverse and legitimately conflicting interests, need to recognize inherent contradictions in any effort to optimize towards one objective or set of constraints, unforeseen and unforeseeable problems arising from inherent instabilities in the technology or environment." Bartlett and Ghoshal (1990) add the accelerating rate of change as a neighboring issue to environmental complexity. Although this research is quite dated there is evidence that this environmental complexity is also increasing today, as reported by the Economist Intelligence Unit report in 2011. It seems that matrix is more apt at dealing with complex and fast changing environments than elementary structures. Sy and d'Annuzio (2005) as well as Davis and Lawrence (1978) find that a matrix organization can help speed up the response to these environmental. In the same direction, Brown and Agnew (1982) find that matrix has the flexibility to meet these changes and the uncertainty presented by the environment. Yet this is only the case in a fully functioning matrix. Indeed one of the often cited disadvantages of a matrix is navel-gazing (Davis & Lawrence, 1978) or the politicization of the organization (Kuprenas, 2001). This means that within the matrix there is no longer a focus on dealing with the complex environment but its focus is turned towards the inside of the organization, losing the added value of being able to deal with the environment better. Ford and Randolph state that the increasing complexity in the technology and environment increases the amount of information a company needs to process. This thought is also shared by other authors such as Davis and Lawrence (1977), who include pressures for high information processing as a key basic condition for implementing a matrix. In the strategy structure fit literature it is assumed that "matrix structures fit higher levels of transnational strategy than elementary structures" (Donaldson, 2009, p. 3), with transnational strategy levels composed of firm internationalization and corporate integration. It seems that matrix would be adept at dealing with such pressures, as explained by Donaldson (2009) who finds that the information processing capacity of matrix structures is superior to that of elementary structures. Galbraith (1971) also wrote that matrix was a solution towards handling complex tasks, which would therefore require more information processing. Wolf and Egelhoff (2011) also found in their comparison of network and matrix organizations, that information processing in a matrix was more predictable and reliable than in a network organization. Some write that matrix organizations are faster and more flexible than elementary structures, such as Burton et al. (2009) who state that matrix can be very flexible and deal with new information and adjust to new situations quickly but the opposite is often cited as a main disadvantage of matrix structures, such as Ford and Randolph (1992) who write that matrix can lead to multinational issues having slower response times or Galbraith (2008) who finds decision delay to be a main challenge. Others find that matrix leads to increased technical excellence, notably through improved knowledge transfer, Burton et al. (2015) find that the transmission from of best practices is a main advantage of matrix and Galbraith writes that the strong lateral relations between divisions or units increases a company's information-processing capacity. Similarly Brown and Agnew (1982) state that the cross-fertilization of ideas combined with the continued work of experts within their own domain leads to further technical excellence within the matrix.

A cited driver of matrix implementation is that companies have increasingly complex strategies and that these strategies will require matching complex organizational forms (Egelhoff and Wolf, 2017). Yet information overload is also often included as a disadvantage of a matrix organization (Galbraith, 2008) and Peters (1979, p. 5) writes that the matrix structure "over-estimates the information processing capacity of most human brains and the problem-solving capability of most social systems". Another driver often cited as key to matrix implementation is the possibility of shared resources. Derven (2010) saw in matrix implementation a way to be more agile and to do more with less resources. Ford and Randolph (1992) found that the flexible use of resources could be an advantage of matrix, and through this, one could imagine that technical excellence would be achieved more easily (Ford & Randolph, 1992). Yet some state that matrix is actually more expensive because of the need for more managers (Donaldson, 2009), or because of more meetings and delayed decisions (Ford & Randolph, 1992). Davis and Lawrence (1978) also state that matrix is more expensive but balance this with the opportunity for increased production. Because of the additional costs there are some risks associated with bad economic situations in a matrix. Derven (2010) finds that people who are worried about their jobs will focus on looking good rather than the success of their projects. Although one could argue that this could be the case in any type of organization. Davis and Lawrence (1978) find that one of the ills of the matrix is the risk of failure when faced with a difficult economic situation that they claim can be prevented with good planning. Overall, Burton et al. (2009) state, quite logically, that the costs for coordination should be outweighed by the benefits of the matrix. On the other hand, in 1976, Sayles wrote that matrix was a "structure with a future". The question now would be what future does the matrix have? Indeed when one looks into the trends often mentioned by consulting companies the key words are "network", "flat-organization" and "teams of teams" (Morgan, 2015 ; Deloitte, 2016). On the other hand Galbraith (2012) seemed to believe that matrix would keep being used more and more, as he wrote that matrix organizations would be developed in the future. This research will have the opportunity to observe a matrix organization in action, hopefully bringing to light further understanding of the value of the matrix in the contemporary MNC.

Many definitions have been given to matrix organizations, with a broad spectrum going from structures with multiple or dual forms of authority, basically two managers (Knight, 1976), to a project organization superimposed on an elementary structure (Anderson and Fleming, 1990). There seems to be three different types of definitions: those who consider it to be a network, those who see it as a project form (or some kind of dimension) superimposed on an elemental structure and those who describe it as a purely project form. The question of whether project management literature is relevant when studying matrix organizations is also quite present. When Ford and Randolph (1992) wrote their literature review they found that the terms matrix management and organization and project management and organization were frequently interchanged. They therefore mix matrix and project organizations in their work and consider them as equal. More recently, Wolf and Egelhoff (2013) state that, in their opinion, project management literature is not relevant.

Table 1: Types of Matrix Structure (own elaboration based on Galbraith, 2008)

Matrix form	Description	Example
Simple (two-dimensional) matrix structures		
Standard	Profit centers superimposed (to a varying extent) on an elementary structure.	P&G: "line boss and functional boss". Time Warner: holding company.
Two-hat	On set of VPs who each wear two hats, i.e. play two roles.	Royal Dutch Shell.
Baton-pass	Leadership is passed between the two matrix managers depending on business needs.	Consumer goods industry: baton-pass depending on the cycle of "revitalization and relaunch".
Complex matrix structures		
Matrix within a matrix	Matrix replicated at successive levels of the organization.	Mars Pet Foods.
Three dimensional structures	The third dimension is often "the consequence of doing business internationally". Companies have, for example, a functional dimension, a product dimension and a geographical region dimension.	Nestle, ABB.
More than three dimensional structures	The fourth dimension can be a customer dimension, with for example, the "front-back" hybrid structure. This structure has the front-end as a customer facing dimension organized by geography, customer segments, or both and a back-end organized around business units and large scale functions.	IBM.

These different kinds of matrix organizations make it all the more difficult to come to one concluding definition of a matrix organization, although it seems that most recent writing tends to concentrate on the concept of a elementary structure with (at least) one added dimension. Wolf and Egelhoff (2012) find three categories of matrix organizations, the function-product matrix, the product region matrix, the function-region matrix and additionally the three-dimensional matrix or tensor organization (Wolf & Egelhoff, 2012). Yet these structures still vary greatly, Sayles (1976), for example, writes that in fact the difference between different types of so-called matrix organizations could be found to be as great as the differences between a matrix and a non-matrix organization. Galbraith shows these variations when looking into more complex structures (at least three dimensional), as will be discussed in the following paragraph. These matrix organizations vary greatly from the classic two dimensional ones. In order to try to clarify these issues, some have defined matrix typologies such as Gobeli and Larson (1986), and Galbraith (2008). They have defined typologies for the matrix, analyzing the structure and placing different matrix organizations in categories, such as "functional", "balanced" and "project" matrix organizations for Gobeli and Larson (1987) or Galbraith (1971) who places matrix between the functional and product organization. More recently, Galbraith (2008) separated forms of matrix into simple (or two-dimensional) and complex (three dimensions or more) structures. Some academics even consider matrix not to be a permanent structure but rather a phase organizations go through when transitioning from an elementary structure to a project based organization (Ford and Randolph, 1992). It is interesting to see the broad range of matrix organizations which already existed in the past. This research will be furthering the understanding of a typology that is only briefly touched upon, namely the holding company matrix.

2.2.2 Decision Making in the Contemporary Matrix Organization

After this overview of existing literature on the matrix organization, a potential view of the contemporary matrix organization will be created. Based on the findings and theorization of the most recent authors on the topic, an outlook for the contemporary matrix organization, using the literature regarding the characteristics of the contemporary MNCs and the recent academic work on matrix structures will be developed.

To start with, one of the often mentioned issues is the speed of decision making in a matrix (Davis & Lawrence, 1977, Goold & Campbell, 2003; Galbraith, 2008; Wang et al., 2012; Wolf & Egelhoff, 2017), which can even develop into excessive group decision making (Sy & Cote, 2004). Moreover, not only might the decisions be slow, they may also be less effective. This could happen if these decisions do not have commitment from all dimensions of the matrix due to, for example, a lack of leadership buy-in (Sy & Cote, 2004). Although the classical matrix organization did not always have a balance of power in terms of decision making, it was the general idea that this should theoretically be the case (Davis and Lawrence 1977). Wolf and Egelhoff (2017) offer two examples of how this tendency to assume that decision making should be balanced can lead to the speed and effectiveness of said decision making being impacted. The first example they describe is of Texas Instruments (Vancil, 1984), where the firm would use its three dimensional matrix to make decisions. When the company grew, the balanced decision making was no longer sustainable, as it led to delays and a drop in firm performance. Another example they cite is that of California Bank (1978), where the balanced decision making led to high costs, poor customer service and slow decision making. In both these cases, the matrix was considered a failure.

Today, Wolf and Egelhoff (2017) found that the mode of decision making in today's matrix organizations is moving away from the balanced-mode, where both dimensions of the matrix have relatively equal power and make the decision jointly, towards a rule-based form of decision making, which pre-assigns decisions, formally or informally, to one dimension or another. This should lead to faster decisions and reduce conflict. However, this does lead to less exhaustive information processing. Therefore they developed a contingency theory, where they recommend that firms use both modes of decision making, taking into account the information processing capacities of both modes. The information processing capacities provide accountability, speed and lower cost for rule based decision making and innovation and thorough evaluation of alternatives in the case of balanced decision making. This should create a more flexible matrix. In the table below they have described their contingency theory for the use of balanced or rule based decision making.

Table 2: Balanced and rule based mode of decision making (Egelhoff & Wolf, 2017, p.133)

	Classical balanced mode	**New rule-based mode**
Influence of the two hierarchies on decisions	balanced	unbalanced
How decision-making operates	Reconciles divergent viewpoints of the two hierarchies through the exchange of information and, when necessary, escalation up the hierarchy	Rules and formally designed processes guide decision- making so there is less overlapping responsibility for specific decisions; escalation is available, but rarely required
Speed of decision-making	Slow	Fast
Nature of information processing	Rich, exhaustive, largely reciprocal information processing	Efficient, largely sequential information processing
Level of conflict	High, driven by shared responsibilities and different goals	Reduced, minimized by more narrowly-defined and non-overlapping responsibilities
Importance of shared values and culture	Very important Without shared values and culture, reconciliation of divergent viewpoints is difficult and too many decisions have to be escalated too far up the hierarchy	Less important Specified rules and processes make responsibilities clear and less overlapping, so shared values/ culture is less important

Egelhoff and Wolf (2017) explain that due to the radically different nature of the information processing capacity of both modes of decision making, contemporary matrix organizations should use both modes based on the requirements of the decision in terms of information processing. They assume that this would result in a better quality of decision making due to the fit between the mode of decision making and the information processing requirements. This would therefore create a more flexible matrix, which could actually surpass any hierarchical structure in its information processing capacity. This would facilitate low-cost and fast decisions when required, thanks to the use of rule based decision making, and a better exploration of alternatives and potential for innovation using balanced decision making. This flexible matrix that they describe seems to differ from both the previous examples of the balanced matrix as well as the solely rule-based organizations which seem to be used in companies today. Indeed companies today can more easily measure the benefits of a rule-based organization, as the advantages are speed, low-cost and accountability, which can become apparent rather easily. In contrast, the advantages of the balanced decision making mode (innovation and evaluation of alternatives) provide less immediate results and are not as easy to evaluate. This is part of why Egelhoff and Wolf (2017) have developed this contingency theory, as it provides theory to support the use of both modes. By using this contingency theory, firms should be able to be more flexible, adapting to the information processing needs of each situation. Furthermore, they explain that there is an added benefit in using the different modes of decision making in order to make MNCs more flexible, as the decision making mode can more easily be changed and modified than the stiffer characteristics of a company such as its hierarchical structure. This allows the firm to adapt to change within their strategy or environment in a more flexible way.

Table 3: Contingency theory for rule-based or balanced decisions (Egelhoff & Wolf, 2017, p.143)

Types of information-processing capacity	Level of information-processing capacities provided by:	
	Balanced mode	**Rule-based mode**
Accountability during decision-making	Low	High
Speed of decision-making (in terms of elapsed time)	Low	High
Economizing on human and monetary costs during decision-making	Low	High
Novelty and innovativeness of alternatives generated	High	Low
Thoroughness with which alternatives are evaluated	High	Low

This concept is very interesting to us for multiple reasons. To start with it offers, as explained above, an opportunity for more flexible decision making in MNCs. Furthermore, this is still a theoretical concept which has yet to be developed and understood empirically. Indeed, these authors mention that they have yet to observe it in any organization but they estimate that it is currently being developed within the contemporary MNC. Being able to observe this in an existing organization could offer insight into how this is applied in the field and offer avenues for further development of the concept. On top of that, as Egelhoff and Wolf also explain, having this type of flexible matrix could be a significant advantage in responding to the requirements for a more ambidextrous organization (O'Reilly & Tushman 2011, Wolf & Egelhoff, 2017). Therefore the next section will describe the views of Egelhoff and Wolf on the potential for ambidexterity issuing from this contingency theory and its use.

2.2.3   The Question of Innovation in a Matrix Organization

This section will look into the question of innovation in matrix organizations. It will start by giving a brief overview of the theoretical ideas existing regarding innovation before going into the model recently developed by Egelhoff and Wolf concerning the role a flexible matrix could potentially play in the ambidexterity of an MNC. When looking into the idea of innovation and matrix organizations, little research on the topic has been found, although some do mention that matrix could facilitate the finding of solutions which are innovative to deal with technical problems which are complex (Sy & Cote, 2004); this idea is yet to be empirically developed.

Innovation is key for MNCs and has often been found to be an important factor for long term success. Because companies who renew and acquire new knowledge are better able to understand their changing environments and respond to them, knowledge has been found to be an antecedent of innovation (Crossan & Apaydin, 2010, Jimenéz-Jimenéz et al., 2014, Tippins and Sohi, 2003). Furthermore, MNCs have more opportunities for knowledge gain as their subsidiaries operate in different markets, with different cultures and potentially different ideas. Therefore MNCs can innovate by gathering and sharing knowledge from their subsidiaries (Almeida & Phene, 2004). However, in order to do this, MNCs need to be able to transfer this knowledge from the different locations, which is a complex task. In general when looking into knowledge transfer within organizations, the research has focused on the HQ-subsidiary transfer (Minbaeva, 2008). However more recently there has been an interest in reverse knowledge transfer; the transfer of knowledge between subsidiaries and headquarters (Rabbiosi, 2011). On top of that, not only does the knowledge need to be transferred, but the receiving party needs to be able to absorb this knowledge and use it to innovate (Andersson, 2003). This is where the importance of learning comes into play.

In our research, we will study the question of innovation, knowledge and learning together, in order to understand the impact that the matrix organization has on the innovative capacities of the MNC. In particular, we will look into the impact that the decision making style used within the matrix affects these processes, based on the model developed by Egelhoff and Wolf regarding rule based and balanced decision making. Furthermore it would be interesting to empirically study what they have theoretically proposed regarding the potential for ambidexterity offered by a flexible matrix. In this section we will give an overview of the theoretical concept developed by Egelhoff and Wolf pertaining to the potential advantages of a flexible matrix organization for the ambidexterity of firms. The question of the exploration versus exploitation challenge of firms is not a new one. These two activities are fundamental for company survival; the first pertaining to the exploration of new ideas and opportunities while the second can be described as continuing operations in order to respond to the current business demands. One could picture this in terms of long term versus short term goals for a company (March, 1991). These two activities are both essential to a company's survival. However, due to often limited resources, companies often find themselves having to make choices, both implicit and explicit regarding these two directions (Egelhoff & Wolf, 2017). Based upon this, the concept of ambidexterity was developed and can be defined as "an organization's ability to be aligned and efficient in its management of today's business demands while simultaneously being adaptive to changes in the environment" (Raisch & Birkinshaw, 2008, p.375). Ambidexterity is being viewed as increasingly important, due to the dynamic and changing nature of the business environment meaning that companies need to both be efficient and reach their short term goals as well as be able to adapt to this dynamic environment in order to survive. The research on ambidexterity is still in its infancy, and there is little knowledge on how to actually successfully implement ambidexterity in an MNC (Raisch & Birkinshaw, 2008). Egelhoff and Wolf explain that, in their opinion, although it is difficult to generalize based on the existing literature, exploration is usually associated to more organic structures and exploitation to more mechanistic structures (He & Wong, 2004). In general ambidexterity is usually achieved by having separate units deal with exploration and exploitation and having a common purpose they interact around. By having these boundaries between the units, the different goals, behaviors and subcultures are protected. It seems that the integration between these units happens in targeted manner, for example through informal networking or the creation of task forces with participants from both units. According to Egelhoff and Wolf, much of the literature focuses on the importance of these informal relations, yet some also found that formal organizational mechanisms were also used (Jansen et al., 2009).

Using the concept of the flexible matrix organization, which can change its decision making style from balanced to rule-based, Egelhoff & Wolf suggest that because they can change the kind of information processing in a flexible way, such organizations have the potential to be more ambidextrous. Indeed, the information processing capacities of balanced-decision making fit the information processing requirements of exploration, and rule-based decision making can be associated to exploitation. If the company has the ability to flexibly change between these two modes of decision making, it could therefore also potentially be more ambidextrous. The flexible matrix structure could create the opportunity for ambidexterity at the highest levels of MNCs. As Egelhoff and Wolf mention, this concept is currently just a theoretical construct which has yet to be observed empirically. Therefore, it would be interesting to see how this concept potentially comes to life in large multinationals, as we will have the opportunity to do in this research.

2.2.4   Relevance and Associated Research Questions

As can be seen in this section, considerable work has been done on matrix organizations over the last fifty years, not only to define a matrix organization but also on the topic of understanding what drives companies to implement such a structure and its success factors. We have seen in the previous section, that the matrix advantages and disadvantages, in particular the issues of decision making and the structure's apparently conflictual nature has been well observed (Davis & Lawrence, 1977, Sayles, 1976). There is however still much work to be done. Indeed, although there is a lot of literature on the topic, only a minority of it is based on empirical data and a lot of it is now quite dated. Furthermore, the findings are often conflictual, and the range of types of matrix organizations which have been studied is very wide.

Overall, it seems that research would greatly benefit from further understanding matrix organizations in today's context. As Egelhoff and Wolf (2017) wrote, it is necessary to restudy the matrix organization in order to understand how they are used in the contemporary MNC. Indeed, it seems that many companies may be using some form of matrix organization and it would then be possible to analyze the drivers of matrix implementation in a modern and empirical context. This leaves a very wide field of possibilities for research. To start with, one of the main issues of the past matrix organizations apparently came from the decision making being reportedly slower and conflictual. Egelhoff and Wolf (2017), the primary researchers on the topic of matrix organizations today propose that the contemporary matrix in fact would benefit from a different decision making model, namely having not only balanced, but also rule-based decision making. Indeed, in the past, matrix organizations were assumed to have balanced decision making styles, whereas it seems that today these structures would benefit from some kind of rule-based decision making. Accordingly, this thesis will focus on decision making in a matrix organization and in particular attempt to further understand the antecedents and consequences of these different modes of decision making as described by Egelhoff and Wolf.

Secondly, it would be interesting to build on the theoretical concepts developed by Egelhoff and Wolf concerning the flexible matrix organization. The idea would be to use these two modes of decision making, on a contingency basis, leading to a more flexible matrix organization. However, as they note, this research is still in its infancy, and remains to be more deeply empirically observed, which leads to the research question the topic. They have developed an interesting theoretical concept on the potential value of such a flexible matrix for innovation. Indeed, the concept of ambidexterity, and balancing the conflicting goal of exploration and exploitation could potentially be facilitated by the information processing capacities of a flexible matrix. This has further value as it not only builds on the more recent matrix literature but will also allow us to further understand the issues mentioned in the classic matrix literature, notably the use of a matrix organization to deal with dual environmental pressures. However, the concept of a flexible matrix still remains to be empirically understood, which we will attempt to contribute to in this research.

2.3 Conflicts, Negotiations and Power Capabilities in the MNC

The closely linked concepts of power and conflict are important when analyzing matrix organizations. The social space of the matrix organization can be considered to be a "contested terrain" (Morgan, 2001) where actors have different goals, practices, expectations and power resources leading to conflicts and negotiations. Indeed, a matrix organizational structure amounts to giving power over certain decisions to two (or more) dimensions, where in a hierarchical structure this power would be allocated to one dimension only. Moreover, according to Sy & Cote (2004), matrix creates a "constant state of conflict". In fact, one of the reasons matrix was abandoned as an organization structure is the excessive conflict and subsequent excessive bureaucracy created to deal with it (Egelhoff & Wolf, 2017). It does seem logical that matrix would naturally create task conflict, as it increases interdependency within two dimensions with different goals, with managers from different functions, (Davis & Lawrence, 1977, Wolf & Egelhoff, 2013) who in certain situations share jurisdictions and economic outcomes (Chi & Nystrom, 1998). In order to understand these concepts within the IB field and, before looking more closely into the implications for matrix structures, the literature on conflict and power will be reviewed. It must be noted that a large part of the literature used concerns itself with headquarter-subsidiary relationship conflict and power relations. This literature is highly relevant to the empirical research of this thesis, as it will concern a "holding company matrix" structure (Galbraith, 2009), which is a matrix where one dimension is made up of the corporate functions (headquarters) and the other dimension is represented by the brands, or subsidiaries. It is therefore conceivable that the conflicts and power relations in this matrix would be comparable to those in a headquarter – subsidiaries relationship. This review will start by reviewing the literature on conflict in MNCs. Next, the literature on power capabilities in MNCs will be explained.

2.3.1   Conflict in MNCs

When defining conflict, most agree that "conflict always entails some kind of opposition, tension or incompatibility" (Blazejewski & Becker-Ritterspach, 2011, p141). Authors however make different emphasis, such as Deutsch (1973) who defines conflict as occurring as a consequence of incompatible activities, or others who focus on the goals and interests incompatibility (such as Jameson, 1999 and Rössing, 2005). Thomas (1992) adds another 2 dimensions: perceptions and process. He theorizes that incompatibilities only result in conflict if they are perceived as frustrating and that at least one of the actors involved acts on said incompatibility. It is therefore likely that many conflicts simply do not occur; if the actor does not notice this incompatibility or does not express the frustration resulting from the incompatibility. Schotter and Beamish (2011) include in their definition of conflict most of these aspects. Although they include the perception of incompatibility they do not include the prerequisite action of at least one of the actors involved in an incompatibility from Thomas's (1992) definition.

> *"Conflict is the awareness on the part of the parties involved of discrepancies, goal incompatibility, or irreconcilable desires. Conflict is based on interest divergence, information asymmetry between actors, or perception gaps of more than one party with an interdependent relationship." (Schotter and Beamish 2011, p. 195)*

Thomas (1992) makes a theoretical distinction between "conflict processes and the structure in which the process occurs" (Thomas, 1992, p266). The process model concerns itself with "the temporal sequence of events which occur as the system operates – e.g. the mental and behavioral activities of the conflicting parts" (Thomas, 1992, p267). It looks into the steps that occur within the conflict process while considering the environmental factors surrounding said conflict as a given. "Conflict management strategies in the processual model concentrates on the modification of actors' perception, motivation and behavior in conflict situations" (Blazejewski and Becker-Ritterspach, 2011, p147). Within this model, four phases of conflict are identified. The first is "frustration", the second "conflict conceptualization", the third "behavior" and the last "outcome" (Thomas, 1992). Conflict management research using the process model therefore plots conflict management actions against the individual phases of conflict (Blazejewski and Becker-Ritterspach, 2011). The structural approach, on the other hand, focuses on the structure and context in which the conflict occurs, on "the more or less stable (slow changing) conditions which shape or control the system's process" (Thomas 1992, p267). In this case, Thomas (1992) sees how the context, including organizational processes, norms and incentives, affects the conflict. Blazejewski & Becker-Ritterspach (2011) extend this concept to include the larger MNC environment: home/host country institutions, socio-cultural, economic and political influences on the conflict.

Conflict can be analyzed on different levels, going from intra-personal, inter-personal, intra-group, intra-organizational / inter-group, inter-organizational and international (Blazejewski & Becker-Ritterspach, 2011). According to Blazejewski and Becker-Ritterspach (2011), the most investigated levels are the intra-group and interpersonal levels, with a focus on cultural diversity, inter-organizational conflict, especially between MNCs and external stakeholders and intra organizational conflict, with a high quantity of research focused on the headquarter – subsidiary relationship. Although conflict is often pictured as negative, this does not necessarily need to be the case. Schotter and Beamish (2011), for example, explain Pondy's (1967) view of conflict as "a normal consequence of managing" that firms should "internalize" rather than eliminate (Schotter and Beamish, 2011, p194). Galbraith (2009) also sees conflict as natural in a matrix organization. Indeed, conflict can be divided into two categories, functional and dysfunctional. Functional conflict is a conflict in which the outcome improves firm performance whereas dysfunctional conflict leads to reduced firm performance (Menon et al. 1996, Schotter & Beamish, 2011). According to Bartlett and Ghoshal (1989), a key element to avoiding conflicts with dysfunctional outcomes is making sure that the managers have the right mindset. Bartlett and Ghoshal (1990) later also address this more specifically in the context of a matrix, calling it "making a matrix in the manager's mind", which will be discussed in more detail when reviewing the literature focused on matrix organizations.

More recently, organizational conflict has been divided into three categories: relationship, task and process conflict. Task conflict revolves around unemotional and rational differences in opinion. Process conflict concerns how a goal should be achieved and finally relationship conflict is about interpersonal incompatibilities and involves emotion. All three of these types of conflict will be found at the same time within a conflict; it is the distributed levels of conflict which are important, that is the proportion of each type of conflict in relation to the total amount of conflict. (Schotter and Beamish, 2011). Task conflict can lead to more effective decisions, due to better group decision quality and acceptance (Simons & Peterson, 2000). However, Simons and Peterson (2000) warn that if this task conflict lasts too long or is too frequent, this could lead to poor decisions, linked to group satisfaction sinking. Another issue, would be that the naturally occurring task conflict turns into relationship conflict which, according to Simons & Peterson (2000), leads to ineffective decisions. Jehn and Mannix (2001) also found that low levels of relationship conflict is associated with higher group performance. Simons and Peterson (2000) find that trust, the expectation that the other will fulfil their commitments and will behave in an ethical, dependable and socially appropriate manner (Gefen et al., 2003), is essential in hindering task conflict from turning into relationship conflict. Jehn and Mannix (2001) add the importance of having similar value systems and open discussion during conflict as a success factor for functional conflict. Egelhoff and Wolf (2013), when studying conflict in matrix organizations further divide task conflict into three categories, most relevant to matrix organizations: goal, authority and evaluation conflict. This will be further discussed in the next section.

Blazejewski and Becker-Ritterspach (2011) identified the general causes for conflicts in MNCs as being the following: the heterogeneity of cultures, the heterogeneity of stakeholder interests, the heterogeneity of institutional contexts and the contested allocation of limited resources. We can also note that one goal of conflict can also be changing or distributing the balance of power (Blazejewski & Becker-Ritterspach, 2011). Conflict can be a way of maintaining or gaining power in a relationship, which is "often viewed as a primary goal of conflict" (Blazejewski and Becker-Ritterspach, 2011, p176) and Blazejewski and Becker-Ritterspach (2011) explain that authors such as Bachrach and Baratz (1969) or Dahl (1963) even state that power relations only come into existence as a response to conflict. In the "power over" view, power can be an antecedent, a cause for conflict, the asymmetrical distribution of power creating potentially conflicting interests. Furthermore, in the "power to" view, power can also be used as a means to resolve the conflict, for example using personal power in order to solve the conflict. It can also be used to structure the conflict, by setting the hierarchy, for example. Moreover, it can shape the methods of resolution as the "powerful also largely determine what is important, fair and just in most settings" (Coleman, 2006, p121). Moreover power may even be able to prevent conflict from occurring or even being perceived (Hardy, 1996)

We will now review the theories which can be used to understand conflict in an MNC. It must be noted that Blazejewski & Becker-Ritterspach (2011), in their comprehensive review of conflict in headquarter-subsidiary relationships, also add theories which will not be comprehensively reviewed here, due to a lack of relevance in the conflict and power issues in matrix organizations. The first theory used is the contingency theory. The basis of this theory is that companies face two "fundamental environmental forces" (Blazejewski & Becker-

Ritterspach, 2011, p148), namely pressure from the headquarters' environment and from the subsidiaries' environment. These forces have also been labeled "forces for global integration" and "forces for national differentiation" by Bartlett and Ghoshal (1989), who also add a need for worldwide innovation to these two forces. These pressures can create conflicting interests leading to frequent conflicts on key strategic decisions. A solution to these issues often suggested in international management research is in fact a matrix organization of some sort (Schotter & Beamish, 2011; Bartlett & Ghoshal, 1989). Secondly, resource dependency theory is based on the fact that power is based on the control of rare strategic resources which are essential to deal with the external environment (Pfeffer & Salanik, 1978). This theory was first used to understand inter-organizational relationships but it can also be used to explain inter-unit relationships within the MNC (Schotter & Beamish, 2011). The physical manifestation of this power within the MNC can be seen through budget and resource allocations within the organization, for example. From this power, subsidiaries can draw bargaining power, allowing them to "influence the division of contested resources" (Mudambi & Pedersen, 2007, p2) and resist control from Headquarters. This allows subsidiaries to 'own' their decision rights and makes it harder to revoke them, rather than the 'loaned' decision rights. Indeed, in a "classic" MNC, the headquarters own decisions and only allow subsidiaries agency by 'loaning' the decision rights, whereas in a more networked view of an MNC, subsidiaries will have more bargaining power. Although some of the aspects of the relationships between units come from the structural aspects of an MNC, which can be explained through agency theory (Mudambi & Pedersen, 2007), the bargaining power drawn from the control of scarce resources is essential to understand the negotiations between the units (Schotter & Beamish, 2011). Looking at these two theories used to understand conflict in the MNC, we can see that this is relevant in the context of a matrix organization. Indeed, the first, contingency theory, deals with the conflicting environmental forces that the headquarters and subsidiaries face. In a holding company matrix organization, one could consider this to be an obvious potential source of conflict. Furthermore the additional dimension of the need for worldwide global innovation (Bartlett and Ghoshal, 1989) once again brings up the issue of ambidexterity, which has already been touched upon in the previous section, with the theoretical proposal by Egelhoff and Wolf (2017) for the use of a flexible matrix to address this issue. The potential use of a matrix organization to address these issues is interesting. Bringing together the dimensions, and therefore the interest of both parties through the use of matrix organization, effectively creates the arena necessary to solve the conflict. Furthermore resource dependency theory is essential when considering a holding matrix organization. Indeed, in this case the subsidiaries control substantial resources, giving them considerable bargaining power. It will therefore be interesting to see how the use of a matrix as a coordination mechanism can enable the headquarters to leverage their power capabilities.

Now if we look into the case of conflict within a matrix organization, we can see that conflict plays a central role in matrix literature. According to Sy & Cote (2004), matrix creates a "constant state of conflict" and Gos (2015), in his mixed literature review on the advantages and disadvantages of matrix organizations, found most researchers deem this a reason against matrix implementation. It seems logical that matrix would naturally create task conflict, as it increases interdependency within two dimensions with different goals, managers from different functions, (Davis & Lawrence, 1977, Wolf & Egelhoff, 2013) and in certain situations share jurisdictions and economic outcomes (Chi & Nystrom, 1998). Indeed, Davis and Lawrence (1977) explain that the large number of interdependencies in a matrix structure contributes to more communication as well as interaction between the different parties and dimensions, thus increasing the chances of developing conflict. They also note that conflicts are more likely to arise between people with different functions and roles, as well as usually different orientations and attitudes (Davis & Lawrence, 1977). This is interesting, as it brings up the question of organizational culture, and the consequences of bringing them together in a matrix. This will be addressed further in the section on culture. Moreover, since the power is divided within the different dimensions of the matrix, it is conceivable that power struggles are more likely to occur (Egelhoff & Wolf, 2017). It will therefore be interesting to look further into the issue of power in a matrix organization, which will be done in the next section. Overall it seems that the different goals and cultures, which are brought together through the matrix organization, leading to interdependency, is the source of intra-organizational conflict in the matrix organization. However, Galbraith (2008) considers conflict to be natural in a matrix organization. He in fact considers conflict to be a sign that the matrix structure is working, and that if conflict does not arise, it means that it is being hidden and dealt with in a dysfunctional way. He therefore sees conflict resolution as an essential and natural part of matrix management (Galbraith, 2009).

The evidence that there is more conflict in a matrix organization than in an elementary structure is mostly supported by case studies and the logic that bringing dimensions with conflicting interests together is bound to increase the amount of conflict in the organization (Wolf and Egelhoff, 2013). There has since been evidence that the amount of conflict is not necessarily higher in a matrix MNC than in an elementary structure MNC. The type of matrix structure may influence this fact, as Wolf and Egelhoff (2013) showed in their study of 82 German MNCs. In their study, they focused on three sorts of task-conflict, most relevant to the matrix organization, which they classified as goal, authority and evaluation. Because many of the reported conflicts in a matrix structure are related to the conflicting goals of the different dimensions (Davis & Lawrence, 1977; Janger 1983; Galbraith, 2009) , which makes sense as the matrix attempts to give value to the goals of both dimensions equally in such a structure, considering conflicts issuing from differing goals seems appropriate (Egelhoff & Wolf, 2017). Then, literature often finds conflict over who has the authority in decision making within matrix organizations (Peters, 1979). Therefore authority conflict is considered. Finally, Egelhoff and Wolf (2017), also add evaluation conflict as a potential source for conflict in a matrix, as they see the fact that people interacting from different dimensions bringing up potential conflicts due to the fact that these individuals will have different conceptual frameworks and perspectives linked to their varying experiences and backgrounds. This is an interesting perspective for this research in particular as we have chosen to look into the issue of culture in a matrix organization, and therefore the potentially differing cultures in the dimensions could be a source of evaluation conflict. In this research Egelhoff and Wolf found higher levels of task conflict (goal, authority, evaluation) only in matrices which combined product divisions and geographical regions. They theorized, as both these dimensions tend to organize as profit centers, that it could be because profit issues are harder to solve horizontally than vertically. Although this study has its limitations, notably that it used only one respondent per firm, it does show that there is still much to be learned on this topic and intra-organizational conflict cannot be outright classified as a barrier to matrix implementation.

Overall, there are diverging views on conflict in a matrix organization. It seems that the fact that matrix organizations have more conflict than elementary structures is in question, based on the recent research by Wolf and Egelhoff. Furthermore, the two views of conflict, as a disadvantage of the matrix organization, and a reason for the abandon of the structure in opposition with Galbraith's view of matrix conflict as a natural occurrence of the structure once again highlights the complexity and heterogeneity of understanding on matrix organizations.

2.3.2   Power in MNCs

As mentioned above, the issue of power is relevant when considering matrix organizations, as the confrontation of multiple dimensions with potentials conflicting goals can lead to power struggles. Furthermore, the balance of power is important to the basic concept of the matrix. Power is closely linked to conflict and decision making in the classic conceptualization of a matrix. In the classic literature on the matrix, while the balance of power often shifts from one dimension to the other, due to changes in strategies, environments and the characteristics of managers, there is still a measure of equal power and influence between the dimensions (Egelhoff & Wolf, 2017; Davis & Lawrence, 1978). However, the CEO of Dow Chemical claimed to have an unstable matrix (Davis & Lawrence, 1977) where the weak dimension had to be supported in order to not lose power. Kuprenas (2001) also reported the issue that the functional side becomes more powerful than project dimension, leading to a lack of project level focus. However, if we consider the flexible matrix, this unbalance of power is deliberate and constantly changing with decision-making assigned to one dimension or the other (Egelhoff & Wolf, 2017). Power is an important, or even the "most central concept" (Clegg et al., 2006, p1) when researching organizations. If we take a micro-political view, organizations can be understood as "fundamentally political entities" (Pfeffer, 1992) and therefore the notion of power must be investigated. In this next section we will start by defining the notion of power and what this means in the MNC before looking into how the actors can leverage their power and finally looking into the potential role of power in a matrix organization.

Over the years, power has been defined in many ways. Dahl (1957) is one of the most relevant authors, who researched power on the community level and linked it to the decision making process (Clegg, 1989; Lukes, 1986; Pfeffer, 1981). This next section will look into the various dimensions of power and in particular the three dimensional view. Clegg et al. (2006) state that power can be viewed from 2 angles. The first, "power over", is a mechanical view of power as negative and prohibitive, being "exercised either when people and things are made to do something that they would not otherwise do or when their preferences, dispositions or natures to do something are arrested or stopped in some way" (Clegg et al., 2006, p191). The second, more positive view of power, "power to", views power as facilitative; it is "creative, it accomplishes acts, and it changes the nature of things and relations" (Clegg et al., 2006, p191). Moodley et al (2016) find that "power is generally defined in terms of a relationship, whereby an agent influences, or attempts to influence, a target with the intended outcome being some form of action or behavioral change". Andersson et al (2007) find two types of definition of power, the first set of definitions answers the questions "power to do what?". This includes definitions such as "power enabling actors in an organization to overcome resistance from other actors" or the "power to mobilize resources to accomplish a certain end" and finally the "power to control premises of actions, such that the power becomes almost unobservable". The second type of definition of power answers the question "who possesses the power?" and where this power originates, either in personal power bases such as reputation or charisma or in power sources such as authority or access to scarce resources (Andersson et al, 2007). Clegg et al. (2006) describe a one, two and three dimension view of power. They first describe the liberal one-dimensional view of power, "getting others to do what they wouldn't otherwise do" which is how Dahl (1957) understood power. Then the reformist two-dimensional power, which adds to the first dimension a second dimension, "agenda setting and issue shaping of preferences". Last, Lukes (1974) conceptualizes the radical three-dimensional view of power, which adds the "hegemony occluding appreciation of real interest" (Clegg et al., 2006, p.213). Within IB literature, it seems that the explicit mention of power and politics tends to be avoided, yet widely recognized (Mudambi, 2011; Pfeffer, 1992). Indeed, in practice, Gandz and Murray found that managers recognized and considered the use of power and politics in their organizations to be common and successful, yet they disliked that fact. However, it seems that politics in an organization may just be a fact to be accepted (Ferris & Kacmar, 1992), and therefore in order to understand them, companies should be treated as political beings (Pfeffer, 1992) and that the presence of politics in the organization must be accepted and understood.

Politics in the organization can be understood using the following definition, "organizational politics involves those activities taken within organizations to acquire, develop, and use power and other resources to obtain one's preferred outcomes in a situation in which there is uncertainty or dissent about choices." (Pfeffer, 1981, p. 7). Ferner et al (2011) also use a Lukesian perspective on power in their article on the transfer of human resource and employment practices in MNCs. They use Hardy's (1996) terminology of the three dimensions of power. The first, the power of resources, which is the power which comes from controlling scarce resources. The second, the power of processes, which influences the decision making processes, sets the "rules of the game", including determining which actors can participate in said decisions. Third, the power of meaning, the "way in which organizational groups legitimize their own demands and 'delegitimize' those of other through the management of meaning and the deployment of symbolic action" (Ferner et al, 2011). The power of meaning is especially important in the transfer of practices as it leads to making visible and challenging previously invisible and taken-for-granted institutional processes.

In the case of headquarter-subsidiary relationship, Ferner et al. (2011) describe the power capabilities of the headquarters and the subsidiaries. For headquarters this includes for example the power to allocate resources among the subsidiaries, shape the way decisions are made and define corporate culture, for the power of resources, process and meaning, respectively. From the subsidiary side, they can achieve power of resources, for example, by bringing in a large amount of the company's profit. Although the power of processes tends to stay within the headquarters, subsidiaries can use their power of resources to influence the decision-making processes, by influencing the way "global policies or practices are designed" (Ferner et al., 2011, p.178). Furthermore, Ferner et al. (2011) also note that practices developed in leading economies, sectors or firms have more resources of power because of their better economic situation, leading to "dominance effects". Through their ability to influence the rules for decision making they obtain power over processes. On top of that, actors from the "dominant side" will assume that their practices are superior, and this may also be the case for the host as the practice could be regarded as a 'best practice' on a global level. (Ferner et al., 2011). These dominance effects can help smooth the transfer of practices as they supply the dominant side with power of resources, process and counteract power of meaning from the host (as the practice is already accepted as a best practice). Within this research we will be using Ferner's terms and definitions of power.

In the context of the transfer of practices in MNCs, Ferner et al. (2011) distinguish actors and their divergent interests. These interests diverge between headquarter actors and subsidiary actors as well as within these groups, between managers and employees, for example in the case of a practice which impacts employee interests in a subsidiary but not those of managers. In this case the managers may help the transfer of a practice, overcoming internal obstacles by acting as a Trojan horse (Tempel et. al., 2006) for the headquarters. The factors influencing whether the transfer of practice will be accepted include the "criticality" of the practice; how disruptive it is to the subsidiary. Another factor influencing whether a practice will be accepted or resisted by a subsidiary manager is the career aspirations of said managers. Indeed, managers with international career aspirations may act in favor of HQ whereas managers who see their future in the subsidiary will focus on the interest of the subsidiary. Based on the interest of these actors they may support or oppose the transfer. This can be done in an overt manner, or the resistance may be less visible. For example the subsidiary may comply in a ceremonial manner only, or adapt the practice, a "hybridization" to better fit subsidiary interests. Indeed, research has empirically shown that subsidiaries may abandon or reject the roles assigned to them by Headquarters (Dörrenbächer & Gammelgaard 2006; Morgan & Kristensen 2006). This can be due to other opportunities within local environments perceived as more lucrative, or as mentioned above, the managers' own aspirations and interest in improving their standing within the organization, or simply a different perception of their role as more independent, leading to initiative taking (Dörrenbächer and Gammelgaard 2011). This can then be perceived by the headquarters either as valuable, as this kind of initiative taking can lead to better local capabilities and knowledge leading to competitive advantage, or viewed as insubordination. Here, the view of the headquarters is important, as the headquarters may then employ tighter control mechanisms in order to ensure that the subsidiary follows the goals of the headquarters and the roles assigned to them. Therefore subsidiaries need to be aware of the power capabilities and the subsequent autonomy and room for initiative that these allow (Dörrenbächer & Gammelgaard, 2006). Another important factor to consider in these power considerations are the intentions of the headquarters. Indeed, the need to deploy power capabilities in order to achieve a certain level of autonomy is contingent on the headquarters intent to not grant this autonomy to certain extent. However, as we have seen in the previous sections, it seems that the role of the headquarters in the contemporary MNC is changing, and the subsidiaries are taking on a more important role, as the value added bottom up contributions is seen as competitive advantage. If we look into the M&A literature, there is an interesting concept which can contribute to our research, the idea of "partnering". Instead of integrating acquisitions (Kale et al., 2009), where the acquirer will leave the operational autonomy of their new subsidiary intact, allowing them to preserve their identity. Kale et al. describe this phenomenon in MNCs from emerging countries. Here the headquarters will keep their acquisitions separate and focus on key synergies which can be obtained while avoiding disrupting the subsidiaries operations. Here they will use key links such as boundary spanners and task forces both to identify and then exploit the opportunities for synergies. We will go into more detail on this concept and how it operationalized in the following sections. For now, looking into the power capabilities deployed by subsidiaries and headquarters it is clear that in a case such as this, the desire for control from the headquarters is very much different to the usual headquarter subsidiary relationship. It will be interesting to further research this topic and in particular discover how a holding company matrix is used to deploy these capabilities.

2.3.3   Relevance and Associated Research Questions

In this section, we have observed that there are different views and perspectives on conflict, and more precisely, the causes and role of conflict in a matrix organization still need to be further empirically understood. Indeed, Egelhoff and Wolf have developed an interesting framework for researching the sources of task conflict in a matrix, which could be further built on to understand how this conflict appears and the role in plays in the matrix. The role of conflict is in fact still up to debate, with the different views of conflict as one the negative aspects of the matrix versus a natural occurrence in such structures, as presented by Galbraith (2009). As such it would be interesting to look into how conflict manifests itself and what the sources of this conflict is in a matrix organization. Indeed, the research as we have described it tends to have a more quantitative approach towards conflict in a matrix, looking into how much conflict occurs compared to an elementary structure.

Furthermore, there is a research gap on the topic of conflict and power in MNCs. Blazejewski and Becker-Ritterspach (2011) suggest further research on this topic, specifically in MNCs and not only within headquarter-subsidiary relationships. Indeed, it seems that the subsidiary – subsidiary relationship remains a "black-box" in IB literature (Schmid & Maurer, 2011) making it an interesting topic for further research. Blazejewski and Becker-Ritterspach (2011) state that one of the areas where further theoretical development is needed in conflict research is the relationship between conflict and power. They explain that power and conflict are closely related in conflict theory (Clegg et al, 2007). They suggest themes such as "the power or resource mobilization strategies actors can and will employ to wage the conflict in their interest", analyzing power distributions in various contexts, finally looking into how conflict impacts the power distribution. This thesis will contribute to that in the context of matrix organizations, where, as explained above, the concepts of conflict and power play a central role. Therefore this thesis will look into the power capabilities deployed by the actors in matrix organization. Furthermore, there is a clear requirement not only for further research on contemporary matrix organizations in general, but also on the specific issue of conflict in a matrix organization (Wolf & Egelhoff, 2013).

2.4 Towards a Dynamic View of Culture in the Matrix

The MNC is a distinct form of organization because it operates in different countries. This has a significant impact on the organization as it leads to greater uncertainty due to the weakly institutionalized context of international activities. Due to this, the international business environment, in comparison to the national environment, is less organized and predictable (Whitley, 2001).

When cultures collide, as has been researched in the case of mergers, acquisitions or international joint ventures, the norms, values and basic assumptions of one group are confronted with different cultural contexts. What has before been taken for granted may no longer be true in this new context. This can cause high levels of annoyance, hostility and stress, potentially leading to negative outcomes in the case of post-acquisition mergers and acquisitions such as employee resistance, low job satisfaction and high turnover rates (Lee et al., 2015). The topic of culture will be addressed, including the literature related to culture in mergers and acquisitions as well as international joint ventures, since these situations could be comparable to those of bringing two dimensions of a matrix together. Furthermore, culture can be used as a strategic tool in the MNC. According to Ybema and Byun (2011), culture can be used as a "symbolic and strategic tool to promote own interests and identity". Depending on the power context, culture may be perceived differently. For example in a headquarter-subsidiary relationship context, country culture may be constructed in a different way by employees depending on if theirs is the home or host country and if they are the managers or the subordinates (e.g. when the Japanese are the bosses in the Netherlands, the Japanese culture is perceived as more hierarchical and when the Dutch are the bosses in Japan, the Dutch culture is perceived as more hierarchical). Moreover, culture can be used to legitimize or oppose the power asymmetry. For example, in MNCs, the management team with the home country culture, may be challenged by subsidiaries on this basis (Ybema & Byun, 2011). In the particular context of a matrix organization, culture has been touched upon, as a potential source of conflict (Davis

& Lawrence, 1977). However the role of culture in the contemporary matrix organization has rarely been empirically researched. The research done by Gos (2015), demonstrated that culture has a role to play in the matrix organization and that it may potentially contribute to the success of such a structure. In fact, he describes culture as a facilitating factor to deal with matrix conflict, an idea briefly shared by Egelhoff and Wolf (2017), where they mention that companies with a strong company culture and shared vision seem to have more limited or improving levels of conflict. However there is still a lack of empirical evidence and a need for more contributions on this topic. Indeed, apart from this finding by Gos and the brief mention by Egelhoff and Wolf, the role of culture in a matrix organization has yet to be developed in depth.

In this next section we will start by providing an overview of organizational culture, before describing the more recent concept of dynamic culture, which not only considers the different levels of culture, organizational, national and professional, but also interests itself in their interaction. Then we will look into the concept of creating a new culture and negotiated culture before finally addressing how these ideas are relevant in the context of a matrix organization.

2.4.1   Organizational Culture

A rich literature on the topic of culture has been developed by anthropologists, necessary in order to understand the ways in which culture around the world varies and how domestic and global management differ (Adler, 2002). According to Adler (2002), one of the most comprehensive and accepted definitions in anthropology is offered by Kroeber and Kluckhohn (1952) and is the following:

> *"Culture consists of patterns, explicit and implicit, of and for behavior acquired and transmitted by symbols, constituting the distinctive achievements of human groups, including their embodiments in artifacts; the essential core of culture consists of traditional (i.e. historically derived and selected) ideas and especially their attached values; culture systems may, on the one hand, be considered as products of action, and on the other as conditioning elements of further action." (Kroeber and Kluckhohn, 1952, p. 181)*

Another definition of culture is provided by Haggett (1975) as "patterns of behavior that form a durable template by which ideas and images can be transferred from one generation to another, or from one group to another" (p. 238). This is interesting as it presses the fact that culture is not innate but rather acquired due to social interactions within a group. Furthermore, it touches upon the durability of culture, meaning that change within culture is a slow process. Furthermore the concept of ideas and images is particularly important. These ideas and images are the basis for acceptable behaviors within a group. Therefore culture is partially represented by the rules in a group, either by laws or social norms (Wilson, 2001).

Looking at the available business literature now, Jones (2007) estimates that Bartels (1967) was the first to understand and demonstrate the importance of culture in business. Soeters and Schreuder found that "there are nearly as many definitions of culture as there are authors writing about this subject" (Soeters & Schreuder, 1988, p.75). There have been many definitions used for organizational culture, such as the "rules of the game" (Van Maanen, 1976; Ritti & Funkhouser, 1968) or "how things are done around here" (Drennen, 1992). Today, when studying culture in MNCs, many use the definition developed by Hofstede, where he describes culture as "a collective programming of the mind which distinguishes one group from another"

(Hofstede, 1980, p. 25). In the literature on organizational culture, two main streams have been mostly documented. The first is the study of organizational cultures, such as the work by Schein (1985) and the second stream looks into the influence of national culture on organizations, such as the work of Hofstede and his widespread research within IBM (Hofstede, 1980, 1983).

The first stream of research focuses on organizational culture which has been in fashion in academic management research since the 1980s. The main idea was that due to increasing complexity and competitiveness, companies could no longer gain advantage through the sole manipulation of their structures, strategies, and material resources, but that their success was dependent on their successful management of the values, attitudes and beliefs which exist within the organization. Indeed, corporate culture is made up of the shared beliefs, values and behavior patterns which are developed and shared within an organization (Schein, 1986; Hofstede, 2001). On an individual level, organizational culture is learned by group members as they enter the organization. This process is both formal, for example through onboarding programs or trainings as well as informal through socialization with already exiting members of the organization (Harrison & Carol, 1991). Historically within organizational theory, research on culture went from considering it as something that an organization "has" to something an organization "is" (Wilson, 2001). Indeed, corporate culture has an important role to play within organizations as it develops the shared identity of the organization's actors and guides decision making. According to Barmeyer and Davoine (2006b, p.230), corporate culture is a "soft, holistic concept with hard consequences". These consequences include the performance of the organization, as a strong corporate culture can contribute to the economic success of an organization (Peters & Waterman, 1982). Organizational culture has become a variable linked to performance and integration, with for example research done on how strong versus weak organizational cultures will affect these elements, effectively making culture a factor of managerial control and effectiveness (Barley et al. 1988; Peters & Waterman, 1982; Wilson, 2001).

Most describe cultures as having two levels (Wilson, 2001), a visible and a non-visible component. The visible part includes elements such as behavior, language and the environment whereas the non-visible is made up of the values, or what Schein calls the basic assumptions. Schein considers the non-visible aspects to be the "essence" of culture (Schein, 2004). These values are made up of what the group considers important and what they think "ought" to be (Wilson, 2001). These values can also be part of the company in an explicit way, through the corporate values or the organizational strategy of an organization, which is what Argyris and Schon have called "espoused values" (1978). However these may not actually be the true values, as they may not be the ones on which the behaviors are based. In this case these values may be aligned with what people will say in a certain situation but not correspond to what they actually do (Schein, 2004). In Schein's (2004) research on organizational culture and its impact on performance, he divides culture into three levels, namely artifacts, beliefs and values as well as assumptions. These three categories are illustrated in the figure below. Artifacts are the most visible elements of culture. These artifacts are made up of all the elements that one will feel hear and see when first entering an unknown culture. According to Hofstede, this level of culture includes symbols such as logos, corporate branding, geographical and physical locations. It also involves heroes of the company, such as founders or charismatic leaders, as well as rituals such as meetings, or how people greet each other. Kemp and Dwyer (2001) also include organizational structures, stories and control systems in this level of culture. Although this is the most visible element of organizational culture, it is also very difficult to decipher artifacts on their own as they are ambiguous. Attempting to understand artifacts independently from the other levels can lead to false interpretation. Schein (2004) uses the example of pyramids; artifacts built both by the Mayans and Egyptians but with very different meanings. Therefore it is important to also study the espoused beliefs and values of an organization, the second level of culture, according to Schein (2004). These values are the beliefs and business strategy of an organization's members. As mentioned above, these values and strategies may however not fully illustrate the culture of organizations, if they only espoused and not actually guiding the behavior. If the values are to a certain extent aligned with the underlying assumptions, the third level of culture, then they can be useful as a tool for bringing the group together, creating a common identity and driving the core mission of the organization. However, it is important to note that not all these espoused values will be aligned with the assumptions, but rather "rationalizations of only aspirations for the future" (Schein, 2004, p. 30). That is why it is important, yet difficult, to also understand the underlying assumptions, which are the unwritten rules of the organization. These rules, if they are strongly embedded, make it inconceivable for people to base their behavior on any other premise. These assumptions come from repeated success in the implementation of certain values and beliefs (Schein, 2004). Schein sees five different types of assumptions (2004). The first is made up of the assumptions of the relationship with the environment. Are we able to impact or influence our environment? The second is assumptions about truth and reality. Is there one truth or solution or just our own interpretation? The third is assumptions about human nature. Are we basically good and will we act accordingly if given autonomy? The fourth is the question of activity.Must we be rational and think before acting or is it better to be decisive and act quickly? The fifth is the assumption of the value of individualism versus collaboration.

When studying a matrix organization, it will be important to keep the three levels of culture in mind, as one can assume that the different dimensions of a holding matrix organization, which have different goals and strategies, and therefore potentially different values, both espoused and basic assumptions, could potentially lead to issues. Furthermore, the clash of these dimensions could also offer an opportunity for the understanding of basic assumptions, as these could be brought to light through the contact of the dimensions.

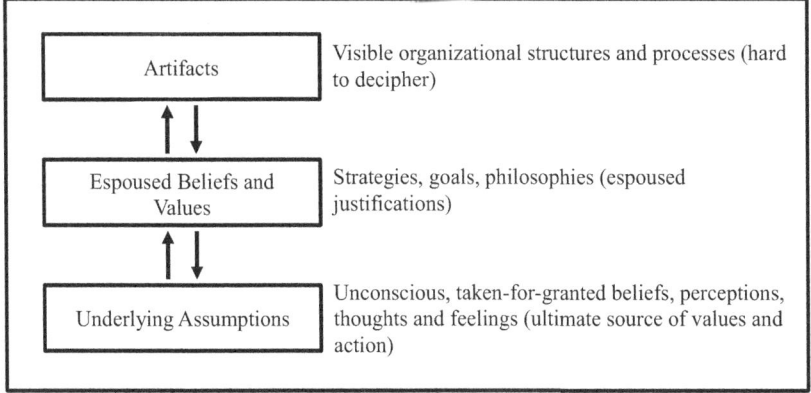

Figure 3: Levels of culture (Schein, 2004, p. 26)

There are different perspectives which have been studied regarding organizational culture. As mentioned above, corporate culture plays an important role in an organization, by giving guidance for decision making and driving a sense of shared identity (Barmeyer & Davoine, 2006b). There are some who have argued that a strong corporate culture is to be desired. In a strong corporate culture, the espoused values are in alignment with the actual behavior, norms and informal beliefs of the group and there is a high level of coherence within the whole organization regarding these values. Here, consensus and consistency on an organization wide basis is a desired state (Schein, 1991, Peters & Waterman, 1982). However, because organizational culture comes from experience and interactions within a group, it is a shared phenomenon. It therefore only exists if there is a group to speak of (Pfeffer, 1981). However, some consider that this group is not just the whole company, and different sub-cultures can be found within one company (Kotter & Heskett, 1992, Wilson, 1997). Here, there is a more fragmented view of culture within an organization, where within the company, boundaries can be drawn between different sub-groups with sub-cultures (Van Maanen, 1991). These sub-cultures can be based on functions, levels, or any other factor depending on the company. Therefore an organization's culture is in fact made up of multiple sub-cultures, which could both co-exist in conflict, harmony or even just indifference (Wilson, 2001). However, this perspective has yet to have been analyzed in depth within existing research (Viegas-Pires, 2013). It has very interesting implications for matrix organizations, as the dimensions coming into contact through this structure could potentially have different sub-cultures. Furthermore, this will also bring us to one of the further topics we will elaborate upon in a later section, namely the issue of boundary spanning in an organization. Indeed one could consider these sub-cultures as boundaries to be spanned.

It seems that the rate of change of organizational culture is rather slow, and may be considered too slow by management or compared to the market (Wilson, 2001). However it does evolve, either due to the change in the members of the organization, the environment or society (Kotter & Heskett, 1992). These factors for cultural change are complex and interlinked and there is debate on how these changes can be managed. Some see culture as an opportunity for managers to strategically influence their organizations (Schein, 1991; Peters & Waterman, 1982). Others see culture, because of its complex and fragmented nature, as very difficult, yet not impossible, to manage (Smircich, 1983). Many, such as Kotter and Heskett (1992), when looking into the key ingredients for cultural change, focused on the importance of charismatic leaders. In particular when looking into the origins of an organizational culture, the role of the founder is often stressed (Martínez-Cañas & Ruiz-Palomino, 2014; Schein, 2004), as being the creator of an organizational culture, by imposing their values and beliefs on the company, before becoming a manager of this culture and, if unable to manage the culture they have created, could become a victim of this culture (Schein, 2004). It is also important, however, to stress other factors such as HR processes including recruitment, remuneration and training will also play a role (Wilson, 2001). Furthermore, organizational structure could also be an important factor for cultural change. This is obviously particularly interesting when studying the implementation of a matrix organization, as the impact it has on cultural change could potentially be observable.

Now looking into the second stream of research on organizational culture, based on the work of Hofstede (1980, 1983, 2001), he defines culture based on five dimensions (power distance, uncertainty avoidance, individualism/collectivism, masculinity/femininity, and long- versus short-term orientation). Hofstede conducted country-by-country evaluations within IBM to filter out nations' "average" culture. Kirkman, Lowe, and Gibson (2006) indicate that Hofstede's research (1980) is the most important resource in the field of national cultural classifications.

Over the past few years, focus has persisted on the central role of national culture. For example, the GLOBE research project is the most recent large-scale venture, with one hundred and seventy investigators from sixty two cultures working on the project (House et al. 2004), with the goal to understand how culture is related to societal, organizational and leadership effectiveness. In this study they use some of Hofstede's cultural dimensions (uncertainty avoidance and power distance) while differentiating new cultural dimensions. The cultural dimensions they use are future orientation, gender equality, assertiveness, human orientation, in-group collectivism, institutional collectivism, performance orientation, power distance and uncertainty avoidance. We will dive further into the topic of national cultures in the research design part of this section, as it will be important to understand the national cultures involved in the case study.

This classic conception of culture considers culture as an objective reality which is therefore measurable. Generally based on the research on national cultures by Hofstede, the concept of cultural distance has been widely used, in particular in the context of mergers and acquisitions. In international business literature, few constructs have gained wider acceptance than cultural distance. Presumably evaluating the degree to which different cultures are similar or different, the concept was applied to the majority of disciplines of business administration, and most especially in the context of foreign direct investments and the literature on mergers, acquisitions and joint ventures. However, even if cultural distance between two entities can be used to study culture in the context of an M&A, reality points to interaction as the key issue, because the distinction between one culture and another has little significance until these cultures come into contact (Shenkar, 2001). Overall, this classic conceptualization of culture, while necessary to develop the field initially, has to be further expanded upon in order to be able to explain culture in organizations with multicultural fields of action. Indeed, Barmeyer and Mayrofer (2008) explain that culture cannot be seen as something fixed that countries or organizations have, but that on the contrary subcultures can be developed on different levels such as communities of interest, departments or professions. Lee et al. (2015) found in their study of Volvo and Samsung that the classic view of culture was useful to predict which kind of issues are likely to happen during the post-integration phase but that the dynamic view of culture, which will be discussed next, will help predict whether or not these issues will actually happen.

2.4.2 Organizational Identity

We have now seen the significant role that organizational culture has to play in MNCs. On top of that we posit that organizational identity will also have an important impact. Organizational identity, much like organizational culture, started to gain attention in the 1980s (Alvesson, 1990). Organizational identity was first defined by Albert and Whetten in 1985, as being made up of attributes which are central, enduring and distinguishing. If an attribute is central, it means that it has changed the history of the organization, without these attributes the organization would not be the way it is today. Attributes are enduring if they are deeply embedded in the organization and its history. Finally, attributes are distinguishing if they allow the organization to distinguish itself from other organizations while also setting a norm or standards for this organization. Overall, organizational identity answers the question "who are we as an organization?" (Whetten, 2006). Organizational identity is what the members collectively think, feel and perceive about their organization, a shared understanding of what distinguishes the organizations and its values and characteristics (Hatch & Schultz, 1997). Although the views of Albert and Whetten are those generally accepted in the field of organizational identity, some have also developed different and varying views on this concept. Ravasi and Schultz (2006) have divided these perspectives into the social actor perspective and the social constructivist perspective. Where the initial view as described by Albert and Whetten sees organizational identity as enduring, others have described identity as a being constantly changing through interactions between the members of the organizational as well as external actors. Here organizational identity is rather viewed as unstable rather than enduring. Gioia et al. (2000) explain that while basics of identity remain, it is how this identity is interpreted which will change. There are many factors which can influence the creation and the reinterpretation or reformation of organizational identity. For example, the foundation of the company, the growth or decline of an organization or a merger can have an impact on the organizations identity (Albert & Whetten, 1985). Furthermore identity change, like culture, can also be used as a strategic tool (Gioia et al., 2000). These changes may however be slow, due to deeply embedded cultures or resistance to change. This change will require buy-in from its members.

The strength of organizational identity can vary. While some have strong identities and inspire strong feelings of oneness with the organization, other companies will not inspire as much identification (Zaheer et al. 2003). According to Kostova and Zaheer (1999), the internal legitimacy of a company will play a role in the strength of identification. Furthermore, Zaheer et al. (2003), note that companies which have a lot of socialization as well as high membership prices, for example in a start-up, could also have stronger organizational identification. When members identify strongly with their organization, in a way that their identification as a member of the organization is stronger than other potential identities they may have (Dutton et al, 1994), their feelings about the company may be more positive. Furthermore, strong organizational identification may be beneficial for the organization as a whole (Ashforth & Mael, 1989; Dutton et al., 1994). People may be more attracted to organizations that have values which they perceive as similar to their own (O'Reilly et al, 1991). On the other hand, organizations with low performance, or which have had many lay-offs may have lower levels of identification. Incidents that disrupt members' beliefs about the attributes of the organization can lead to identity threats, which challenge how the members categorize and perceive themselves. These threats can bring about emotional responses, as described by Zaheer et al. (2003), which can be expressed through feelings of "us" versus "them" for example, as they describe in the case of identity threats within a merger of equals.

As mentioned, organizational identity is the relationship between an employee and the company, the oneness of the employee with the organization (Mael & Ashforth, 1992), while culture, as has been explained in the previous section is made up of the norms, values and behaviors within the organization. Strong identities and strong cultures are often found together. However although organizational identity is related to organizational culture they are separate concepts (Hatch and Schultz, 1997). Hatch, Schultz and their colleagues have contributed much work to linking organizational culture, organizational identity and organizational image. Ravasi and Schultz (2006) point out that although the role of organizational culture in providing substance to organizational identity, how culture actually affects identity has not yet been largely explored, and there has been little empirical research done regarding the identity-culture relationship. It is important to note that although identity, culture and image and their relationship are treated together by these researchers, organizational image tends to lie in the external perception of the organization, therefore it will not be particularly relevant for our research, and omitting to develop the concept further is intentional. Hatch and Schultz (1997) find that organizational culture must be taken into consideration when attempting to understand organizational identity. Indeed, activities and beliefs, which are grounded in organizational culture, will impact how people define and experience themselves. As stated by Bingöl et al. (2013), "organizational culture provides the context in which organizational identity is developed". And, the other way around, it seems that strong identification by the members may support a strong organizational culture (Bingöl et al. 2013). Moreover, organizations may have multiple identities, and some identities may be specific to a department, function or other sub-group within the organization. This can lead to issues, as managing multiple identities is complex, and having them could lead to identity conflict. However, these multiple identities may offer benefits, such as increased flexibility when dealing with the increasingly complex environment. Managers can have three strategies when dealing with multiple identities. The first is to simply focus on fostering one identity, while leaving the others unattended. The second is to accept the pluralism of identities and deal with them either by compartmentalizing the organization (for example through departments) and the third is to attempt to find synergies between these identities (Pratt & Foreman, 2000).

The final point we would like to make in this section, is to explain why this question of identity is important to address within a matrix organization. Indeed, as has been seen above, an organization can have multiple identities, and this is expected to be the case when setting up a holding matrix organization. Based on the paper by Zaheer et al. (2003), we would liken our set-up to the situation found in a merger of equals. Indeed, as has been mentioned we have found literature on M&A to be relevant to our research. As Zaheer et al. mention, organizational identity may be as important as organizational culture when looking into the integration process of a merger. We will address culture in M&A at a later stage, in the section on socio-cultural integration. Zaheer et al. (2003) explain that even if organizations have similar cultures, strong organizational identities could lead to issues within the integration. Furthermore, the assumption that both organizations should be equal, as it is a merger of equals, could lead to more issues regarding culture and identity, as the expectation of equality may lead to high expectations of equality in all things. They found examples of mergers of equals where cultural incompatibility was low, but there were still many issues and identification as "us" and "them" for a long time after the merger had effectively taken place. This shows that there is an important role to be played not only by culture but also identity within M&A. Therefore they recommend that managers should be aware of potential identification issues when undertaking a merger. This will be particularly interesting to observe in our case, as a holding matrix organization can be comparable to this merger of equals situation, where the identification of the actors will play a significant role within the organization.

2.4.3 The dynamic View of Culture

In the classic view described above, culture is imprinted on our minds subconsciously (software of the mind) and therefore cannot be easily changed. Furthermore it is seen as homogenous and monolithic; it is expected to find a similar set of values for each individual within the same cultural group. (Lee et al., 2015). Moreover the classic conception of culture views national culture and organizational culture as two separate entities. For example, many researchers posit that international mergers and acquisitions are bound to lead to more cultural issues than domestic ones as employees must deal with double-layered acculturation, both organizational and national. However, it must be noted that a study of domestic and international mergers and acquisitions did not find any evidence of this said double layered acculturation, but on the contrary found the domestic integration, and namely employee resistance to be higher in the domestic M&A (Lee et al, 2015). In much of the research on national culture, it is assumed that national cultures are static and homogenous, however "culture can be dynamic, heterogeneous and strongly contextualized" (Barmeyer & Davoine, 2019, p4). In this case, culture can be defined as "sets of symbols and patterns of meaning and interpretation that are shared or partially shared among a group of people"(Yagi & Kleinberg, 2011, p632). Moreover, in this view culture is negotiable and dependent on the social context rather than fixed principles (Barmeyer & Davoine, 2015). Overall this view of culture does not have strong boundaries and definitions based on nationality or organizational entities, but rather prescribes careful examination of communities of meaning (Lee et al, 2015).

Furthermore, while the classic culture literature considers national culture and organizational culture as separate entities altogether, more recently national culture is seen to influence organizational cultures (Barmeyer & Mayrhofer, 2008). Expanding on this even further, Leung et al. (2005) describe a dynamic, multi-level construct of culture. They explain culture as being a multi-level construct, with various levels, each fitting within the next. These levels start with individual, then group culture, organizational culture, national culture and finally global culture. On top of that, the culture within each of these levels is shaped and reshaped, both by top-down and bottom-up processes, where each level will influence the one above it or below it.

According to Lee et al (2015), social identity theory can be used to explain how culture and identity are linked. In social identity theory, when people identify themselves within a group (or in this case a cultural group), they compare in-group from outgroup characteristics, most often favoring in-group culture as they draw self-esteem from their belonging to said group. Therefore in the case of mergers and acquisitions, if the employees from the acquired company do not accept there relatively lower status as "acquired" they will attempt to keep their old group identity. Therefore they will focus on the cultural differences between "us" and "them", in an in-group favoring way. Lee et al (2015), based on Hogg and Terry (2000) explain that two social factors can be used to deal with this issue, namely that acquired employees not only accept their new group identity but also find it to be attractive. The first factor is that the "stability and legitimacy of intergroup status is high", meaning that acquired employees accept their status of acquired employees. The second is that the "the possibility of social mobility is high" (Lee et al. 2015, p583).

This concept offers a dynamic view of culture, where the boundaries are not necessarily determined by national or organizational boundaries and where culture is constantly transformed and reinvented as people interact with each other and "acquire or discard a shared sense of identity" (Lee et al. 2015, p584).

2.4.4   Integration and the Emergence of New Culture

In this next section, we will use literature on mergers, acquisitions and joint ventures. Indeed this is relevant when studying matrix organizations, because combining different dimensions of the matrix can be considered as similar to a situation of M&A or joint venture. Furthermore, if one uses the newly emerging M&A attitude of partnering (Kale et al. 2009), where the acquirer will allow its acquired entities to remain relatively independent, especially in the case of strong brands on new markets, therefore retaining their own identity, the areas of cooperation within the MNC will be very much comparable to a holding company matrix organization. Therefore looking into the concept of socio-cultural integration and negotiated culture, topics studied in M&As and joint ventures, could be interesting. Once we have explained these concepts we will see how they can apply to the areas where the dimensions of a matrix organization meet.

The topic of culture and its effect on the performance of mergers and acquisitions has led to mixed results. While some find that cultural differences lead to issues, others that they have no impact while, finally, some find that cultural differences add value (Brock, 2005). Globalization and an increasingly competitive environment has been linked to the expansion of the international activities of companies, with the value of total foreign direct investment (FDI) growing more than tenfold between 1990 and 2012 (OECD, 2015). Firms which internationalize face multiple options, including exporting, joint ventures, and mergers and acquisitions (M&A). M&A is the most common form of foreign direct investment (OECD, 2010) and can be defined as a strategic deal between two or more independent companies who chose to share their resources to reach a common goal (Barmeyer & Mayrhofer, 2002). The rates of cross-border Mergers and Acquisitions (M&As) remain high, making M&A a popular form of development today (Cartwright and Schoenberg, 2006), with the value of M&As in 2018 amounting to 3.88 trillion USD (Statista, 2019). However, M&As often fail to reach their goals. There are many documented factors for the disappointing success rates of M&As, including the strategic rationale for the M&A, the strategic fit between the businesses of the companies involved and the process of the integration (Cartwright & Cooper, 1992; Cartwright & Schoenberg, 2006). Although there have been decades of research on this topic, the success factors and the reasons why M&As fail so often are still not fully understood (Stahl et al. 2013). Many different approaches have been used to study M&A, and have developed separately in different disciplines (Cartwright & Schoenberg, 2006) which has led to high fragmentation (Rossi et al. 2013). One of the key topics (related to M&A) is the performance of the M&A. For example, Larsson and Finkelstein (1999) created a model for M&A success, using synergy realization as the construct to measure this. Here they state that the key antecedents to synergy realization is combination potential (assessed in terms of similarities and complementarities) and organizational integration which positively affect synergy realization; as well as employee resistance, which negatively affects it. Bauer and Matzler (2014) elaborated a model where M&A success is the product of strategic complementarity, cultural fit, and the degree and speed of integration. They find that strategic complementarity also has a positive impact on the degree of integration and cultural fit. Cultural fit is related positively to M&A success yet negatively to the degree and speed of integration. Finally the degree of integration positively impacts the speed of integration. As can be seen in the two models above, the integration phase within an M&A plays a determining role in M&A success and firm similarities or lack thereof and the characteristics of the deal only explain some of the M&A issues (King et al. 2004). The integration stage, which lasts for years after the closure of the deal, is therefore essential for M&A success (Steigenberger, 2017). Jemison and Haspeslagh stated that "all value creation takes place after the acquisition" (1991, p129) and Larsson and Finkelstein (1999) found the integration stage to be the strongest predictor of synergy realization (which they use to measure M&A success), yet it would seem that firms underestimate the importance of this stage. Moreover, this topic has received little empirical focus in M&A literature (Ellis & Lamont, 2004). When studying the integration process by reviewing the literature on the topic, Steigenberger (2017) found four categories of topics which affect (both positively and negatively) the integration phase. The first is the context of the M&A, which includes the relatedness of the firms involved, both internal and external, cultural distance, integration experience and the employee perception of the M&A. The second are the "structural interventions", this includes both the depth and speed of integration as well as operational integration, such as system alignment, resource allocation or reward systems. The third are the leadership and communication-based interventions, the "human-side" of the integration. This includes mobilization (steering the integration), mitigation (smoothing this process), and managing cultural distance and leadership styles. Finally collective sense-making and negotiations play a role. There are various micro-political struggles involved in the integration process making the integration the result of political bargaining and collective sense-making.

It has been assumed that different integration approaches are required for different types of acquisitions for a long time now (Ellis & Lamont, 2004). The most popular classification of integration strategies (Steigenberger, 2017) comes from Haspeslagh and Jemison (1991). It is a matrix which uses strategic interdependence and need for organizational autonomy as the two dimensions. They identify 3 categories of integration approaches "absorption" (low need for organizational autonomy – high strategic interdependence) "preservation" (high need for organizational autonomy – low strategic interdependence) and "symbiosis" (high need for organizational autonomy – high strategic interdependence). Marks and Mirvis (1998) also classify the different integration strategies in a similar way, based on the degree of change in the two firms, into five categories: absorption, reverse merger or assimilation, preservation, best of both, and transformation. High level of integration might be essential to obtain synergies yet loss of autonomy associated with the integration process can be negative for the performance of the M&A (Rossi et al. 2013) M&A research has in the past been focused on strategic and financial factors, and failed to explain the factors that impact M&A performance (King et al., 2004). Cultural differences have been blamed for the failure of domestic and cross-border M&A (Teerikangas & Very, 2006). Now an emerging field of research on this topic is the sociocultural and human resource issues. (Stahl et al. 2013). Social-cultural integration can be defined as : "a process of combining two previously separated workforces, where different management actions take place, which shape the process in order to influence the outcomes favorably, that is to generate trust (versus distrust), satisfaction (versus dissatisfaction), cooperation (versus conflict) and a shared identity (versus fragmented identities) among the members of the combining organizations" (Viegas-Pires, 2013). Unsuccessful post-acquisition integration can be attributed to the cultural differences and poor cultural fit between the organizations that are merged (Teerikangas & Laamanen, 2014; Viegas-Pires, 2013).

As previously explained, organizational culture can be defined as the beliefs, values and assumptions shared by the members of an organization (Schein, 1985). Research has focused on the impact of these organizational cultural differences on the performance of domestic M&As, as well as the importance of cultural fit. Cultural differences are often associated with bad results in domestic M&As. However, the results are mixed (Teerikangas & Very, 2006). Some found complementarity and therefore organizational culture distance, to positively impact M&A performance (e.g. Krishnan, Miller & Judge, 1997; Larsson & Finkelstein, 1999, Very et al. 1997). Others find no consequence or negative consequences on M&A performance (e.g. Marks, 1982), with for example cultural issues being blamed for the failure of the Daimler-Chrysler merger (Schuler & Jackson, 2001; Steigenberger, 2017). Finding synergies in the case of an M&A often requires the reorganization of the companies involved. This reorganization can be more complex in the case of cross-border M&A (Barmeyer & Mayrhofer, 2002). National culture can be defined in a similar way to organizational culture (Teerikangas & Very, 2006) but the fact that national culture operates on a deeper level, because it is learnt earlier on (Hofstede, 1980), must be taken into account. Moreover, national culture is often measured using national borders and an average of the data within them, which doesn't account for the plurality of cultures which can be found within one country (regional, minorities, etc.) (Teerikangas & Very, 2006). Some state that cross-border M&As tend to be more problematic than domestic M&As because the national cultural differences are added on to the organizational differences. This is what is referred to as the cultural distance hypothesis where coordination and communication are more of an issue the greater the cultural distance (Kogut

& Singh, 1988). Indeed, the companies involved in cross-border M&A are embedded in national cultural and institutional contexts, where companies will face issues linked both to national and organizational cultures (Søderberg & Vaara, 2003). Moreover, the development of trust is made easier by similar norms and values both on the national and organizational level (Williams, 2001). There is however a debate about how this impacts the performance of M&As (Stahl et al. 2013). Some find more integration problems associated with national cultural differences, as well as other human resources issues (top management turnover, stress, negative attitudes). Therefore Viegas-Pires (2013) proposes that national cultural differences impede socio-cultural integration. However, these cultural differences may also provide competitive advantage if leveraged (Aguilera & Dencker, 2004, Larsson & Lubatkin 2001), by providing access to resources that are not easy to imitate (Morosini et al. 1998, Barmeyer & Mayrhofer, 2008). There is also more synergistic potential if cultures are different, the differences meaning that the companies can learn from each other, generating more knowledge, and therefore more added value (Morosini et al. 1998). Moreover, people are more likely to be prepared to accept differences if the perceived theoretical cultural distance is higher (Weber et al. 1996). Björkman et al. (2007) find that the best case is if the cultural differences are "moderate" enough for synergies and learning but not too much so that people can still understand each other and capabilities can still be transferred. Overall, the relationship between national and organizational culture distance and M&A performance is still complex and relatively unclear, making it difficult to predict the impact of culture on the results of an M&A (Teerikangas & Very, 2006).

One of the potential reasons for the lack of consistency in the findings on the culture – performance relationship can be explained by the lack of consideration for further kinds of culture, or sub-cultures within the M&A integration process such as industrial, functional, professional, and occupational cultures (Viegas-Pires, 2013). The level of the cultural challenges will depend on the integration strategy chosen. For example, when looking at the classification made by Haspeslagh and Jemison (1991), the M&As which require high strategic interdependence (symbiotic and absorption) will have more cultural clashes (Teerikangas & Very, 2006). Moreover, Teerikangas and Very (2006) also find that preferred acculturative mode (integration, assimilation, separation and deculturation), which depends on the degree of multiculturalism and relatedness of the two firms as well as their histories, will mediate the impact of the cultural issues on the performance of the M&A. Furthermore, the impact of cultural issues will be different depending on the progress of the integration, as the integration goes on, it is likely that the cultures of the two firms will become closer (Teerikangas & Very, 2006).

In order to avoid potential issues due to cultural differences, some recommend giving the acquired company a high level of autonomy and keeping the level of integration low. On the other hand, some state that acculturation through social control leads to cooperation between the employees of both firms. Larsson and Lubatkin (2001) found, regardless of both national and organizational cultural differences, that social controls (socialization rituals such as introductions programs, celebrations, training, etc.) had a positive effect on acculturation. Barmeyer and Mayrhofer (2008) in their case study of EADS (European Aeronautic Defense and Space company, a French, German, Spanish merger) showed that intercultural management is essential to overcome conflicts, where intercultural management (Barmeyer & Mayrhofer, 2002), helps go from conflictual coexistence to "interculture". Companies must actively communicate on their perceived view of cultural differences and cultural learning interventions facilitate the integration process by developing employee perceptions and attitudes. Moreover, the constitution of the integration teams is important. Integrations teams can include members from both firms as well as external consultants. Mixed teams show that all interests are being considered, not only those of the acquiring firm, but these teams are likely to have more issues with decision making (Piske, 2002). Barmeyer and Mayrhofer (2002) also recommend mixed teams and maintaining balance in the working teams.

HR has an important role to play in integration (Barmeyer and Mayrhofer, 2008), especially in the case of cultural differences (Child et al., 2001), as these differences will affect the company's policies and processes on many levels. Many HR activities are important in the integration phase of an M&A, including training programs, retention, appointing integration managers (Sarala et al., 2017), forming mixed teams, keeping balanced membership in these teams as well as in the delegation of responsibilities and the allocation of salaries (Barmeyer and Mayrhofer, 2008). Furthermore, it seems that flexibility in HR practices may be essential to adjust to the changing needs during the integration (Sarala et al. 2016). The different national and institutional environments the companies are embedded in will make aligning HR practices more complicated (Sarala et al. 2017). It is normal to have some localization in HR practices (Aguilera & Dencker, 2004), however these differences may be used as a tool for resistance, especially if they reflect power unbalance (Sarala et al., 2017). Overall there is still a lack of comprehensive understanding on the use of HR tools in M&As and their consequences, and in particular, the role of external actors, such as unions, needs to be studied further (Sarala et al., 2017).

Furthermore, the creation of a new organizational culture, or "negotiated culture" has been recently described in international joint ventures (Brannen & Salk, 2000; Barmeyer & Davoine, 2019). This new culture will appear through mutual understanding and adjustment processes from both parties. Brannen and Salk (2000) have identified four categories which can be used to understand negotiated practices. When the practice from one group is adopted by the other group, the category has been named "compromise by one group". When both groups compromise, the category is "meeting in the middle". When both groups create a new practice which is not based on one's groups practice, it is "innovating something new for both groups". The last category, "division of labor", occurs when each group performs tasks separately. However, national culture still has its place here, as Brannen and Salk (2000) posit that national culture serves as an initial anchor for the team members and that the new working culture is then shaped though the social negotiation within the group. In this view of culture, groups with common cultures are not created because their members share a set of value standards but because these people identify themselves with this cultural group, this in an often deliberate way. Therefore research needs to go beyond studying culture itself and its dimensions and look into the social interactions through which culture is created and recreated (Lee et al, 2015).

2.4.5   Matrix Organizations and Culture

In this next section we will attempt to see how the concept of culture can be addressed in a holding company matrix organization. We will start with the impact of culture on synergy creation, as within a holding company matrix, which has relatively independent dimensions, like in a partnering M&A (Kale et al., 2009), synergies are an important goal. Then we will look into the literature on managing culture in an MNC before developing the idea of a matrix organization as a coordination modus for cultural integration.

Brock (2005) studied the impact of national culture in creating synergies. Using a classic view of culture and focusing on the dimensions of individualism and power distance, Brock (2005) focused on the impact that cultural differences in these dimensions had on cultural integration and resource sharing. He found that integration and resource sharing, on top of structural and financial fit, are necessary to the creation of synergies. The following table based on the results from this study, shows in which cases (based on 103 acquisitions in New Zealand and Australia) these cultural differences were reported to have an impact on integration and resource sharing, and subsequently, synergy creation. Brock (2005) explains this conclusion through the fact that individualism may be more "anchored organizationally" influencing factors such as accountability, autonomy, leadership, performance based evaluation, and so on. Managers in companies lower on individualism may be more used to receiving orders from above rather than having decision making delegated to them, which may make integration more difficult for the subsidiary. Organizations with high power distance scores tend to be centralized and have autocratic leadership, which may complicate resource sharing. Moreover, centralized decision making can isolate top management making it more difficult to make the most of resources found at lower levels. On top of that, if the subsidiary is used to a decentralized form of decision making this may further complicate resource sharing. Overall, based on this study it seems that cultural differences in terms of individualism create issues both in terms of resource sharing and integration whereas power distance differences only complicates resource sharing. However, as Brock (2005) himself notes, these dimensions and their value today (the initial research by Hofstede is over 20 years old and based only on IBM employees) is often debated. Yet these two dimensions (power distance and individualism) seem to have survived the test of time and are still relevant today.

Table 4: Effects cultural differences on synergy creation (own elaboration based on Brock, 2005)

Parent company (acquiring)	Subsidiary (acquired)	Consequence on integration
Lower on individualism	Higher on individualism	More integration problems
Higher on individualism	Lower on individualism	More integration problems More resource sharing problems
Higher on power distance	Lower on power distance	No real impact on integration seen More resource sharing issues

As discussed in the previous paragraphs on this topic, culture is often seen as a problem to be dealt with. Blazejewski and Becker-Ritterspach (2011) explain that current research finds that teams which are culturally more diverse tend to have higher levels and more intense inter-personal conflict. Moreover, this diversity may increase the chances of the conflict manifesting itself. Ayoko et al. (2002) find that international teams "suffer more conflict, higher turnover and more communication difficulties". It is therefore important to manage culture and the processes involved when two (or more) cultures are likely to clash. However, Kanter and Corn made the interesting point below:

> *"Cultural differences do not automatically cause tensions. But when tensions do arise – often due to situational factors such as lack of communication or poor performance – people blame many of the organizational difficulties they encounter on cultural*

heterogeneity – on the presence of others who seem different rather than to the context within which these problems took place" (Kanter & Corn, 1994).

Therefore cultural issues must be managed, but it must be taken into account that the cultural issues may be perceived as greater than they actually are, as they can be used as scapegoats for "everyday" organizational issues. Moreover, there have recently been those who find cultural differences to be an advantage. Lee et al. (2015) found in their review of literature that there are many cases where national culture differences were viewed as positive. When taking a resource based view, for example, national culture differences can be seen as an opportunity by providing access to critical repertoires and routines which did not exist within the company beforehand (Barmeyer & Mayrhofer, 2008). Moreover, from an organizational learning perspective, cultural differences can also be valuable as they tend to lead to an increase in the acquiring company's knowledge base, and helps stimulate organizational learning as well as decrease organizational inertia. Finally, it seems that the cultural differences in a merger and acquisition may not be a critical issue.

Table 5: Convergence and divergence in international management (Barmeyer, 2000, p.38)

	Convergence	Divergence
Contender	Differences will disappear	Differences will remain or increase
Consequence	Cultural homogeneity	Cultural heterogeneity
Risk	The negation of culture may cause misunderstandings and conflicts	The overestimation of culture can become the principal element of conflict
Management	Management methods are universal and can be transferred and applied in different contexts	Management methods are principally marked by their culture of origin and encounter resistance in their application in other contexts
Mergers-acquisitions	Cultures will tangle and be diffused; consequently, the stronger culture will have more influence and be applied	Cultures resist change; consequently, adjustments and intercultural compromises need to be made.

To start with, the performance of a merger or acquisition may not be dependent on the cultural distance between the firms involved but rather on how well the processes within the post-acquisition are managed. Furthermore, organizational culture is more likely to be an issue than national culture. Indeed many researchers did note more negative aspects of organizational culture differences within domestic mergers and acquisitions. They posit that the reason behind this could be that the cultural sensitivity from the acquiring firm is higher towards foreign acquired firms than domestic ones (Barmeyer & Mayrhofer, 2008). It is therefore most relevant not how different the cultures are, but how these differences are managed and that the way companies manage both the formal, organization aspects as well as the informal socialization aspect of the integration process are relevant to the acculturation process. Barmeyer and Mayrhofer (2008) in their case study of EADS, mentioned in the section on socio-cultural integration, showed that intercultural management is essential to overcome conflicts. Larsson and Lubatkin (2001) found, regardless of both national and organizational cultural differences, that social controls (socialization rituals such as introductions programs, celebrations, training, etc.) had a positive effect on acculturation.

The question of convergence, or the harmonization of systems, versus divergence, which preserves the plurality within the organization has been focused on within the research on the topic of mergers and acquisitions. This debate mainly focuses on three areas within the organization: corporate culture, organization and human resources management (Barmeyer & Mayrhofer, 2008). In order to avoid potential issues due to cultural differences, some recommend giving the acquired company a high level of autonomy and keeping the level of integration low. On the other hand, some state that acculturation through social control leads to cooperation between the employees of both firms (Lee et al. 2005).

Barmeyer and Mayrhofer (2008) state that communication and intercultural competences are particularly important and should be developed. Companies must actively communicate on their perceived view of cultural differences and cultural learning interventions facilitate the integration process by developing employee perceptions and attitudes. They describe the intercultural learning process Barmeyer's (2000) model pictured below. Furthermore Barmeyer and Mayrhofer (2008) note the importance of a common project and understanding of the value of the merger as well as efficient management of human resources. Forming mixed teams and keeping balanced membership in these teams as well as in the delegation of responsibilities and the allocation of salaries are also important.

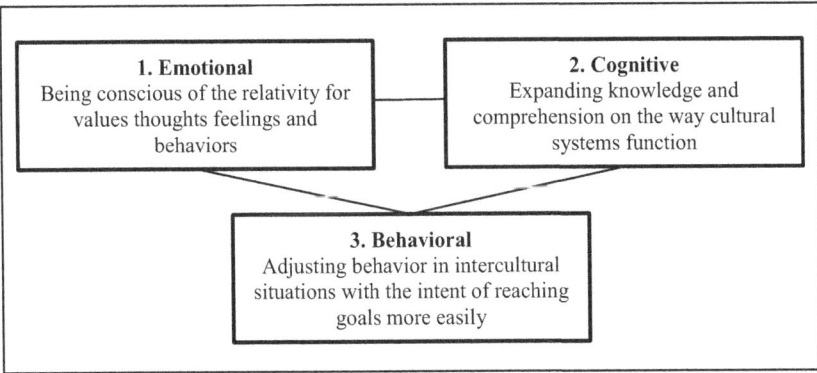

Figure 4: The process of intercultural learning and training (Barmeyer, 2000, p271)

In order to bring two or more companies together, it is clear that boundaries need to be bridged and linkages created. Mechanisms of control and collaboration need to be leveraged to ensure successful collaboration and integration of the firms. In fact, one could consider using a matrix organization as an integration strategy, using the structure as a coordination modus for integration. There has to our knowledge been no research on the use of matrix as a coordination modus for integration on a company wide basis. It has however been described on a smaller scale in the case of the specific task forces involved in the integration process (Meckl, 2004). A matrix organization has already been defined as an elementary structure with (at least) one added dimension (Wolf and Egelhoff, 2012). The two-dimensionality of the structure, which leads to the ability to have a dual focus, can be used to balance the needs of specialization and the needs of coordination. Moreover in an uncertain environment with conflicting interests such as the one in the case of an M&A, matrix is said to have the flexibility to deal with complex and rapidly changing situations (Brown & Agnew, 1982; Sy & d'Annuzio, 2005; Burton et al. 2015). Indeed it seems that this organization is able to process more information, therefore being more flexible and faster than elementary structures (Burton et al., 2009). In line with the "changing nature of the corporate HQ in MNCs" (Birkinshaw et. al, 2017, p. 426), where the HQ, while still owning the subsidiaries, has a less dominant role than in the past, acting more as a coordinator of resources and an enabler for effective cooperation and subsidiary capability development, one could consider the holding company matrix as a potentially appropriate structure for integration.

2.4.6   Relevance and Associated Research Questions

In this section we have seen that the existing literature on culture in MNCs can be relevant for research on matrix organizations. Indeed, the idea from the classic view of literature of two different cultures coming into contact would be pertinent for the context of a holding matrix organization, confronting the two organizational cultures of the dimensions. The linked concept of identity will also be a very interesting addition to research on matrix organizations, as one could imagine that the set-up of a matrix organization could potentially lead to a so-called identity crises. This is why this research will attempt to understand how cultural and identity issues come to life in a matrix organization. Furthermore, the dynamic view of culture, which considers culture to not only be a static reality, but rather a fluid and changing phenomenon, which is influenced and influences multiple levels from professional to national culture can also be interesting to observe in the case of a matrix. On top of that, the fact that the importance of culture has been elaborated upon in the literature on mergers and acquisitions supports the idea that it would be relevant to study culture in the context of a matrix. Indeed, key topics addressed in the merger context, such as synergies, is also important within a matrix, as was identified when looking into the advantages of matrix such the flexibility of resources and the possibility for dual focus on exploration and exploitation, ergo potential synergistic activities. Through this, the potential use of a matrix as a coordination modus for this integration will be developed within this work. Linked to the previous section on power, it will make sense to add to the understanding of the role of culture and identities in the matrix organization, the power capabilities which are used in order to influence the negotiated culture.

As was mentioned in this section, the cultural implications of a matrix organization have yet to be explicitly and empirically studied, therefore allowing for plentiful opportunities for further research. Consequently this work will bring a first look into the impact of culture on the matrix organization and how a matrix organization could potentially be used as a coordination modus for cultural integration. Furthermore, linked to the research on power in the MNC, this thesis will propose an empirical understanding of the power capabilities leveraged by actors in order to influence the practices in MNCs, or negotiated culture in the matrix organization.

2.5 The Role of Boundary Spanning in the MNC

Going beyond the global integration versus local differentiation challenge that MNCs face, Bartlett and Ghoshal (1998), theorize that MNCs must also deal with the need for global innovation. Dealing with these three forces simultaneously can lead to high levels of fragmentation and conflict within the MNC. The mechanisms they recommend to use include structures, formal coordination mechanisms, systems and processes. The mechanism they most recommend is socialization. They explain that the use of only formal mechanisms is not sufficient, but it is the mind-set of the managers which will contribute most to bringing these conflicting forces together. Within this thesis, we will deal with the issue of socialization of the actors, as informal coordination mechanisms using the concept of boundary spanning.

MNCs are not coherent and integrated global operations but are a group of units acting in different local environments and sometimes with divergent goals and practices. The units perform relatively homogenous tasks within specific areas of the organization. Within the unit the efficiency of the information processing will be high, whereas processing information between units or between a unit and the environment will be more difficult (Tushman & Scalan, 1981). This creates boundaries within the organization which can be functional, geographical, temporal, cultural or linguistic in nature. These boundaries are the place where friction can occur and inter-unit relationships may be more difficult. (Barner-Rasmussen et al., 2014). MNCs, due to their international nature, incorporate far more internal boundaries than domestic companies (Casson, 1997), but by offering diverse knowledge and capabilities it can also generate opportunities (Doz et al. 2001, Schotter et al, 2017). This leads to the need for boundary spanners and boundary spanning activities. Boundary spanners are critical to link disconnected parts of the organization and are essential to knowledge transfer and creation as well as innovation (Marrone, 2010). Boundary spanning can therefore be defined as "a process shaped through the interplay of the contextual issues that make a boundary problematic" (Yagi & Kleinberg, 2011, p629), or more simply, as a set of communication and coordination activities performed by individuals within an organization and between organizations to integrate activities across multiple cultural, institutional and organizational contexts (Schotter et. al, 2017). In the context of a matrix organization, boundary spanning is important, as the dimensions of the matrix naturally involve boundaries, and these boundaries need to be spanned in order obtain value from the interaction between the two dimensions. Gos (2015) found boundary spanners to play an important role in the success of matrix organizations. He addressed this issue using the concept of matrix guardians, who he describes as people who play an essential role in fostering cooperation between the dimensions and mitigating conflicts, which is essentially a boundary spanning role. However, in the study researched by Gos, these boundary spanners were unofficial and often hidden within the structure, which he posits may be one of the reasons why the importance of these individuals, whether we name them matrix guardians or boundary spanners, has yet to be discussed in matrix organization research.

This next section will look at the concept of boundary spanning in the MNC. It will start by defining boundary spanning, then explain the boundary spanning activities before looking at boundary spanners and skills required, and finally boundary spanning objects will be explained. The final part of this section will explain the role of boundary spanning in the matrix organization.

2.5.1 Boundary Spanning Activities and their Antecedents

As has been described in the section regarding MNCs, these global organizations are complex. The geographically dispersed activities that they perform lead to entities being embedded in both local contexts and the HQs corporate context. The complexity linked to this dual embeddedness leads to a wide range of boundaries within the MNC, which explains why today's work in MNCs is increasingly complex, combined with changing environmental conditions, increasing global competition and flatter work structures, leading to collaboration across boundaries being essential to the organizations' performance. Work efforts need to be coordinated and disconnected units need to be linked in order to achieve economies of scale by transferring best practices (Cross et al. 2015, Marrone, 2010). Tasks can no longer be done independently or sequentially; they require "interdependent and coordinated action across various parts of the organization" (Marrone, 2010). The high uncertainty, high competition environment that organizations evolve in requires innovation, adaptability and the fast development of high quality products to be able to survive (Marrone, 2010). Therefore, the boundary spanning capacities of a firm have been found to be important to the success of the MNC.

Boundary spanning can be studied between an organization and its environment (Tushman, 1977), where boundary spanners link the "organization's internal network to external sources of information" (Tushman, 1977, p587). Most of the earlier research viewed organizations as a whole and studied their boundary spanning activities with the organization's environment. More recently, the boundary spanning activities between teams within an organization has been studied (Ancona et al. 1992; Marrone, 2010) and there has also been research on the boundary spanning activities of dyads (Barmeyer and Davoine, 2019) or between individuals within an organization (Barner-Rasmussen et al., 2014). However, although boundary spanners can be found on all levels of the organization, this does not mean that all employees should become boundary spanners. Indeed, boundary spanning is a time consuming and communication across boundaries can be inefficient and inaccurate. Therefore too many boundary roles would be inefficient, and they should exist only where needed (Tushmann, 1977).

Boundaries in the MNC have both a division and identification role (Ernst & Chrobot-Mason, 2010). They allow for the division of the organization into parts, making up the sum and dividing up the labor, be it in divisions, functions, or subsidiaries. Furthermore they provide an identification opportunity, by creating an "us" and a "them". The extent of this identification varies depending on the organization, with for example a strong corporate culture leading to strong identification. Strong identification is positive as it has been linked to organizational performance, however it also makes it more difficult for actors outside of the Group to make a connection (Guiso et al. 2017, Schotter et. al. 2017). Naturally, MNCs span different national and cultural borders, simply by operating in different countries. Geographical distance increases the need for coordination (Schotter et al., 2011) and also leads to a higher probably for dysfunctional conflict (Armstrong & Cole, 2002). National boundaries can be seen in both a formal and informal way. To start with, institutional differences such as the labor market and national laws mark the differences between the countries within the organization. These boundaries may also be mirrored within the organizational structure, for example if the MNC is set up based on geographical regions. On top of that, cultural boundaries have been proven to bring boundary spanning challenges, even in the case of culturally close groups (Schotter et al., 2017). Dille et al (2018), describe the fact that organizations' idiosyncratic time may differ from each other, because their notion of time is embedded in the processes, policies and routines of each organization. Stjerne et al. (2019), use the IOP (inter-organizational project) as a basis for research, as it is characterized by conflicting goals and will involve organizations with different temporal understandings and regularities (Dahlgren and Söderlund, 2001). Stjerne et al. (2019), introduce the notion of temporal boundary spanning as key to resolving temporal tensions. They identify three activities: framing, synchronizing and hyping, which help to deal with temporal tensions.

In this next paragraph, we will review the different literature streams on boundary spanning activities. Aldrich and Herker (1977) describe two boundary spanning roles: information processing and external representation. The information processing role selects, transmits and interprets the information from the environment coming into the organization. The external representation role includes all functions that "involve resource acquisition and disposal, political legitimacy and hegemony and a residual category of social legitimacy and organizational image" (Aldrich and Herker, 1977, p220). Ancona et al. (1992), divided boundary spanning functions into three categories: ambassador, task coordinator and scout. Ambassadorial activities aim to protect the team, secure resources and promote the team to other groups. The task coordinator role aims at coordinating the activities of the two units, by negotiating, coordinating and giving feedback in order to bring the two parties closer together. The scouting activities provide access to information beyond the boundary, obtaining information about the market competitors or technology. Tushman and Scanlan (1981) on the other hand view boundary spanning activities as a two-step process, whereby the boundary spanner must first obtain the information and then disseminate it.

Barner-Rasmussen et al. (2014) have more recently described boundary spanning functions in four categories, which we will be using to understand boundary spanning in this thesis. The first, (information) exchanging, includes delivering and gathering information across internal boundaries. The authors note that positions such as expatriates or top management, employees with network or liaison roles, are more likely to engage in this type of boundary spanning. The second, linking, occurs when "boundary spanners use their personal networks to enable previously disconnected actors to link up across internal boundaries" (Barner-Rasmussen et al., 2014, p888). Third, facilitating requires assisting in the interaction across-boundaries of two parties. Finally, intervening includes "resolving misunderstandings, managing conflicts or building inter-group trust" (Barner-Rasmussen et al., 2014, p888). Barner-Rasmussen et al (2014), note that these functions in the order they were described increase in complexity and in how demanding they are to perform.

Schotter et al. (2017) propose a rubber band model to understand boundary spanning. They explain that boundary spanners link the two units while still allowing for enough flexibility or give for the units to adapt to other forces when necessary. The boundary spanners use their position within both organizations in order to replace formal control. This allows the organizations to be able to stray somewhat from the formal course of action if necessary while being kept in line by the 'rubber band' that is the boundary spanner, making sure that they do not stray too far away from the formal guideline. This allows for balance between integration and innovation. Schotter et al. (2017) see this rubber band theory as increasingly valuable in complex environments, with multiple rubber bands dealing with forces from different directions. This is particularly interesting when one considers the question of ambidexterity and the flexible matrix. One could imagine that these boundary spanners acting in this rubber band model could also contribute to the flexibility of the contemporary matrix organization.

2.5.2   Boundary Spanners, Skills and Objects

In order for the MNC to be able to respond to both global and local challenges, it needs be flexible and must be able to manage its boundaries. This however requires investment on the companies' part, as it must encourage its people to act as boundary spanners and make sure they have the skills required in order to perform the needed boundary spanning activities (Schotter et al. 2017). Therefore, this next section will look into these organizational boundary spanners as well as the skills required.

Barner-Rasmussen et al (2014), define boundary spanners as "individuals who are perceived by other members of both their own in-group and/or relevant out-groups to engage in and facilitate interactions between the two groups". Boundary spanners and boundary spanning activity can be encouraged and driven by an organization, by giving competent employees the opportunity to develop their network and knowledge of other units through rotations, training and transfers. Moreover the climate must be created where boundary spanning behavior is encouraged and rewarded (Tushman and Scanlan, 1981). In international business research, the boundary spanners which are researched are often expatriates working in subsidiaries or subsidiary managers, where the boundary spanning activities are actually embedded in their formal positions within the organization (Barmeyer & Davoine, 2019). This is also the case for matrix managers, who are lead to deal with issues in two dimensions of the organization due to their formal position within the structure. Some boundary spanners are created by the organization specifically to deal with difficulties, Tushman (1977) for example when studying R&D laboratories mentions developing special boundary roles for people who are capable of translating information across boundaries. Moreover, Tushman and Scanlan (1981) note that formal status will facilitate boundary spanning activities. This will be interesting to study in a matrix organization, as the structure "creates" boundary spanners, or at least boundary spanning functions. These individuals would therefore be the prime candidates for being highly effective boundary spanners. However, Barner-Rasmussen et al. (2014) found that boundary spanners can be found on all levels of the organization, in an informal fashion. The most effective boundary spanners were not always in the most expected functions (such as subsidiary managers and expatriates) but they could be found on all levels of the organization. In this case, their personal skills drove their boundary spanning abilities rather than their position within the organization. Boundary spanners are rare resources for an organization, as their ability to correctly "translate" vital information across boundaries is a role that is difficult to routinize, leading the organization to have to rely on these boundary spanners and therefore making their position valuable (Aldrich & Herker, 1977). Furthermore, Schotter and Beamish (2011b), found that dysfunctional conflict occurred less in the presence of boundary spanners.

Although boundary spanning activities have been associated with stress and conflict for the boundary spanners (Aldrich & Herker, 1977), it may seem that in fact boundary spanning activities are associated with higher levels of job satisfaction, due to the status and power accumulated through boundary spanning activities as well as the personal growth drawn from working in and with multiple environments and units. Au and Fukada (2002) in their study of expatriates found that those who had boundary spanning roles had the perception of more personal power. They also found that expatriates who engaged in more boundary spanning activities had higher levels of job satisfaction. Moreover, due to the valuable, and hard to routinize skills they bring to the organization, boundary spanning is likely to be associated with promotion and rewards. Promoting boundary spanners rewards this activity and may also give these individual the opportunity to broaden their scope of boundary spanning activities (Tushman and Scanlan, 1981). However, collaboration is time consuming and can lead to overworked employees. In fact, leaders often underestimate how much their employees are overburdened by collaborative demands. This overwork can lead to reduced performance and productivity as well as burnouts and therefore harm the organization (Cross et al. 2015).

There has been little research on the characteristics of these actors who perform the boundary spanning activities in MNCs, and it is still uncertain whether these characteristics can be developed or intrinsic to the actor (Jemison, 1984; Williams, 2002). However, more recently Barner-Rasmussen et al. found that if given development opportunities and organizational support individuals could increase their boundary spanning capabilities through increased social capital (Barner-Rasmussen et al., 2010). Indeed, Barner-Rasmussen et al. (2010) looked into the resources necessary for boundary spanning. They start by explaining that a key requirement for boundary spanning is the spanners possession of social capital, as in the resources which can be accessed thanks to membership in a group or network relationships. They focus on individual level social capital which comes from interpersonal connections between different areas of the MNC. They see this capital as being the sum of three distinct yet interlinked dimensions: structural, relational and cognitive (Nahapiet & Ghoshal, 1998). They found that the more social capital an individual possesses the more likely they are to perform boundary spanning activities and play important roles in bridging the MNC boundaries. First, the structural dimension applies to physical connections, including structure and connectedness. Here one could imagine that the presence of a matrix organization, effectively bringing together people from each dimension could play a role in the capital possessed by the individuals. Boundary spanners need to be well connected within the organization both internally and externally (Tushman & Scalan, 1981). The relational dimension refers to the behavioral obligations and assets which are found within relationships, which includes norms, expectations, trust and identification. Individuals must be perceived as being competent in their work as well as having the required communication skills and background to communicate (Tushman & Scalan, 1981). Here trust is usually the way that this dimension is operationalized (Tsai & Ghoshal, 1998). Indeed, trust generation is a known role of boundary spanners (see Edelenbos & Klijn, 2007; Klijn et al., 2010), and is included by Barner-Rasmussen et al. (2014) in their "intervening" category of boundary spanning activity.

The cognitive dimension is made up of the shared paradigms including shared goals, systems of meaning in language and codes of conduct. Here cultural and linguistic skills will play an essential role. Barner-Rasmussen et al (2014) found that cultural and language skills in boundary spanners were positively linked to their ability to perform boundary spanning activities, for all functions, that is exchanging, linking, facilitating and intervening. Tushman and Scalan (1981) also found that because units develop their own specific technical verbal and non-verbal language, this could lead to misunderstandings when communicating across boundaries, which lead to a need for translation. Moreover, Barner-Rasmussen et al (2014) found that these skills also contributed to boundary spanning versatility, that is, individual were able to perform more of these boundary spanning functions when they were more skilled in in cultural and language skills. Finally they also found that language skills were more important in order to be able to perform the two more complex functions of facilitating and intervening. Boundary spanners need to be able to translate the information across the boundaries, that is they must be able to understand perception gaps between the two parties, for example between the headquarters and the subsidiaries within an organization (Schotter & Beamish, 2011). A global mindset is also deemed to be essential to the boundary spanning in MNCs (Levy et al., 2007; Vora et al., 2007). The complexity and contradictions embedded in MNCs cannot be resolved by structure but need to be built into employees' way of thinking (Bartlett and Ghoshal, 1989). It has been argued that a 'global mindset' is required to span MNC boundaries successfully. Having this perspective is a 'way of being' rather than a skill according to some (see Arora et al., 2004; Evans et al., 2002, 2010), which would let the people deal with the issues in a constructive way rather than fight for one or the other (Furusawa & Brewster, 2019). This also requires the ability to communicate and work in complex situations as well as multiple cultures and be able to manage ambiguous situations and conflict (Furusawa & Brewster, 2019; Schuler, 2004).

Overall in their research, Barner-Rasmussen et al. also found that an important factor in the boundary spanning capacities of individuals was the number of types of social capital that the individual possessed, and that by increasing this, they increased the chances of successful boundary spanning activities. Based on this they created a typology of boundary spanners, ranging from conduits, with two or less types of social capital, ambassadors and finally transcenders who have four types of social capital. Overall transcenders are the most important individuals in bridging boundaries. This will be particularly important in a matrix organization as they will have the capacity to bridge the multiple dimensions of the organization.

Boundary spanning is an essential topic when talking about matrix organizations. When implementing a matrix, an organization brings two or more organizational dimensions together, spanning the boundaries of these two dimensions, creating links that would not naturally occur in a functional or divisional structure. The matrix structure formally creates boundary spanners at the junction of these two dimensions. In order for the matrix organization to function effectively and efficiently, the two dimensions need to be able to work together when needed. The ability for the people working in the junctions of the two dimensions to effectively perform boundary spanning activities is therefore essential to the success of the matrix structure. There has been however, little research done on the nature of boundary spanning activities of actors within a matrix organization, or their effectiveness. Tushman (1977) studies the importance of boundary spanning for innovation. He bases his research on the premise that the communication across boundaries tends to be inefficient and inaccurate, and that effective information transfer across these boundaries is important for innovation. This will be interesting to look into when considering the ambidexterity of a matrix organization. Boundary spanning, however does not always have only beneficial or functional consequences. Indeed information seeking may be slow going, and reducing efficiency and innovation in the party waiting for said information. Moreover if the information received is incomplete or inaccurate, this may also affect performance (Marrone, 2010). Cross et al (2015) also warn against a "blanket approach" towards collaboration, excessive and unfocused collaboration which will overload employees and stall innovation, therefore harming organizational performance. The hierarchy and formal structures can become overloaded when they are used to drive multiple changes, which require mutual adjustment, simultaneously. Cross et al. (2013) recommend using boundary spanners, and their influential positions in the organizational network, to create direction, commitment and alignment to leverage complex change efforts. We posit that the use of a holding matrix organization could also support in focusing the boundary spanning efforts, both by generating opportunities for boundary spanning through collaboration projects and by concentrating the boundary spanning activities within these relevant areas.

2.5.3   Relevance and Associated Research Questions

Overall, in this section we have seen that boundary spanning is an essential mechanism within the MNC, in order to bring together the dispersed areas of the organization. However, it has yet to be developed in the context of a matrix organization. This is potentially due to the rather recent nature of literature on boundary spanning. We have seen that boundary spanners can be active on all levels within the organization and they can have a formal boundary spanning role, or an informal one. They have a key role in organizations as they allow for bridging between unlinked parts of the organization, which will evidently be important when considering the dimensions of the matrix organization. This thesis will therefore start to understand how boundary spanning is deployed in the matrix organization and the role played by boundary spanning in the matrix. On top of that the literature has found that organizations can encourage or support boundary spanning activities, usually based on the example of expatriation. One could assume that the matrix organization both requires boundary spanners and their activities as well as may potentially encourage boundary spanning activities and help focus them in the relevant parts of the organization. It will therefore be interesting to see how the matrix structure impacts the boundary spanning activities within the organization. Finally, the boundary spanners draw on their social capital in order to perform boundary spanning activities, and their boundary spanning activities are contingent on the amount of types of social capital they possess. It will be interesting to further develop this idea and add to the understanding of the required skills and capacities of boundary spanners, as this research is not yet plentiful.

This thesis is taking on a novel view of matrix organizations, using the concept of boundary spanning to further understand how the matrix functions. This will be a potentially significant contribution to the way matrix organizations are researched.

2.6 Research Questions Emerging from the Literature Review

In conclusion, within this first section, a research framework to further understand matrix organizations in a contemporary MNC was developed. In order to facilitate the understanding of this research, the research questions and sub-questions, elaborated based on the identified research gaps in the literature review are available in the annexes. This work started by reviewing the literature on MNCs and the evolution towards the contemporary MNC and the particular challenges it presents, notably due to the changing role of subsidiaries and headquarters. Here the idea that the matrix organization could be a potential solution to deal with the issues raised within a contemporary MNC was raised. Then the review dug deeper into the heart of the topic, reviewing the existing knowledge on matrix organizations and pointing out some interesting gaps in the literature, which is due to multiple factors. The first being that matrix organizations followed a management hype, leading to a lot of enthusiastic literature followed by the inadequate implementation of matrix structures in practice which subsequently led to a downturn in research on the topic. Furthermore the matrix structures in the literature tend to be very broadly defined making it difficult to draw conclusions. A topic in particular which this thesis will build on is the question of decision making in the matrix. Indeed, the most prominent current authors on the topic have developed a theory pertaining to the use of rule-based decision making in the matrix organization which this thesis will attempt to develop. Furthermore, the newly developed theoretical concept of the role of matrix for the ambidexterity of a firm was touched upon, which will be built on further in this research. Then this review looked into conflict, a central concept in the matrix organization, as excessive conflict is often blamed for the abandon of these structures. Here it was found that there are conflicting views on the role of conflict in the matrix and a need for further empirical research on the causes for conflict in a matrix organization was identified. In particular, this research will add to the understanding of matrix organizations through the use of a micro-political perspective, taking into account the power capabilities deployed by the actors in conflict situations in a matrix organization. Then this research delves into a very popular topic within IB research, notably culture and its role in the MNC. This research will apply the understanding of culture and identities to a matrix organization and study its role within this particular structure, as it effectively brings together two dimensions, leading implicit assumption that it will also bring together two cultures. In fact, although it may seem "implicit" as mentioned above, the role of culture has been mentioned in the context of matrix structures, but not extensively studied, meaning that this section is in fact novel to matrix research. Finally, this thesis will add the concept of boundary spanning to research on matrix organizations. This has not yet been done, but it could be particularly relevant as one could consider the different dimensions as boundaries, and therefore the activities happening where the dimensions meet could be boundary spanning activities. This thesis will attempt to understand how the boundary spanning activities are not only performed in a matrix but also how the structure affects these activities. Furthermore this work will also contribute to the knowledge on boundary spanning skills within a matrix organization. Overall this framework builds on the existing research on matrix organizations while also adding other IB concepts which have been shown to be potentially useful in order to further understand these complex structures. In fact this framework can contribute to the literature on matrix organizations in itself, as it offers a novel view on elements, such as culture and boundary spanning, which can be used to assess a matrix organization and its effectiveness. This framework will be developed in an empirical way in the upcoming section which will focus on the research design of this work.

3 Research Design

In the following chapter, we will provide a description of the research paradigm behind this research, as well as explaining the methodological choices made to conduct this study. Furthermore, we will also provide a description of the case study and give a review on the national contexts the company evolves in, as well as defining the holding matrix organization and the cross-brand project. Through this we will develop an analysis grid for our empirical research.

3.1 Methodology

3.1.1 Research Paradigm, Ontology, Epistemology and Methodology

Research paradigms are "overall conceptual frameworks within which some researchers may work" (Healy & Perry, 2000, p.118). Alternatively, a research paradigm can be described as "a set of basic beliefs (or metaphysics) that deals with ultimates or first principles. It represents a worldview that defines, for its holder, the nature of the "world", the individuals' place in it, and the range of possible relationships to that world and its parts" (Guba & Lincoln, 1994). Simply put, a paradigm is a worldview which is shared by a community of researchers (Deshpande, 1983; Healy & Perry, 2000). According to Guba and Lincoln (1994), a paradigm is made up of three elements: ontology, epistemology and methodology. Ontology is, according to Healy and Perry (2000) the "reality" that researchers investigate. Epistemology links the ontology, the "reality" and the researcher (Healy & Perry, 2000). Methodology is the technique used to investigate the researched reality (Guba & Lincoln, 1994; Healy & Perry, 2000). The methodology here, a case study, will be discussed in the following section. Scientific research paradigms can be synthesized into four categories: positivism, realism (or post-positivism), critical theory and constructivism (Guba & Lincoln, 1994; Healy & Perry, 2000).

Positivism considers that there is one quantitatively measurable reality and it is still the most used within science (Healy & Perry, 2000). The researcher is an objective observer, detached from the object being studied and the world it evolves in. The methodology used within this paradigm is predominantly quantitative and the context does not play a role (Guba & Lincoln, 1998). This paradigm is most appropriate for theory testing rather than theory building (Healy & Perry, 2000). The critical theory paradigm is different to the positivism paradigm in that it accepts multiple realities and context is important. Reality is shaped by historical values and "crystalized over time" (Guba & Lincoln, 1998, p. 109). The researcher is linked to the object being studied, and the methodologies most used are not quantitative but dialogic and dialectical (Guba & Lincoln, 1998). Furthermore, this paradigm is appropriate for theory building (Healy & Perry, 2000). Constructivism is similar to critical theory in that it also accepts multiple realities and is also a theory building paradigm (Healy & Perry, 2000). In this paradigm reality is subjective and constructed by the interaction between the investigator and the research object (Guba & Lincoln, 1998). Postpositivsm or realism is close to positivism in that it considers reality to be "real" but however answers some of the criticisms towards positivism by considering it to be imperfectly apprehensible. This paradigm can be both theory testing and theory building where context plays a role.

This research is within the post-positivism, also named the realism paradigm, as this paradigm allows for the study of complex social phenomena (Healy & Perry, 2000). In this paradigm, "a

© Springer Fachmedien Wiesbaden GmbH, part of Springer Nature 2020
J. Shahani, *Limits and Opportunities of a Matrix Organization*, Auto
Uni – Schriftenreihe 149, https://doi.org/10.1007/978-3-658-32261-8_3

participant's perception for realism is a window to reality through which a picture of reality can be triangulated with other perceptions [...] realism relies on multiple perceptions about a single reality" (Healy & Perry, 2000, p. 123). Within this paradigm, qualitative research methods, in particular case studies and interviews (Guba & Lincoln, 1994) can be used. Furthermore, research within this paradigm "assume that the accounts participants produce in interviews bear a direct relationship to their "real" experiences in the world beyond interview situation" King (2004a, p. 12).

3.1.2   The Choice of Case Study Research

According to Yin (2009), there are three conditions which help determine which method is most appropriate. The first condition is the type of research question, the second is the extent of the investigator's control and the third concerns whether the focus is on historical or contemporary events. This research corresponds to the requirements for a case study, as the research questions (as described above) are how and why questions. Furthermore there is no need for the researcher to control behavioral events and finally the focus is on contemporary events (Yin, 2009). Moreover, the contextual conditions are very much significant and relevant in order to understand the phenomenon being investigated, which Gibbert et al. (2008) point out is a key difference between the case study and other research methods.

The case study can be defined in two parts (Yin, 2009, p.18):

1. A case study is an empirical enquiry that:
   - investigates a contemporary phenomenon in depth and within its real-life context, especially when
   - the boundaries between phenomenon and context are not clearly evident

2. The case study enquiry:
   - copes with the technically distinctive situation in which there will be many more variables of interest than data points, and as one result
   - relies on multiple sources of evidence, with data needing to converge in a triangulating fashion, and as another result
   - benefits from the prior development of theoretical propositions to guide data collection and analysis.

There are various sorts of case studies. The first sort of case study is the multiple case study. This has its advantages, since theory building is facilitated by the opportunity for comparison and a higher level of generalization. However, the single case-study also has its strengths. Although generalization and theory building may be more difficult, the single case study may allow for more depth of analysis (Almond et al., 2005). This single case study can either be holistic, meaning that it has a single unit of analysis or embedded, with multiple units of analysis. The single case-study is an effective research design under certain conditions. Yin (2009) lists 5 rationales for the single case-study: it is a critical case in order to test a theory, it is an extreme or unique case, or on the contrary it is a representative or typical case, it is a revelatory case and it is a longitudinal case.

This research is a single case study, with multiple embedded units of analysis. Indeed, within one multinational, the TRATON GROUP, this research has been done on multiple departments, which will be described in more detail later. Arguments can be made that this case is representative and revelatory. Representative, because the context of a multinational company with multiple brands attempting to obtain value through cooperation is rather common today. Revelatory because the use of a matrix organization as an integration mechanism, or even simply how a holding company matrix functions has not been explored. Within the single case study, both the holistic and embedded approach have their strengths and weaknesses. When there are no subunits at hand and the topic of the research is holistic, then the single unit of analysis makes sense. However, there is a risk that the research will have a level of abstraction which is too high. In order to avoid this, multiple units can contribute to focusing the research. Here however, the researcher must make sure to also return to the holistic level, and not limit the analysis to the subunit level. In order to do this it is important to identify what the unit of analysis is (Yin, 2009). In this case, it is an organizational study, with the R&D and HR department used as the two main sub-units, within which multiple projects are studied, these effectively being sub-subunits. This is illustrated in the figure below. Thanks to these units of analysis on the project level, it allows for an in-depth analysis of the projects and their issues. Indeed, in this way we are able to interview the project members on key deciaions and on

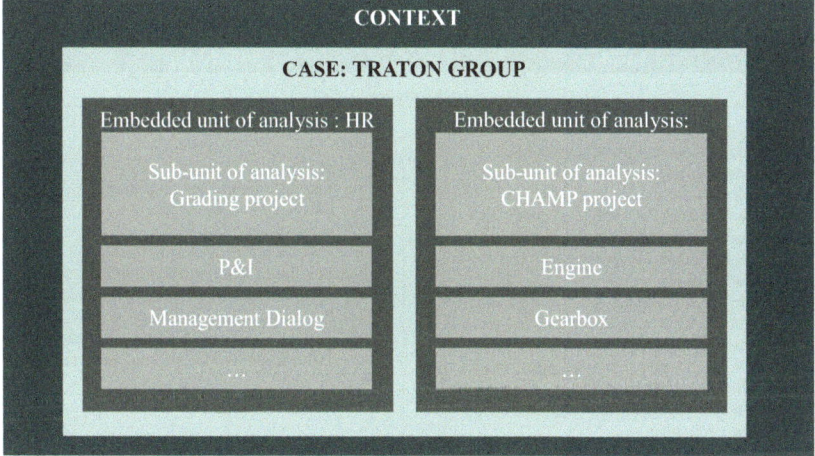

Figure 5: Embedded case study, based on Yin (2009)

concrete events, before abstracting the findings to a department level and then summarizing the the findings from these two departments together.

The fact that the researcher works at TRATON allows broad access to data and information, allowing deep investigation into this single-case. It is however clear that the fact that the researcher is embedded has some risks. Indeed, the fact that the researcher was working within the company itself can lead to a bias, both positive and negative towards the data found. There are advantages and disadvantages to being a participative researcher, as described by Bonner & Tolhurst (2002). Access and understanding of the environement appear as a clear advantage for embedded researchers, but bias can be present. Bias can be found for example when selecting the interviewees, it can be linked to the preferences of the researcher for concepts, kinds of people, therories, etc. Bias can also be linked to the ability of the researcher, as well as their knowledge and skills (Norries, 1997). Furthermore, the fact that the company is named, can be both an advantage, as it allows transparency and the opportunity to describe and explain the case in detail, and a disadvantage as one could consider that there would be certain reluctance to describe negative situations. Furthermore, the embeddedness not only within the TRATON GROUP, but more particularly within the TRATON holding could also lead to a bias towards the cooperation and collaborative role of said holding. In order to counteract these potential biases, certain steps were taken. The study itself has certain design qualities which help eliminate bias. To start with, the interview guideline, which is the basis for the qualitative interviews in this research was tested. It was tested on one German person and one Swedish person and adapted based on their comments as well as the interview itself. For example, if questions were difficult to understand, or leading or if they were not open enough, they were changed. On top of that, the study takes multiple perspectives, with interviewees from different brands, different nationalisties and experiences as well as managers and non-managers. There are also multiple units of anaylsis within this work, different projects which help reduce the risk of bias.

Table 6: Insider versus Outsider Researcher (Bonner & Tolhurst, 2002)

Insider	Outsider
Advantages	
<ul><li>Not seen as 'strangers' but members of group.</li><li>Incorporate traditionally ignored or unrecognised perspectives into theory.</li><li>More economical – know the culture, language (jargon), familiar with local conditions.</li><li>Less inclined to construct stereotypes.</li><li>Easier to gain acceptance, trust and cooperation.</li><li>No decision needed whether to go native or not; question of understanding the group is minimised.</li><li>No lengthy preparation necessary as already in 'field' or study setting.</li><li>Involve yourself fully with the participants and their activities.</li></ul>	<ul><li>Free of commitment to the group.</li><li>Advantage in observation and analysis of events and structures</li><li>Can see properties lost to the insider because of familiarisation and discover something of value to theory or to his hosts</li><li>Seen as objective observer.</li><li>May be more privy to some sensitive information because of temporary stay.</li></ul>
Disadvantages	
<ul><li>Not seen as researchers but advocates by some.</li><li>May be biased towards interpretation/findings.</li><li>May initially have difficulty re-establishing ties with local 'culture'.</li><li>Unknown researcher qualities.</li><li>Reliance on participants with whom the researcher feels comfortable.</li><li>Focusing on the dramatic events rather than the routine.</li><li>Experiencing role conflicts.</li></ul>	<ul><li>Experience 'culture' shock which may delay or interfere with research.</li><li>Take time to establish trust or may never be seen as trustworthy.</li><li>'Cultural' or linguistic (jargon) distance may desensitise researcher to group's needs/meanings.</li><li>May receive 'expected' responses rather than true attitudes or knowledge.</li><li>Lengthy time required understanding the 'culture' and language (jargon).</li><li>Less economical – may need to hire and train 'experts from the field'</li></ul>

Moreover, as a researcher steps were taken to reduce the risk of bias. Being aware of the risk is a first step, which is supplemented by other measures. The first supervisor served as a neutral sounding board, with regular feedback, bringing perspective on findings which could be perceived differently from the inside. Furthermore, the company supervisor and the first supervisor had regular discussions, ensuring that the academic understanding of the data was respected. On top of that, as mentioned above, feedback was also gathered from other external sources outside of the company, for example at conferences. Finally, the way the data was gathered and systematically analyzed using the template analysis method in an anonymous way also supports against bias.

3.1.3   Seals of Quality and Ethics

Every research method has issues and can be criticized, and this is particularly true of the case study method, potentially due to a lack of rigor in past cases (Yin, 2009). Criteria have been developed in order to judge the quality of research designs in order to ensure rigor within the chosen methods. In particular for case studies, one can use the four widely used tests: construct validity, internal validity, external validity and reliability (Yin, 2009).

Internal validity or "logical validity" has been the most used in experimental and quasi-experimental research (Yin, 2009). It concerns whether the researcher makes a compelling, plausible and logical argument for the results of the research (Gibbert et al. 2008, Yin, 1994). This is relevant during the data analysis phase (Gibbert et al. 2008). It is mostly an issue when the researcher attempts to prove a causal relationship. Furthermore, especially in case studies, these issues occur when there is inference made, when an event which is not observed but rather reported (for example through an interview) is used as evidence (Yin, 2009). There are multiple tactics to ensure internal validity such as: including pattern matching, formulating a clear research framework, explanation building, addressing rival explanations, using logic models (Yin, 2009), theoretical and literal replication, in-depth questions, emphasis on "why" issues and describing the context of the case (Healy & Perry, 2000). Within this case, pattern matching has been done, meaning that the empirical results found were compared to those expected from the literature. Furthermore, this research draws from multiple theoretical fields, contributing to the creation of the research framework, and allowing for theory triangulation. Basing research on theory also contributes to validity. Furthermore, the questions asked were developed in depth and there was an emphasis on why questions, as recommended by Healy and Perry (2000). On top of that the context of the case, and the opportunity to analyze it in depth due to the embeddedness of the researcher in said context also fills one of Healy and Perry's criteria.

Construct validity can be defined as the "quality of the conceptualization or operationalization of the relevant context". This is relevant during the data collection phase (Gibbert et al. 2008, p.1466). Basically, the researcher needs to avoid using subjective measures in order to provide an objective reflection of reality. There are multiple ways of making sure of this, the two most used being having multiple sources of evidence, which is also referred to as triangulation of data and establishing a clear chain of evidence (Gibbert et al. 2008, Yin, 2009). There are however also other methods which have been noted, such as having key informants review the draft report (Yin, 2009), using existing theory and having a case study database (Healy & Perry, 2000). In this case, in order to ensure construct validity, the data collected comes from multiple sources including interviewees from the different brands and on different hierarchical levels within the same project. Furthermore the interview data is complemented by internal documentation and reports. Here there are therefore data sources (different interviewees from different angles) and types of source (interview and documentation) therefore ensuring the first point, data triangulation. Moreover, all the data collected has been clearly and electronically filed, and all documents dated, meaning that there is a clear archive with all the exiting versions of all data and research process, therefore ensuring the chain of evidence. All these documents are stored in the same folder, effectively, the case-study database. On top of this all published results are reviewed by multiple parties within the company, following the publication process related to the publication of company data. One of the key reviewers here, related to the HR department was also interviewed after all the initial HR interviews were done in order to establish validity. On top of this, the results regarding HR were presented at an academic conference (Atlas-AFMI, Fribourg, 2019), where academics not co-authoring the paper, reviewed the draft and gave feedback on the paper; one of the points mentioned by Gibbert et al. (2008) as a measure of methodological rigor for case studies.

External validity can also be referred to as generalizability, and is one of the most criticized aspects of single case study research, as mentioned above. This concept in based on the expectation that theory not be built only in context but also be generalized to other settings (Gibbert et al., 2008). Case studies, single or multiple cannot be used for statistical generalization. However, they do allow for analytical generalization, allowing the case study to be a starting point for theory development (Eisenhardt, 1989). Yin (2009) recommends using theory in single case studies in order to ensure validity, as well as using replication within multiple case studies. One could argue when doing a single case study, that if reliability is ensured (as will be discussed in the next section), then a single case study could be replicated in other contexts, therefore allowing for generalization over time. Furthermore, Healy and Perry recommend identifying research issues beforehand in order to develop an interview protocol which provides data regarding these issues specifically.

Finally, the main idea behind reliability is the following: if someone were to do the same research in the same context again, then they should come to the same conclusion. It is therefore important to maintain transparency, through measures such as having a case study database which has already been mentioned above, a case study protocol detailing how the research was conducted, and a description of the case selection and interview procedures (Healy & Perry, 2000, Yin, 2009). In this case, within this thesis a detailed description of the research is provided, answering the criteria for reliability, as well as the case study database with all the data. Overall, within this research, steps have been taken to ensure that this single-case study is rigorous, by using the internal validity, construct validity, external validity and reliability criteria.

Research should be conducted with the highest ethical standard (Yin, 2009). It is important to make agreements about needed anonymity and confidentiality (Hartley, 2004) by gaining informed consent and making sure to protect the privacy and confidentiality of the participants. Moreover, the participants should be protected from any harm and should not be deceived and special precautions should be taken when conducting research that involves especially vulnerable group (for example children). This is not the case within this research as the people interviewed are employees of the TRATON GROUP and there is no deception involved. Within this research, in order to ensure ethical standards and to comply with the regulations at TRATON, the following steps were taken. The research design was approved within the company by the direct manager as well as the company data protection officers. Moreover, in accordance with the regulations, the works councils of all entities were informed of the study. Then each interviewee received a declaration of consent form on which the anonymity and confidentiality modalities were explained, the voluntary nature of the study reiterated and contact of the manager was available in case of complaints. An example of this form can be found in the appendix. The interviews were recorded and transcribed. Once transcribed, the recording were permanently deleted. In order to protect anonymity of the participants the names of the interviewees were removed and a number was assigned to them on the transcript. Furthermore any mention of colleagues or other people were also removed from the transcript.

At the end of the study it is important to make sure to close the project well. This includes reminding the informants about the timeline of the research and when results will be made available as well as how these results will be shared within the organization (Hartley, 2004). Within this research, all the interviewees will receive a report presenting the results of the research in a business oriented manner, as well as an electronic copy of this thesis. Furthermore it is planned that this research will further be used within the TRATON organization, notably within training seminars.

3.2 Case Description and Context

3.2.1 Case Study Overview

The TRATON GROUP is a 100% subsidiary of Volkswagen AG. The TRATON GROUP owns the brands MAN, based in Germany, Scania, based in Sweden and Volkswagen Caminhões e Ônibus based in Brazil as well as a digital brand, RIO. Although the Group is very new, set-up in 2016, the heritage brands MAN and Scania both have over 100 years of automobile and transportation industry experience. However, Volkswagen Caminhões e Ônibus is much younger and RIO is brand-new. TRATON aims to become a global champion (Volkswagen, 2018) and has a clear expansion strategy, because although the company has a strong presence in Europe and Brazil, it wishes to expand worldwide. In order to reach this goal, the company was set up as a matrix organization, as illustrated below. Although the reporting structure of the company is in fact very complicated (as can be seen in the figure below), the focus of this research will be on the TRATON holding and the three main brands Scania, MAN and VW Caminhões e Ônibus, with a particular interest in the role of the holding and the two big historical brands, MAN and Scania. The relationship with the associates and cooperation partners such as Navistar, Hino and Sinotruk will not be elaborated on. The context this company evolves in plays a significant role, and will be highly relevant to understand the phenomenon observed, therefore justifying the use of a single case study (Yin, 2009). This has been developed in the previous section "justifying the use of case study research". The research field can be seen as a "contested terrain"(Dörrenbächer & Geppert, 2011; Morgan, 2001) as it confronts companies with long histories, strong corporate cultures, national cultures, as well as different standards, legal environments, practices and actors.

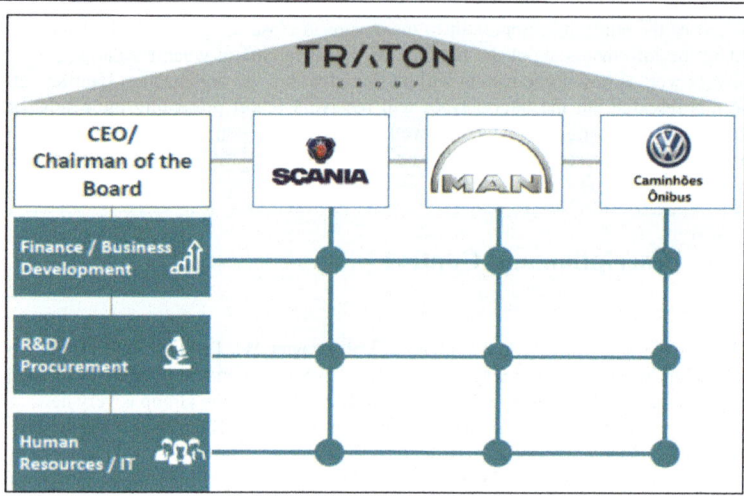

Figure 6: The TRATON GROUP matrix (TRATON internal document, 2019)

The TRATON holding counted around 150 employees at the time of this research, based in Munich, Braunschweig (Germany) and Sodertalje (Sweden). Scania counts around 52,000 employees, based in around 100 countries. The headquarters of Scania are based in Södertalje (Sweden), where most of the Research and Development activities are concentrated. There are however some Research and Development activities in Brazil and India, too. There are production sites in Europe Latin America and Asia, as well as regional production centers in Africa, Asia and Eurasia (Scania annual report, 2018). Scania is one of the leading global providers of sustainable transport solutions, with production in Europe, South America, and Asia. The company offers city buses, intercity and travel coaches, heavy-duty vehicles for long-distance and distribution transport, as well as construction vehicles. Scania is also a leader in networked services in the commercial vehicle industry. In addition, the company offers a variety of supplementary sales and services aligned with its product range (TRATON Website, 2019). MAN is the brand based out of Munich and counts around 36,430 employees (MAN annual report, 2018). MAN is one of Europe's leading commercial vehicle manufacturers. The company has production sites in three European countries as well as Russia, South Africa, India, and Turkey. In addition to vans, MAN builds light- to heavy-duty trucks for distributors and long-distance vans, construction vehicles, as well as city buses, and intercity and travel coaches. Its product portfolio is supplemented by comprehensive sales and services (TRATON Website, 2019). Volkswagen Caminhões e Ônibus is the much smaller brand based in Brazil. Volkswagen Caminhões e Ônibus is a provider of light- to heavy-duty trucks and bus chassis—customized for markets such as Latin America and Africa. The commercial vehicle brand has a comprehensive sales and service network in Brazil and its neighboring countries. Volkswagen Caminhões e Ônibus also offers after-sales services and custom digital solutions for growth markets (TRATON Website, 2019). RIO is the digital brand of the TRATON GROUP and is not a focus of this research. RIO is the global brand for digital services in the transport industry. Its goal is to increase efficiency and profitability in freight transport through data-driven intelligence. To achieve this goal, RIO offers the first open, vendor-neutral, and cloud-based platform for freight transport.

The platform bundles digital solutions for the entire supply chain and delivers valuable recommendations for action in real time (TRATON Website, 2019). This brand is very new and at the time of the research was still building up and recruiting and therefore there were no operational projects which could be analyzed. Although there are officially three brands within the TRATON GROUP, the reality for a lot of the projects was that VWCO, due to the fact that it is much smaller, and used to be part of MAN plays a different role. It seems that the role of VWCO is perceived in the same way by both departments. As they are a smaller entity, they do not have the capacity to participate in all these cross brand projects. However, they do present some interesting challenges. For example, the realities of the market in Brazil are very different to the European ones, which can cause issues when setting up standards, which can be seen in HR concerning bonuses for example. On top of that the geographical and time zone distance, which is small between Sweden and Germany, is much greater for Brazil. These issues will however not be the focus of this research, which will concentrate on the two bigger brands in the Group, MAN and Scania.

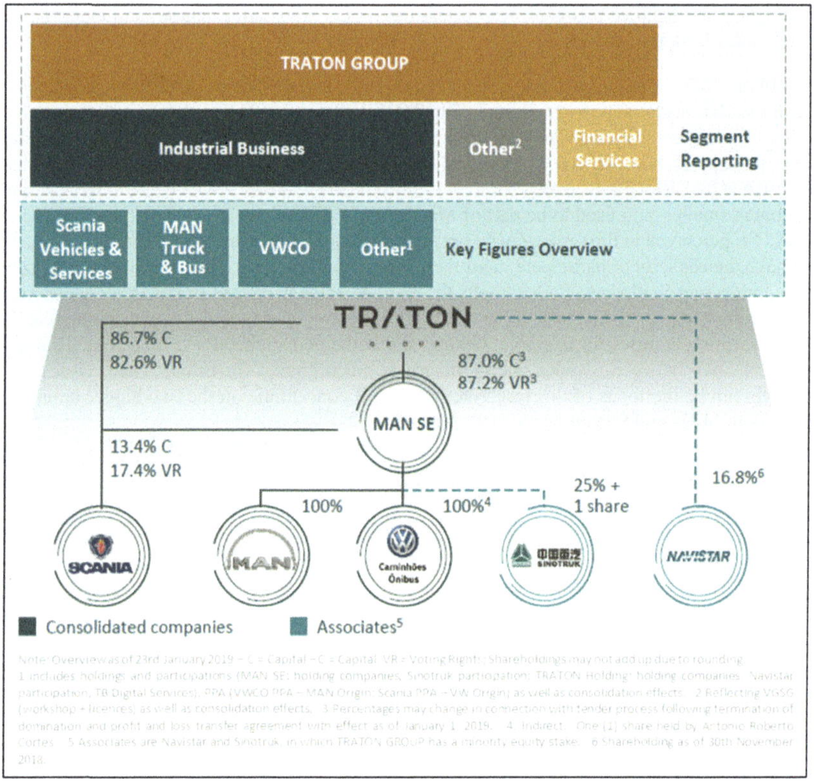

Figure 7: The TRATON GROUP reporting structure (TRATON internal document, 2019)

Figure 8: The TRATON GROUP brand positioning (TRATON internal document, 2019)

3.2.2 National Contexts

In the case of this research, it is obvious that the issue of culture will need to be addressed because the specific environment and contextual conditions of this case, namely a matrix organization formed by a holding bringing together (for the main part) two brands from two different countries, which may lead to not only national but also organizational culture clashes. Although we will focus on organizational cultural differences within this thesis, it is important to note that organizational cultures are embedded in national cultures. This is why it is important to understand the context which the two main brands of the TRATON GROUP are embedded in. Indeed, although there are pressures for convergence, especially with globalization, MNCs remain embedded in their home-country configurations (Ferner et. al. 2001). The institutional and cultural context of the MNCs home country can therefore be expected to play a significant role. As the institutional and cultural context of the two big brands within the case will be relevant, the next section will give a brief overview of these German and Swedish contexts. In terms of German and Swedish culture, although they are geographically close, cultural differences can still be found. They are however often considered to be relatively small (Muller et al., 1999). Barmeyer and Davoine (2008) note that cultural differences in countries which are close, using the example of France and Germany, these issues tend to be neglected and underestimated. Indeed, they point out that in the cooperation between neighboring companies, differences in the working methods and way of thinking of the parties tend to be ignored. However, in the same way as the French and the Germans have been socialized within different value systems as pointed out by Barmeyer and Davoine, so have the Swedish and the Germans. They will have different social norms and sense-making frames. The fact that these differences tend to be neglected can lead to potential misunderstandings and misinterpretation by the parties involved in the cooperation (Barmeyer & Davoine, 2008).

Both Sweden and Germany can be classified as coordinated market economies, where institutions play an important role in market regulations (Hall and Soskice, 2001). Sweden as a country internationalized relatively early due to the country's small home market, with a lot of big firms such as Volvo being less concentrated within Sweden. German MNCs on the other hand have been slower at internationalizing, prioritizing exporting rather than producing abroad (Hayden & Edwards, 2001; Ferner et. al, 2001). The Swedish learn English from a very early age (Birkinshaw, 2002), and Swedish television is rarely dubbed, so any Anglo-Saxon content would often be viewed in English (Goodman & Graddol, 1996). Germany also scores well on this regard, although not as well as Sweden, where Sweden ranks first in English proficiency according to the EF English Proficiency Index, Germany ranks 10th.

Moreover, a defining feature of Germany is its system of industrial relations. Collective bargaining and "mitbestimmung" or "co-determination" play an important role in Germany's business system (Lane, 2000), some may even say that is a determining factor of its management model. The works council plays an essential role within the company and has considerable power in Germany, much more so than any other country in Europe (Barmeyer & Davoine, 2008). For companies over 2,000 employees, the works council even has a strategic role as they can take part in all corporate decisions (Barmeyer & Davoine, 2008). Co-determination also plays a role in the Swedish context, as per the Swedish co-determination law of 1976 (Germany's co-determination law is incidentally also from 1976). The two countries differ in that in Sweden the representatives will be appointed or elected by the union whereas in Germany the works council is elected by all the employees (Muller et. al, 1999). Muller et al (1999) also noted that the unions in Sweden (as well as the Works Council in Germany) also have a significant impact on organizational decision making. However large companies (such as Volvo for example) were not open to this (Hayden & Edwards, 2001) and the industrial relations in Sweden are said to be evolving (Hayden & Edwards, 2001).

Using Volvo Construction Equipment as an example in the context of an M&A, Lee et al (2015) found Volvo's organizational culture as being consistent with Hofstede's conclusion on Sweden. In particular, they found low power distance, including a flat organization horizontal relationships and bilateral informal and verbal communication. Birkinshaw (2002) also comments on the lack of hierarchy, or low power distance, in Sweden and uses the example of a graduate student openly challenging a professor (Birkinshaw, 2002). Hayden and Edwards (2001) also note the democratic approach of Swedish management. It is important to reach a consensus within teams (Hayden & Edwards, 2001; Lewis, 2001). In order to do this, the Swedish have a tradition of open communication and a calm way of solving disagreements. The Swedish managers tend to not issue orders but rather give guidance to their employees (Demir & Söderman, 2007). For example, "most lower-level Swedish employees expect to make most of their own decisions about day-to-day operations." Volvo once gave groups of employee's total responsibility for producing cars, including allocating tasks and rewards and scheduling (Adler, 2002, p187). Moreover, in Sweden it is seen as fully acceptable to bypass the hierarchy, for example in the context of presenting an idea the employee would directly go to the person who would need to be consulted (Hayden & Edwards, 2001). Germany scores equally low in terms of power distance according to Hofstede (2010). Germany has culture of consensus and concertation, with strong standardization and compartmentalization of responsibilities controlling the company. The relationship between colleagues however be quite formal (as opposed to the Swedish informality) where each person has his or her own role and territory (Barmeyer & Davoine, 2008) and managers in Sweden were found to be more democratic and practice more participation than those in Germany (Muller et. al, 1999). Finally, Adler (2002), found the role of the manager to be considered rather differently in Sweden and Germany, based on the question of technical expertise. Sweden scored the lowest regarding the question "it is important for managers to have at hand precise answers to most questions their subordinates may raise about their work", whereas Germany's score was much higher regarding this question.

The way the Germans work is often described as structured, be it in meetings where the agendas are fixed well in advance or the way employees consider their time with a strict barrier between their professional time and private time, communication also tends to be formal and fact-centered as well as detail oriented (Barmeyer & Davoine, 2006a, 2008, Barmeyer et al. 2019). Demir and Söderman (2007) used Berglund and Löwstedt's (1996) four cultural characteristics of the Swedish. They note the homogenous nature of the Swedes, the fact that they are reserved when it comes to trust and social situations, a tendency towards conflict avoidance but with an open and direct way of expressing opinions and finally the fact that Swedes believe in planning. They note that this can be understood as risk and uncertainty avoidance in opposition to Hofstede's view (2010). Westerberg et al (1997) also found tolerance for ambiguity as a main characteristic within Swedish firms and Lee et al (2015) found weak uncertainty avoidance to be a characteristic at Volvo, with elements such as pay and promotion based on individual performance and less emphasis on hard work. Lee et al (2015) found that Volvo was strongly individualist, in line where individual performance is valued, functionally identified jobs and weak loyalty towards the organization. However Birkinshaw (2002) and Demir and Söderman (2007) note that Swedish society is strongly egalitarian. Swedish managers tend to maintain egalitarian relationships, avoiding competition with their peers and tend to rely on their team members for input and initiatives (Lewis, 2000) Sweden, according to Birkinshaw (2002) has a strong collectivist culture, such as the Japanese for example, making the group more important than the individual. For example, the concept of "lagom" or "average" is valued over competitiveness in the school system.

Germany and Sweden have followed a similar path in terms of HR trends including centralization followed by service and market orientation since the 1980s and now a shift of responsibility towards the line management (Muller et al., 1999). However, Mueller et al (1999) found in their study that it is less likely that the German line manager have power over HR decisions than the Swedish ones. Ferner et al (2001) that the HR function in German MNCs has a more "administrative-legalistic tradition of personnel management" (than the Anglo-Saxons), adopting a strategic role at a slower pace (Ferner et al, 2001, p109). The Swedes report more use of formal career plans, high flyer and international experience schemes than the Germans while the Germans report more use of assessment centers, succession plans and planned job rotation (Muller et al., 1999). It is also noted that Germans have a preference towards bonuses as performance related pay whereas the Swedes are more likely to use salary differentials. Another distinctive trait in German MNCs is the use of vocational education or dual paths, where formal and practical training is integrated (Barmeyer & Davoine, 2008, Ferner et al, 2001).

Finally, we will look at the cultural scores of Sweden and Germany in the two most popular large scale research on national culture differences, the first led by Hofstede and the second being the GLOBE research project. The results of Hofstede's research scores are illustrated in the figure below. The dimension where the Swedish and German culture seem to differ most significantly is masculinity.

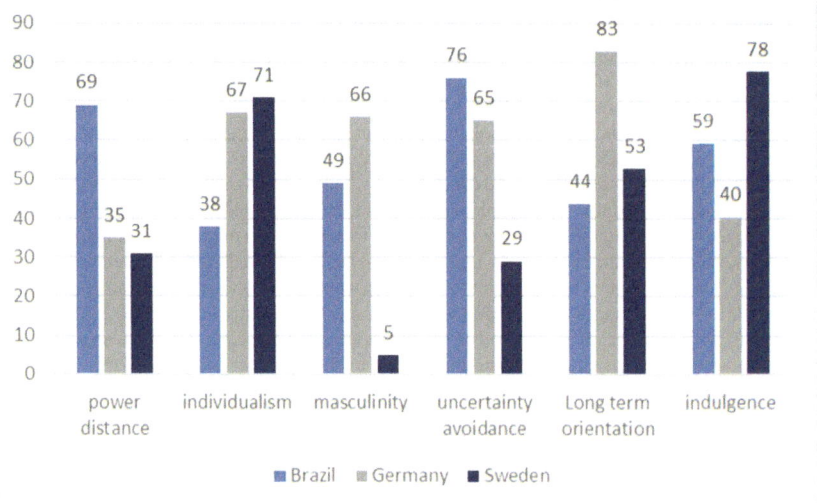

Figure 9: Cultural dimension scores (based on Hofstede 2010, 2015)

Overall it can be expected that the different organizational and national cultures, as well as institutional contexts may create issues. Blazejewski and Becker-Ritterspach (2011) explain that current research finds that teams which are culturally more diverse tend to have higher levels and more intense inter-personal conflict. Moreover, this diversity may increase the chances of the conflict manifesting itself. Ayoko et al. (2002) find that international teams "suffer more conflict, higher turnover and more communication difficulties". It seems that boundary spanners and their activities may have a moderating role in these conflicts, indeed Schotter and Beamish (2011b), found that dysfunctional conflict occurred less in the presence of boundary spanners. Moreover, Barner-Rasmussen et al (2014) found that cultural and language skills in boundary spanners were positively link to their ability to perform boundary spanning activities, for all functions, that is exchanging, linking, facilitating and intervening. Tushman and Scalan (1981) also found that because units develop their specific technical verbal and non-verbal language, this could lead to misunderstandings when communicating across boundaries, which lead to a need for translation.

3.2.3   The Strategic Choice of HR and R&D as a Field of Study

R&D is accepted to play an essential role within the MNC, if not the most essential role, for example Nobel and Birkinshaw (1998) stated that R&D is the raison d'être of the MNC. Indeed, in technology-based companies, R&D is seen as a fundamental driver of value creation (Bodner & Rouse, 2007). Furthermore, R&D has a particular financial value for a firm, as was shown by Johnson and Pazderka (1993) who found that based on their research of the stock market, R&D spending was viewed as an indicator for growth and profitability. Overall in 2018, over 350 billion dollars were invested by UNCTAD's top 100, with automotive MNCs being one of the biggest spenders.

Human Resources play an important role in the success of matrix organizations as HR policies influence the human capital (having competent people who thrive in a matrix context, e.g. people who can influence without authority, are collaborative, are capable of building high-trust networks and inter-personal relationships), social capital (no silos, high-trust personal networks) reward systems and culture, to form a "matrix-supporting package" (Galbraith, 2009). Moreover, Human Resources can play a role in the matrix by dealing with power struggles by adjusting pay levels and changing job titles for example. Training can also contribute to supporting matrix success (Sy & Cote, 2004). A big part of matrix success is the people that make up the firm, as Sy and d'Annuzio (2005) write: "to triumph over complexity and succeed, companies must ensure that their employees are well-equipped to fight this battle." One topic that has been much written about in literature is how to manage in a matrix. Matrix management is seen as critical to matrix success by many authors, such as Bartlett and Ghoshal (1990) who write that "the challenge is not so much to build a matrix structure as it is to create a matrix in the minds of our managers". Ford and Randolph (1992) explain that matrix could create "insecurity for functional managers and erode their authority". Ford and Randolph also question the ambiguity in authority and responsibility created by the matrix organization. They write that many argue that ambiguity is harmful but Goodman (1967) says ambiguity preserves organizational flexibility but note that this is controversial and this work has been criticized as a misinterpretation of data. Davis and Lawrence (1978) identify three unique critical roles within a matrix, each of which has special managerial requirements: the "top manager", the "matrix boss" and the "two-boss manager". It seems that the role of the "two-boss managers" may be particularly important and all the more challenging. Donaldson (2009) writes that "the manager who is subject to two bosses is often based in a foreign subsidiary" and therefore the difficulties of the matrix may be felt more by these managers. Moreover, there may be more "role conflict, stress and job dissatisfaction" (Donaldson, 2009) for managers in a matrix than for those in elementary structures. Burton et al. (2015) also explain that the two boss managers, the ones who work at the junction points, are very important to the success of a matrix; they will therefore need a very specific set of skills. They write that "if a problem occurs at a junction point, it has the potential to ripple across functions and product groups" and call this "the jellow effect". Indeed, for them, the management of junctions is one of the three key factors to matrix success. Burton et al. (2015) explain that "events and actions at the junction points will make or break the organization" and therefore for these managers communication and a willingness to transfer knowledge is essential. Moreover, "matrix managers at the junction want both effectiveness and efficiency but are caught in the middle of this potential conflict." They need skills in negotiation and managing emotions, dealing with uncertainty and ambiguity, sorting out and quickly understanding large scale data and it's implication for decision making, understanding the bigger picture to enhance total firm profits and understanding the organizational culture. (Burton et al., 2015). On top of this, Burton et al. (2015) identify three necessary managerial skills: managers should be able to "focus on the entire firm as well as one's function or division" have an "acceptance of uncertain environments" and "have a willingness to consider complicated trade-offs and negotiate realistic solutions with a focus on results", they also call these leaders "producer leaders", leaders who can delegate and have tolerance for uncertainty. Sy and D'Annuzio (2005) see resistance to change as a key leadership issue, and state that those leaders who are unable to accept change must be removed. Beyond listing the necessary managerial skills needed in a matrix, Sayles (1976) states that "matrix management is not consistent with the traditionally accepted and comfortable 'principles' of good organization and good management", Ford and Randolph (1992) write, similarly, that matrix violates the single line of authority, therefore violating the principles of organization. Sayles (1976) interestingly sees this as an element in favor of matrix because this is what is required in today's "complex managerial environment". The question of whether the necessary skills go against today's principles of good management remains to be seen. Going in this direction, Burton et al. (2009) write more recently that "individuals who have been successful in a hierarchy may not be comfortable or successful in a matrix".

A neighboring topic that Burton et al. (2015) have looked into are the issues that arise for individuals and teams within the matrix, a topic which has been less researched than matrix management. Indeed, the nature of the matrix can lead to ambiguity, especially over "resources, technical issues, pay and personal assignments" (Ford and Randolph, 1992) which can understandably lead to problems. Moreover, matrix can be more "costly for individuals in terms of role ambiguity, conflict and stress" (Ford and Randolph, 1992). Burton et al. (2015) cite the following elements as main challenges for people working within a matrix: "too much or lack of correct information", "heavy workloads" "conflicting goals & superiors", "time orientation differences" and "incentives incompatibility". Yet Ford and Randolph (1992) found "increased individual motivation, job satisfaction, commitment and personal development" to be an advantage of matrix organizations and Brown and Agnew (1982) find "opportunities for personal development through broader experience and greater responsibility". In which cases this is true and counterbalances the challenges of a matrix, remains to be seen. Burton et al. (2015) add that matrix has a "high-tension" and "high-readiness to change" climate, therefore employees must have adequate resources to deal with change and have an open attitude towards it. They explain that this tension helps to drive performance as people deal with fluctuations in trust and conflict but that this is a very competitive environment to work in. Therefore people who do not like a competitive environment will have a tendency to leave the matrix.

One matrix advantage found by Ford and Randolph (1992) is the "flexibility in use of Human [...] resources". In order to maximize this and deal with the challenges associated with matrix organizations for both managers and non-managers, it seems that some processes are essential.

When Sy and d'Annuzio (2005) looked into the main challenges of the matrix they found that a list of five problems: misaligned goals, unclear roles and responsibilities, ambiguous authority, lack of matrix guardian and silo focused employees. They wrote that all these elements were related to employee performance. Their suggestion for a successful matrix organization was therefore having an effective employee evaluation system. Burton et al. (2015) find that many matrix organizations fail because the incentive does not support the complexity of the matrix. Therefore "incentive systems should support the activities at junction points". Profit or gain sharing has to be a significant part of an incentive system in a matrix and people should be rewarded on the basis of collaboration, "people should feel that individual performance can make a difference for the group outcome". They also note "the smaller the target group the more likely the gain-sharing scheme will have the anticipated effect".

Derven (2010) notes the importance of learning in the matrix in order to obtain the relevant skills. He recommends that organizations have "embedded matrix best practices into leadership development programs", "leverage leader-led learning, where executives visibly support the behaviors that will promote the matrix", "specific training on the matrix and promoting best practices" , "incorporate matrix learning into onboarding materials" and "teach critical behaviors, including collaboration, communication skills, conflict management, team alignment, emotional intelligence and building cross-functional networks".

Communication is also an important success factor to a matrix organization. Ford and Randolph (1992) wrote that most of the advantages of a matrix came from improved communication. Burton et al. (2015) state that there needs to be "close inter-relationship among all the activities" in a matrix and Burton et al. (2009) explain that "management must invest in developing cross-organizational coordination" such as lateral relations, liaison roles and coordinating committees. Moreover, knowledge development and sharing is a key contingency in the matrix structure, therefore IT needs to be used to manage information intelligently (Burton et al., 2015).

3.2.4 Defining the Holding Matrix Organization and the Cross-Brand Project

The holding company or H-form of the firm, as defined by Williamson (1975), differentiates itself from other organizational forms by not having an internal capital market. The H-form's main difference when compared to the M-form is that the headquarters do not perform strategic or controlling functions, as the responsibility for these lie in the divisions. Therefore the competition between the divisions is instead focused on the resources provided by the holding company. Because of this, H-forms can more easily add or remove divisions by selling or acquiring them (Weir, 1995; Williamson, 1975). The case of the holding company matrix has been little developed. Galbraith (2009) provides the example of Time Warner which is organized as a holding or conglomerate matrix with very independent divisions. This independence is indeed what differentiates the holding company matrix, which is like the "usual" matrix made up of corporate function crossed with profit centers, with however increased independence for the profit centers and a reduced role of the corporate functions. In our case, the holding company matrix is such that the dimensions of the matrix are made up of brands, Scania, MAN and Volkswagen CO, which were previously independent before being acquired by the Volkswagen Group, at different points in time. The two biggest brands, Scania and MAN then continued to operate rather independently under the umbrella of the Volkswagen Group, focusing their synergy efforts on a few projects and responding to requirements which the Volkswagen Group would set on all its brands, with varying levels of success. The goal behind the creation for the holding was to identify and coordinate further synergy efforts, using the matrix organization to intervene in a horizontal capacity.

Schweiger et al (2003, p128) characterize transnational project teams and networks using the following criteria: They are (1) involved in creative tasks, i.e., the creation of new knowledge incorporated into products and services, (2) functionally heterogeneous, (3) nationally heterogeneous, (4) virtual in the sense that all team members are not co-located in the same geographic territory, i.e., they are physically dispersed and (5) their formation is either "improvised" or emergent or stimulated through a top-down "business planning" process. Here we define a cross-brand project in a similar way, using the same criteria, only adding that in order to be classified as a cross-brand project, there must be team members from at least 2 brands. The relationship within these teams may vary, in some cases it may be a relationship of equals, for example when developing a new process, method or product together, whereas in other cases it may be more of a supplier-customer relationship, for example in R&D if one brand is developing a product for another brand. When looking at how authors describe the characteristics of IOPs (Inter-organizational project), one could clearly consider the cross-brand project, as described within this research, to be an IOP. An IOP can be defined as a "nexus of activity" or a strategic venture which requires various organizations to collaborate in order to achieve a goal (Jones & Lichtenstein, 2007). These projects can be used in order to develop new products, initiate organizational change or build organization capacities (Stjerne et al., 2019). The collaboration and cooperation between these different organizations with potentially conflicting interests, identities and processes can lead to difficulties (Dille & Söderlund, 2011). Because of this, the occurrence of goal conflict is likely and negotiation efforts are required in order to cooperate successfully. Since they offer the possibility for the use of multiple perspectives and complex problem solving, IOPs are being used increasingly (Lundin et al., 2015). Stjerne et al. (2019) explain that because of the fact that IOPs involve a diverse set of parties and organizations, common ground is required in order to promote cross-border interactions and facilitate the integration of knowledge as well as to overcome differences in cultures, languages, views and understandings (Bechky, 2003; Lenfle and Söderlund, 2018; Vijk et al., 2008); and to resolve various problems related to coordination (Mors, 2010). This form of project has been described by Manning (2017) as an innovative organizational form and researchers have stated that more research is need on the topic of IOPs. When looking at this short description of IOPs, it is easy to see that all the points made reflect those of this case, even if the organizations here are part of the same Group. Therefore one could consider the findings of this thesis as direct contributions to the literature on IOPs. In fact, it even answers the call for more research on the governance and dynamics of such structures (Stjerne et al., 2019). Brannen and Salk (2000) have identified four categories which can be used to understand the different types of projects, or negotiated practices. When the practice from one group is adopted by the other group, the category has been named "compromise by one group". When both groups compromise, the category is "meeting in the middle". When both groups create a new practice which is not based on one's groups practice, it is "innovating something new for both groups". The last category, "division of labor", occurs when each group performs tasks separately. In this last case, this is no longer considered to be a cross-brand project as each brand would operate separately. The three previous cases can however occur, and have occurred within the projects studied in this research.

MNCs today are no longer just trying to control their foreign subsidiaries but are attempting to cooperate with them. In order to do this, projects have a central role (Mendez, 2003). Transnational projects teams and networks have an increasingly important role to play in facilitating these horizontal coordination activities (Schweiger et al., 2003). A transnational project can be defined as a "cross-border organizational unit composed of members of different nationalities, working in dispersed business units and functions, thereby possessing knowledge for solving strategic tasks in the MNC" (Adenfelt & Lagerström, 2006). These projects are critical because within an MNC today and in order to be able to innovate, the company must be able to leverage skills and competences from within the whole company, across borders and functions (Schweiger et al., 2003). Coordinating projects across borders presents a specific set of challenges, as the interests and priorities of the actors involved may differ, potentially leading to behavioral problems within these cross-border teams, such as free riding, evasiveness, non-response, non-participation and lower effort (Sapsed & Salter, 2004). Collaboration between the various parts of the organization or between different organizations requires alignment from the actors within these parties. Although project management literature traditionally considers projects as isolated occurrences, more recent literature has considered projects to be embedded within the context of the wider permanent organization. Therefore the properties of the organization, such as its norms and values, will have an impact on the project (Klimkeit, 2013).

3.3 Data Collection and Analysis

3.3.1   Data Collection

Interviews represent one of the main avenues for data gathering in case studies (King, 2004), as is the case within this research. Therefore it is important to have an effective sampling strategy in order to ensure that the interview partners are the correct ones. In order to do this, the position of the researcher, working within the TRATON holding, was a clear benefit, as it allowed for the creation of a network within the firm. Within the HR department, the main cross-brand projects were identified fast, as they were the main projects being worked on by the HR team within TRATON. Once that was done, the main brand counterparts were identified and contacted based on information provided by the TRATON holding HR colleagues. For the R&D department, this exercise proved to be more difficult for a couple reasons. To start with the people informed were no longer direct colleagues but rather people from other departments, furthermore, R&D projects tend to be both confidential and involve many more people than the HR projects. This therefore made it more challenging to gain access. However, 19 interviews were obtained with employees from all brands within R&D.

This research is based on data from 42 qualitative interviews, which were conducted in English, both face to face in Germany and Sweden as well as with Skype and on the telephone, between March 2018 and April 2019. These interviews lasted approximately from 30 minutes to 90 minutes and were recorded and subsequently transcribed. The interviews were conducted with employees from the following brands, all part of the TRATON GROUP: TRATON SE, TRATON AB, MAN SE, MAN TB, Volkswagen Caminhões e Ônibus, and Scania. The main criteria for the interview partners is that they work within Human Resources or R&D and are participating or have participated in at least one significant cross-brand project.

Table 7: Interviewees per brand (own elaboration)

Brand	Number of HR interviewees	Number of R&D interviewees
MAN SE & MAN TB	7	6
Scania & VWTB AB	10	9
VW Caminhões e Ônibus	2	1
TRATON SE & AB	4	3
Total	23	19

In the case of HR, making the most of the relatively small range of projects, after the initial wave of interviews at Scania and TRATON AG, a list of main ongoing projects was established and used to identify the potential interviewees at MAN SE, MAN TB and Volkswagen Caminhões e Ônibus. This will support data validity, as each project has at least two interviewees and/or secondary data supporting the information given by the interviewees. Data saturation is reached through a relatively high number of interviews within a small group of potential interviewees. In comparison to HR, where the projects tend to be quite small, R&D has projects with over 100 participants, working over a number of years. Furthermore, access to these interviewees was harder to come by, as the network and contacts needed to be established. Some of these interviews were part of the core projects which we analyzed as will be seen within the empirical findings section, whereas other interviews, which did not concern these main analyzed projects were used to gather general understanding rather than information on specific project issues.

Each interview was semi-structured, using a guideline containing 21 main questions and 43 follow up questions. The guideline can be found in the annexes. The first part focuses on learning about the interviewee, their current job as well as the cross-brand projects on which they and committees they are part of. The second part asks the interviewee about their perception and understanding of the TRATON GROUP matrix. After the first wave of interviews it was felt that data saturation was reached on this topic and that the data collected here, although interesting from a company perspective, had little relevance to the research. The second wave therefore concentrated on the third part, which uses a project the interviewee has recently worked on in a cross-brand context as a focal point and is centralized around decision making and conflict within this project. The last questions ask the interviewee if they would be interested in the results of the research, and what specifically could be of value to them.

These interviews were then transcribed in MS Word. These interviews were transcribed into a template, which mentions the date and duration of the interview as well as if the interview was held face to face or by telephone or video-conference. The interviews were transcribed literally, and the grammar and sentences of the interviewees, who are not native English speakers, was not corrected. Punctuation was included to facilitate the reading of the transcripts, and only the spoken words were transcribed.

3.3.2 Data Analysis

Then these transcripts were analyzed using the template analysis method, developed by King (2004). This method is not a clear-cut single method but rather a group of various techniques to analyze textual data. This method is rather flexible which therefore allows each researcher to adapt to the specific context of his/her research. Template analysis is suitable for analyzing large quantities of data and comparing different perspectives and angles from various sources, which is suited to this international cross-brand study. In order to use the template analysis method, a priori codes were developed, the most important topics and themes, based on the expectations from the literature. This led to a fairly extensive table of codes and sub-codes which can be found in the annexes. The interviews were then transcribed and analyzed using this table. This analysis was done using Microsoft Excel. Once a small number of interview was coded using this table, the coding table was adapted, some codes were added, deleted or modified in order to better suit the data. This is quite normal and in fact important, in order to extract all value from the data analyzed, for example Miles and Huberman (1994), point out that the adaption of the coding table is important. After this initial phase, the initial coding table is elaborated and applied to all the data. A record of the modification of the coding table, as well as the reasoning behind the decisions was kept in order to have an audit trail (King, 2004) for future reference. However, this is not the final stage, and the table is adapted in parallel with the coding of the data. For example, in some cases, the codes decided upon were very rarely used, because the data was not available, like for example the code "dispositional trust" which was in one of the adaptations of the coding table. Therefore it was removed. Furthermore, in one of the most recent versions of the analysis grid, the codes were divided into issues and facilitating factors. This was also changed as making the differentiation proved to be impossible, with certain codes falling in both categories making the differentiation therefore irrelevant. Another occurrence was that some pieces of data seemed to be "uncodable" based on the initial analysis grid, which led to the creation of a new code to fit the data. Furthermore in some cases codes were added due to new literature. For example, the concept of temporal boundary spanning, based on a paper published in 2019 was added later into the coding table. The initial grid as well as an example of how it was adapted can be found in the annexes. The final table is then used for interpretation and discussion of the data.

A final analysis grid, summarizing the codes has been developed in order to present the results of the analysis. This grid has been developed and matched to our research framework developed in part one. In this section, the analysis structure which will be used to present the empirical findings will be explained.

To start with, the question of the mechanisms of control and coordination, focused in particular on the processes and role distribution has already been addressed in the past research on matrix organizations. This case study will help clarify and contribute further empirical evidence to how these processes and the governance structures can support the success of a matrix. This category is particularly pertinent as not only does it relate to decision making which is the next section, but will also consider the issues of balance of power in the matrix as well as touch upon the question of culture, since processes are an observable manifestation of culture.

We have chosen to focus on a decision making and conflict as a key factor for analysis. The complexity of decision making in a matrix organization has been made clear in past research and has been an important part of the most current research on the topic. The main issues raised by classic matrix literature include the speed of decision making, where the matrix reportedly has slower decision making than an elementary structure. This would be interesting to observe in a contemporary matrix organization, as this is one of the oft cited downfalls of such a structure. Furthermore, the issue of balance of power in decision making within a matrix has been a clear topic for discussion. In this regard, we would wish to further contribute to the research done by Wolf and Egelhoff on decision making in the matrix and further understand the theoretical concepts developed by these researchers notably on the question of rule-based decision making and its use in a matrix organization. On top of that, we would like to observe the potential task conflicts appearing within decision making, using the sub-categorization also developed by the aforementioned authors, with the matrix in mind, which is goal, authority and evaluation conflict. The presence of relationship conflict, if occurring will also be noted.

Next, and once again with the desire to build on the most recent research in matrix literature, we will look into the question of learning, knowledge and innovation. As has been described in part one, Wolf and Egelhoff have described a purely theoretical framework regarding the opportunities of a matrix for ambidexterity. By looking into projects and especially R&D projects, we would expect innovation to be an important topic for the organization. Therefore it would be interesting to see how the potential for innovation is affected by the matrix organization and if we can find empirical evidence to the theoretical concepts we have described in the literature review. In particular, as is developed in the theory, it would be pertinent to link the decision making which occurs, therefore considering the findings from our first category, and the potential for innovation observed within the projects.

Furthermore, the issue of culture and identities is part of our grid. The reason behind this is that they are strong topics within the international business stream of research on multinationals but not yet been addressed strongly in the context of a matrix organization. This research will therefore help identify how these typical MNC issues are present in the case of matrix organizations. The idea here is to see if the respondents perceive cultural differences and how they are manifested in the matrix organization. Interestingly, in the questionnaire, there is no direct mention of culture or specific question regarding culture, therefore the fact that it came up frequently, as will be explained in the empirical section, shows that it is a topic which deserves to be considered in this context.

Furthermore, in the research on MNCs, boundary spanning has emerged as an important facilitating factor for the coordination of a firm's activities. Therefore it is relevant to consider boundary spanners and their activities. Here the goal is to find out what activities are performed in the context of a matrix organization and how they are done. This will give us the opportunity to further understand the matrix through the lens of boundary spanning. The skills and knowledge required to perform these activities will also be analyzed. This too is a topic which has not been addressed in the context of a matrix organization, neither in a theoretical way, nor in an empirical way. Therefore this case study presents a good opportunity to make a first step and explore the realm of possibilities regarding the role of boundary spanners in a matrix organization.

Table 8: Final analysis grid (own elaboration)

Mechanisms of control and coordination
Decisions and conflict
Learning, knowledge and innovation
Culture & identities
Boundary spanning

Overall this grid will help us answer our research questions in structured way, bringing to light the key matrix elements within our case and allowing us to measure them up against the findings from the theoretical research.

4 Empirical Findings

This chapter will analyze the empirical results of this research. This will be the base for the findings and potential theoretical contributions which will then be presented in the subsequent section. Overall, the next section will present the results from over 40 interviews, within three brands and the holding, looking into two departments and with a detailed look upon nine cross-brand projects. It is the heart of the research and also its strength, as the access offered, thanks to the embedded researched is extensive. This allows for a deep empirical understanding of the case study, which will subsequently be distilled into further theoretical contributions on the topic of matrix organizations. Within this section the thesis will start by analyzing the HR projects and their role within the matrix organization. In order to provide an understanding of these projects, it will start by describing the HR organization within the TRATON GROUP, as well as the role of the HR function and the scope of the work done. Furthermore, it will explain the governance structure which has been set up to manage the cross-brand HR organization. Then it will dive deeper into each project individually. In order to provide a structured and comprehensive analysis, the description and analysis of the projects will follow the grid previously developed based on the literature review and elaborated upon in the research design section. It will then follow this same structure for the R&D organization, before summarizing the empirical findings of this research. Using this structure will allow this chapter to provide a comprehensive analysis of the data, while potentially contributing to scientific research. As a reminder the grid developed focuses on the following elements which were developed based on the desk research, creating a framework for analysis of the matrix organization. This framework is divided into the following categories, namely "mechanisms of control and coordination", "decisions and conflict", "learning, knowledge and innovation", "culture and identities" and "boundary spanning". In order to do this, each project will separately be observed through the lens of this framework in order to extract the main ideas from the data. This systematic use of the research framework applied to both departments of study will allow for an in-depth understanding of the issues and facilitating factors identified within this case study. Furthermore it also allows for comparability between the HR and R&D findings.

4.1 HR Project Analysis

4.1.1   The HR Function Governance and Chronology

Starting from the top with the HR board member, this paragraph will briefly describe the current HR organization within the TRATON GROUP. The board member for HR at TRATON is also the board member for HR at MAN T&B, he has a double function. Below him comes the "Human Resources & HR Strategy Manager" who has a team which grew from relatively small in 2016 (7 people) to 30 people in 2018 divided into three teams, HR strategy, HR Operations and Administration. This growth came naturally with the build-up of the holding which also went from 5 people in 2016 to around 150 people in 2018. Furthermore, as the MAN holding was then brought together with the TRATON holding, the holding can be considered to count over 300 people. Nearly all of the HR cross-brand work is done by the HR strategy team. The HR operations team is made up of business partners for the Holding function and the administration team also focuses solely on supporting the TRATON holding. Each brand also has its own board member for HR (for MAN it is the same person as the TRATON HR board member), as well as all their HR departments. The HR head of TRATON is the chairman of the HRMC and then also part of the CHRO, creating a link between the two bodies. In the CHRO

© Springer Fachmedien Wiesbaden GmbH, part of Springer Nature 2020
J. Shahani, *Limits and Opportunities of a Matrix Organization*, Auto
Uni – Schriftenreihe 149, https://doi.org/10.1007/978-3-658-32261-8_4

we have the Board member for HR and he is in the Truck board, so he is the link there. At MAN the HR function is also rather big and is organized in the following way. The HR board member, who is also the HR board member for the TRATON GROUP, has 5 functions below him within the MAN organization. The MAN Academy, the Top Management HR function, the Organization HR processes and IT department, Politics and Labor relations as well as HR operations. The Scania corporate HR function counts around 600 people. On top of this corporate HR function, each other function has their decentralized operational HR function, which reports directly to the relevant function. For the HR holding function, the role is not to fully harmonize the HR strategies of the three brands, but rather to find areas with synergistic potential. This is done by the HR strategy team, this team of around 5 people at the time. Each of these 5 people coordinate a certain number of projects, generally in the same area of HR work. For example, one person is in charge of personnel development, another person looks after the grading project, another coordinates the HR IT projects, someone leads the Global Assignment and international cooperation projects and another person coordinates labor relations and diversity and the employee survey.

Table 9: HR governance structure (TRATON internal document, 2017)

	CHRO Meeting	**HRMC**
Tasks	<ul><li>Decide on strategic HR topics according to decision scope</li><li>Representation of Truck Board and group interests</li><li>Escalation via Truck Board Meeting</li></ul>	<ul><li>Conceptual work on strategic HR topics</li><li>HR Competence Management and deep dive into strategically relevant topics and best practices</li><li>Reports to CHRO Meeting via Liaison Office</li></ul>
Participants	CHROs & link (holding HR manager)	2 per brand
Frequency	<ul><li>Bi-weekly video call</li><li>At least twice per year physical meeting in conjunction with Strategic HRMC</li><li>VICO at the end of HRMC Workshops</li></ul>	<ul><li>Bi-weekly telephone call (in conjunction with Liaison Office)</li><li>4 workshops/year: 2 Concept workshops and 2 Strategic HRMC (all in conjunction with CHRO sessions)</li><li>Different locations at all brands (1 in Germany / 1 in Sweden per year)</li></ul>

In order to facilitate the work between the brands, a governance structure has been set up. It takes the shape of an "HR management committee" which is made up of two HR top managers for each brand and led by the head of the holding HR. This committee generally meets up three times a year and the current status as well as needed decisions of ongoing strategic projects are presented. They also have regular calls or video conference meetings, on a quasi-weekly basis. Above this is the CHROs (board members for HR from each brand) also meet up regularly, generally one or two days after the HR management committee, to further approve decisions.

The Holding HR manager creates the link between these two levels, as he also participates in the CHRO meeting.

The first project that we will address is the management grading project. The reason we address this project first is that it creates a basis that facilitates many other HR processes, including rotations or global assignments, compensation and personnel development. These companies had different ways of grading their positions and the goal of the project was to decide on and implement a common grading system for management within the whole group. This project was run with one team member from each brand, each nominated by their own HR board member to be part of the project team. The challenge here was to find a common grading system for mangers that would be useable in an international context. The second project is the implementation of a management dialogue on a group wide level, in order to create a joint standard for evaluation. It was decided that there should be a common management dialogue for all brands. This would allow for comparable performance evaluation within brands, again supporting other HR processes along the way. The third project is the development programs within the TRATON GROUP. These programs are specifically designed to develop cross-brand cooperation skills. There are multiple development programs on all the levels of the organization, from the trainee program at an entry level to the executive program for top managers. These programs are complementary to the already existing development programs within the brands, adding or completing the current offer rather than replacing it. The fourth project is the diversity strategy within the TRATON GROUP. The topic of diversity was first raised within the TRATON Holding and it was suggested that this was a topic with synergistic potential. The fifth project concerns the Global Assignment toolbox. The goal of this project was to broaden the offer of potential assignment types by designing policies which would enlarge the scope of the current opportunities for assignments.

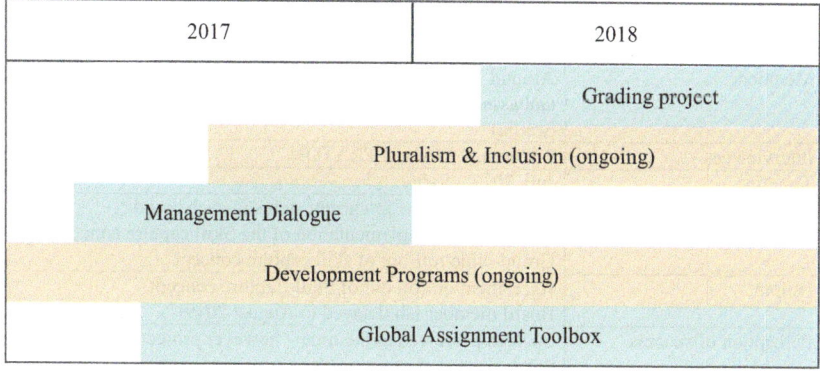

Figure 10: HR project timeline (own elaboration)

Now that we have provided a brief overview of these cross brand projects, we will go into detail using the framework to analyze how each of these projects functioned and the matrix issues associated. Within this next chapter we will describe the five main cross-brand projects which were described by the interviewees. Here we will explain the goals, the value and the issues related to each project. Then we will analyze and explain the results. Each project is also summarized in a table at the beginning of the section. The data from the secondary projects will be used within the transversal analysis but the projects in themselves do not hold much interest.

The RIO employee move and the new compensation logic at TRATON AB were two projects which were in fact very operational and did not have cross-brand scope. The Common health project was just one workshop which was never followed up upon. StiBa is in fact a well-honed process from VW, it is the "Stimmungsbarometer" or Employee survey which happens every year. Here the TRATON GROUP just has a network of coordinators and attempts to harmonize the basics of the survey, such as the survey period and the communication message. There is however no further impact. Finally, the Executive Group Compensation, although potentially interesting in terms of strategic impact had only one respondent, therefore not giving a full overview of this project. Therefore this information from this interview will also only be used within the overall data analysis.

Table 10: HR projects overview

Grading project	
Goals	Harmonized management grading for the TRATON GROUP.
Members	1 person per brand + consulting company.
Interviewees	1 VWCO – 1 Scania – 1 TRATON
Timeline	April 2018 – December 2018
Phases	1. Select grading systematic 2. Implement grading systematic
Output	Grading implemented for all brands.
Perception of success	Successful, with some results different to expectations, especially at VWCO.
Pluralism & Inclusion Project	
Goals	Meet the future challenges when it comes to a diverse workforce, in order to deal with the upcoming competence gap. Main strategy: the skill capture concept.
Members	Around 7 to 10 people from all brands. For the roll out, ambassadors of the concept are then used (around 30 for Scania)
Interviewees	2 Scania, 2 MAN, 2 TRATON
Timeline	July 2017 – today
Phases	Information share on current status in each brand Alignment on implementation of the Skill capture concept Group-wide roll-out of skill capture concept
Output	Agreement on roll out of Skill Capture concept. Board member lab delayed to August 2019
Perception of success	Success perceived at the time – however project currently delayed.
Management Dialogue project	
Goals	Implement a common performance evaluation system for managers within the TRATON GROUP.
Members	Around 8 to 10 people from all brands – 4 main people involved.
Interviewees	1 Scania, 1 TRATON
Timeline	Developed in 2017 – used yearly in December and January
Phases	Designing the template

Implementation (with Scania having a pilot year first)	
Output	Implemented management dialogue in all brands with brand-specific adaptations (e.g. leadership principles)
Perception of success	Perceived as successful – especially in the second year where all brands have an aligned template
Development programs project	
Goals	Develop Group development programs on all levels, in addition to existing brand programs
Members	Around 10 people from all brands and external suppliers (e.g. business schools)
Interviewees	3 Scania, 1 TRATON, 1 MAN, 1 VWCO
Timeline	2017 – today
Phases	Trainee program Executive Elite program Other programs (e.g. leading the future)
Output	Successful Trainee program and Executive Elite program
Perception of success	Successful – trainee program appreciated
Global Assignments Toolbox project	
Goals	Increasing international mobility within the group, especially between the brands
Members	Around 10 people from each brand
Interviewees	1 Scania, 1 TRATON, 2 MAN
Timeline	May 2017 – July 2019 (pilot phase started)
Phases	Information sharing – gap analysis Development of 3 potential mobility tool ideas (cafeteria approach, SIA, young professionals) Focus on SIA
Output	SIA policy approved and to be implemented
Perception of success	SIA policy responding to need – successful

4.1.2   Group Grading

To start with, this section will give an overview of the grading project, describing the goal and the results of the project. As described by the interviewees, the goal of this grading project was to find a common grading system for managers that would be useable within the whole TRATON GROUP and within an international context. Each of the companies within the TRATON GROUP had different ways of grading their positions and the goal of the project was to decide on and implement a standardized grading system for management within the whole group. This does not mean that the grading within each brand would be fully harmonized, but rather that each brand uses the same logic to grade their positions. A systematic which could be applied to all brands needed to be found, and then this methodology would be used to evaluate each position within the brands. The goal is that position which have the same scope and content should have the same grading within the whole TRATON GROUP.

> *So I don't want to be responsible for every management position in the brands, which doesn't make sense but definitely for the group executives we need to be responsible. (Int. 16)*

This project is important for the Group as it creates a basis that facilitates many other HR processes, including rotations or global assignments, compensation and personnel development as well as management planning. For example in order to be able to have a common bonus system for management, the definition of a manager needs to be harmonized, or if a development program is designed for the whole group for a certain level of management, these levels need to be comparable in order to be able to pick suitable candidates. One interviewee saw the grading project as a basis for facilitating rotations between the brands. She saw the rotations of people, in order to foster integration as the end goal of this project. The common grading would facilitate this exchange of people.

> *The main situation is that we would like to promote more rotations between the brands. The best way integrating is to bring the people to your side, understanding why you are acting like that and then when the person is back they understand the diversity, the pluralism, of thinking. That's why we are trying to have the same grading, the same bonus system (Int. 20)*

In the past, MAN and VWCO were using the internal VW Grading systematic "Strata", whereas Scania was using another systematic coming from Mercer. The project team benchmarked existing grading providers in order to evaluate the most appropriate grading systematic for the TRATON GROUP. In order to evaluate the providers, criteria were defined, with in particular a focus on the possibility to benchmark own positions with the market and the possibility to use the systematic internationally. Multiple providers of grading systems were measured up against each other, including the systems being used at MAN and Scania, but also other providers. What was noted is that Strata (internal VW) did not fulfil the criteria of being international and being able to benchmark with the market. Furthermore, one interviewee noted that the VW systematic also required some form of approval from VW in Wolfsburg. In the end the system chosen was the one in use at Scania, the Mercer systematic, as it obtained the best grade based on the evaluation of potential providers.

> *We have always used the VW systematic for that, that was very strict and very Wolfsburg based, so you have a proposal that must be approved by Wolfsburg (Int. 21)*

The Mercer Grading systematic is more focused on the output, or impact of the position rather than on the internal specifications such as the number of headcounts below the position. The criteria are for example the impact of the function, the communication necessary and the knowledge needed to perform this function. Furthermore the scope of the function is considered, depending on if it has a global responsibility or only a domestic and national responsibility. All these factors impact the grading of the position. This is the main difference compared to the VW system which was previously in use. In the VW system, the size of the department managed by the positon was very much a focus, rather than the impact the position has on the organization and its success.

> *With the old concept you were very much also focused on size matters (Int. 16)*

Once the grading systematic was agreed upon, the individual position within the group needed to be graded. Here according the interviewees, it was important that peer functions within the whole group have a comparable grading. This phase of the project is when the most issues explained by the interviewees seemed to happen. Indeed, how the grading gets applied to the functions within the brands obviously has a big impact, so each brand would probably wish to have their positions graded as high as possible.

Overall however, although for some functions the results were not as expected, especially on the Brazilian side, as their positions were graded lower than expected, the project team members agree that this project has been a success since a grading systematic was chosen and all the positions were graded based on this systematic.

> *It was very successful, I think we had a great product, and we followed the timeline. We proposed a common grading provider to the Truck Board. And they went on our proposal so it was very successful. (Int. 9)*

In this next section, we will describe the findings based on the framework developed thanks to the theoretical analysis and described in the methodology section.

4.1.2.1 Mechanisms of Control and Coordination

In the first part, which has an internal focus, where the decision is made by the small project team with the approval happening within the various committees, there were some issues identified by the interviewees. The first issue was that the team members were used to a certain systematic and were not prepared to be open to other alternatives. The solutions used for this were twofold. To start with, one of the team members, who was very attached to the Strata systematic was removed, and replaced by a more neutral party. It is interesting to note here that the main power capability that the holding uses is the power of processes, by changing the team members. Traditionally in an MNC and in the case of HQ-Subsidiary relationship, one would also expect the power of resources to be deployed. Indeed by choosing the team members, the holding is strongly able to influence the decision, as seen within this case. Following this, a scientific approach was taken by designing essential criteria for the grading systematic at TRATON and measuring the various options against these criteria to choose the most appropriate one. This was important within this project as using this scientific approach allowed the team members to consider the options in a more neutral way. There are also escalation possibilities within the TRATON organization, in the case that the conflict cannot be resolved within the cross-brand team. Although these were not formally used as a conflict resolution mechanism, or not to the extent that the interviewees mentioned it, however as seen above, top management was involved and influenced the decision making process informally. Furthermore, the two governing bodies, the HRMC and the CHRO were used to approve decisions agreed upon in the cross-brand team. This allows for hierarchical legitimization of the decisions made.

This project was run with one team member from each brand, each nominated by their own HR board member to be part of the project team. However, the brand and the holding team members play a very different role within this project. The holding member acts as a project manager and receives all the data from the team members. The holding also sets the frame for cooperation, planning the meetings, for example, and also being the main point of contact to the external consultants. The holding has the responsibility for making sure the result is good, meaning that the grading allows for comparable functions with comparable responsibilities across all brands. The brand members hold the knowledge and information, including organizational charts, KPIS, financial data for all the functions and supply it to the holding. They are also the link to the rest of their own organization. One interviewee mentioned that she also had to make sure to think about if any further projects would be impacted by their work within the grading projects and share the information when necessary.

> *The holding, we need to ensure that the positions across brands are also comparable and therefore doing the harmonization for this (Int. 16).*

4.1.2.2 Decisions and Conflict

During this phase, there was time pressure to agree on a common systematic. Therefore in order to obtain the alignment, the team members had to travel to have meetings or workshops regarding this topic. This of course involves financial costs as well as time investment.

We had a tight timeline to agree on a common job grading provider (Int. 9)

In order to grade the positions, information was collected by the brands and then analyzed by the team members. The interviewees stated that the attempted to have all the "hard discussions", encouraging productive conflict thanks to an open climate in order to make the best decision. Once the project group was aligned, input was sought asked for from the HR managers of each brand, and they were able to adjust the grading accordingly. Once these positions were graded in a preliminary way, these results were brought to brand management. According to the interviewees, once the positions were graded using the systematic, discussions became more difficult. Indeed grading is a very sensitive topic as it will potentially be linked to status or salary of the top managers. Therefore each brand would naturally wish to have their positions graded as high as possible. Although some positions were reportedly easy to grade, in other cases the supervisors of the positions being graded had higher expectations for the grade associated to their manager's positions. Therefore the project team members had to negotiate the grading of the positions, by explaining how the positions compared to the market grading of similar positions and how they were comparable across the brands. By having this information at hand, the team members were able to convince the managers, as they had real data based on these criteria. On the other hand some positions were also renegotiated by the brands, as the information that the team had was not complete, or had not been considered to its full value at the time of the initial grading. In that case a further round of grading was required and the positions were adapted accordingly. So the interviewees noted that the difficulty was to deal with the expectations that the executives had regarding the grading of their management position in relation to the grading which was associated to these positons based on the systematic.

If I say "I have here in my organization, a high-level top management" and when you compare with a benchmarking of the market and you compare this with other companies, this is not the top management this is middle manager. (Int. 21).

One interviewee also noted that the reason behind these rather tough negotiations is that thinking ahead, there would potentially compensation and benefits which would be associated to this grading on a Group level. Therefore in the future, the manager's bonus for example could be affected by the grading associated to their function within this project.

It is interesting to note a passing comment that one interviewee made, that this project only affects the higher positions, this project concerning only the top management levels of the brands. When going down in the organizations, the freedom to adapt, grade and compensate the positons lies with the brands. This will be interesting to consider when looking into the flexibility offered by this kind of organization. By imposing a common systematic on the higher levels, there is a desire for group comparability, but local adaptation is supported on the lower levels.

The freedom you have of course on the lower levels (Int. 16)

In order to steer the decisions within this projects, and in addition to the HRMC and the CHROs which serve as governance bodies for the HR function within TRATON, a separate steering committee was set up especially for this project. However, it seems that the HRMC and CHRO were the most used governance bodies in the decision making process within the governance project. These two governance bodies were used in order to align the decisions made on the team level, they effectively legitimized the decisions made by the cross-brand team.

So this is something where we used the CHRO-meeting which I think is very useful and helpful that those issues and topics can be put in one meeting, to align on this. (Int. 16)

4.1.2.3 Learning, Knowledge and Innovation

Thanks to this project, the team members had learning on multiple levels. The Scania employee mentioned that she was able to have a more global view of Scania, thanks to seeing her company within the context of the TRATON GROUP. So instead of seeing the individual Business Units within Scania she had to consider Scania as a whole global entity, in comparison to the TRATON GROUP. Furthermore, all the interviewees mentioned the value of learning from each other, either in terms of sharing best practices or simply learning about the different brands. Finally the interviewees also noted that working within this cross-brand project allowed then to understand more about the TRATON GROUP and the other brands and their business models.

But working within the matrix organization, in a common project you need to have the global hat on, you see the global need for Scania not the local need for each business unit (Int. 9)

In particular, for VWCO, it was mentioned that working with the two bigger brands, Scania and MAN, was a learning opportunity. This was felt by the interviewee that learning about the processes and structures of the other brands, especially because VWCO is still "young" compared to the other two, led to potentially interesting learning for VWCO.

I think it's really interesting at the moment to join all of these discussions and co-create this TRATON GROUP with them. (Int. 21)

In terms of innovation, one could not say that this grading systematic is a breakthrough innovation as many other companies today are using it. However, for the TRATON GROUP as a whole this approach is innovative, as it differs significantly from the systematic being used within the VW Group. It is much less the case for Scania as they were already using this systematic. One would however suppose, that without the use of this cross-brand project approach, the VW systematic would have further been used within the Group. We make this supposition based on the fact that the initial project leader, who would have therefore made the decision in a hierarchical organization, was initially very much attached to the VW systematic. However, by analyzing the situation and the needs of the organization and the strategy, that being to become a Global Champion, which implies comparability and competitiveness on the market the team members moved away from this idea and towards this more innovative approach. Indeed, as the interviewees explained, the need to be flexible and efficient as well as compete on the market were defined criteria which did not fit the systematic in use at VW.

For Scania it is much more easy because since 2015, they have been working already with MERCER to evaluate their positions so they were already ahead of this topic and their Board members already understood the scoring system and also the differences in scoring (Int. 16)

4.1.2.4 Culture and Identities

As it was explained above it seems that choosing the grading provider went rather smoothly. The team members defined the criteria and then evaluated potential providers, including the existing ones within the brands, based on these criteria. However, there were still some issues observed during this phase.

> *So everyone was involved and we had discussions, of course, but figures are quite easy to see the results. (Int. 9)*

These issues which were reported by the interviewees can be linked to the culture and different identities of the brands. For example, the fact that some team members found it difficult to picture moving away from the current grading systematic towards a new one. At the beginning of the project it seems that certain team members could only see using the VW Strata system as an option for a common grading provider. This can be considered a form of evaluation conflict, a conflict which stems from the different frameworks of the brands, therefore what is "good" is judged based on this framework. Here the presence of Scania in the team allowed the team members to see another perspective and move away from the current status, which was in hindsight considered sub-optimal by the team embers, towards a different approach, better suited to the organization's need. Furthermore the team members needed to be open to these other options and accept the input of new information.

> *Because most of the people in the meeting has been working with the VW Strata system and I from Scania have been working with another job grading system, so of course there was some, I won't call it conflicts, but some discussions when we had different views of job grading providers (Int. 9)*

The interviewees noted that the complexity of aligning the grading systematic within three different brands with three different cultures led to the need for more alignment. This alignment was required not just in their organizations, as is usually the case, but between the brands, where it was mentioned that each brand has a distinct corporate culture, in how they meet, how they exchange data, and how they work together. They further explained that it was more challenging to match the processes they were developing to these three different brands. The interviewees explained that this led to slower decision making.

These cultural differences were felt particularly strongly from the Brazilian side, due to a radically different market situation to the other two brands, both European. Indeed, one of the criteria used in order to grade the positions is the revenue of the company, which is integrated into the "size" criteria, together with the headcount the manager is responsible for. It was initially planned to use the 2017 revenues as the base for this criteria. As the markets in Europe are relatively stable, this was no issue for MAN and Scania. However in Brazil, the market is much more volatile and the VWCO was recovering from a crisis. The interviewee explained that in Brazil, some years are very good and some years can also be very bad in terms of revenue, therefore using the 2017 numbers only did not offer a figure which reflected the realities of the Brazilian market.

> *In our market one year you have 20% plus, and then in the following year, you have 20% minus. That was really a challenging situation, how to make these three business models have a comparable chart for that. (Int. 21)*

4.1.2.5 Boundary Spanning

During the whole time the objective of the project remained the same, to have a harmonized and comparable grading systematic for managers within the TRATON GROUP. Some adaptations were made, however. Within this project one issue came from the different Brazilian context and volatile market as explained in the section on matrix organization issues. Therefore the calculation based on the revenue of the company was adapted to be an average of the past years rather than just using the previous year data. In order to come to this result, the relationship and understanding of the Brazilian market from the HR Board member was leveraged. Indeed, the board member had experience working as the production board member in Brazil so was able to understand the situation and defend the interests of VWCO. Here it is mainly conflict due to conflicting interests, or a heterogeneity of stakeholder interests, between the holding and the brands, namely on the holding side having a harmonized and comparable grading, versus getting the highest possible grading for their managers on the brand side. Here the heterogeneity of institutional contexts (Blazejewski & Becker-Ritterspach, 2011) played an important role in the case of Brazil, as the very different economic situation compared to other brands led to dispute. The brand was able to leverage top management involvement and understanding of the situation to get their point across and accepted.

He was previously the board member for production and 2009 -2012, he worked here with us the board member for production of VWCO, so he knows the business (Int. 21)

Another element that helped solve the conflicts over the Brazilian and European issues, was the understanding of the team members, which according to the VWCO interviewee was facilitated by some of them coming to Brazil and experiencing it first-hand. It is important to note this importance of location and coming to the physical location of the counterpart. It was also mentioned that the main decisions were taken together, face to face in Munich. One respondent even joked that working in Munich would make it easier for her to work in this context.

It could also be interesting to note that within this project the external consulting firm was not only a provider of the grading systematic, they also had a moderating role, where if the team members were unable to come to an agreement they would intervene. Indeed, by intervening when the team members were unable to come to a decision, they could use their position as experts and their external view to support the team's decision making.

When discussions went too deep and we couldn't agree the external consultant could just untie the knot and solve it. (Int. 9)

The one skill that was strongly remarked upon in this project was the ability to take a step back and have global view of the issue. It is so important that not having this ability led to the change in team membership. There is also evidence of these cross-brand projects changing or having an influence on the organizational culture of the brands. The interviewee on the Scania side noted decreased formality from the German counterparts, and provided a concrete example of how this has evolved as the project went on. Through this project, and thanks to meeting in person, a network was created, allowing the colleagues to contact each other in informal ways. The interviewees explained that through the socialization opportunities provided by the project, they were easily able to pick up the phone and contact the team members regarding any questions or issues.

I could receive and email from [head of TRATON HR], instead of [head of TRATON HR] emailing [my manager] and [my manager] is emailing me (int. 9)

4.1.2.6 Key Findings

We will now summarize the findings from this project, while reflecting on the potential theoretical implications of these conclusions. The goal here is to anticipate the potential value that these findings will have on the overall research. This will then be further analyzed more in depth in the contributions section.

To start with, considering the value and potential contribution of this project, this example gives us good insight into the matrix supporting processes which can be provided by HR. Indeed, this project has the potential of facilitating rotations, development program nominations, and potential bonus harmonization and so on. As we will discuss further when looking into the facilitating factors of a matrix organization, these advantages just cited, such as rotations and development programs, will prove to important socialization areas, which will act as facilitating factor for the cross-brand cooperation. Therefore, one could see this grading project as an important base for collaboration.

When looking into the mechanisms of control and coordination, one process that the holding leveraged in order to steer the direction of this project, is the question of team membership. Indeed, when the project was not advancing, some of the members were changed in order to move the project along. This is an interesting example of how the holding can leverage the power of processes within these matrix projects. Another process which was an important factor in the success of this project was the scientific approach taken by the team to determine the criteria both for the choice of the provider and for the grading systematic itself. This ensured the team could make an informed choice regarding the grading provider and that they had a solid base for discussion when going into negotiations with the brands regarding the grading of their positions. Finally, an important element used within this project were the committees, namely the HRMC and CHRO meetings, which were used to legitimize the decisions taken within the project group. The membership of these committees is important, as it is made up of top managers for HR from all brands, having their approval is an important factor for legitimization within this project.

When looking at the decision making processes within this project, the decisions were initially made in a balanced way. The brand representatives collected information and brought it back to the team where it was analyzed. One interviewee made a point of mentioning that the "hard discussions" were taken intentionally. In a way conflict was triggered within the working group, in order to find a solution which encompassed all the different perspectives and potential differing opinions. This is theoretically one of the main advantages of balanced decision making. Furthermore, this project, like most within this case, had an ambitious timeline, leading to pressure for the team to deliver. This is not surprising as most projects tend to have deadlines, however we will further develop on the role of deadlines as facilitating factors in this research. Finally, one of the points which brought about conflict were the expectations of the brands for their managers. This project has a high impact, as the grading of the managers will be a symbol of the importance of each brand, naturally leading to all brands wanting to have their positions graded as high as possible. This is an interesting point which will bring us to look into the issue of the balance of power in the matrix organization. Indeed, here we can see that the brands will attempt to leverage the results of this project to make sure their brand is on top. To counterbalance this, the project team has a very detailed and scientific grading approach, with very clear criteria, allowing the team to argue in one direction or the other.

Now we will observe the learning and knowledge which was gained and shared through this project. We have gathered some potentially interesting information. To start with, within his project, the important knowledge required was held by the brands. Therefore the team members had to gather it and bring it into the cross-brand project team where it would be analyzed. This adds value to our research as it helps to highlight the role of the headquarters and the role of the brands further. Moreover, this knowledge is a potential resource which can be leveraged by the brands as a power capability. On top of that, the interviewees mentioned that they had learnings on three levels. The first level is brand self-reflection, which was gained through understanding of their own processes and behaviors when confronting them with those of the other brands. The second level, which was more focused on knowledge sharing, came from sharing best practices within the cross-brand project. The final level of learning for the cross-brand team member was further understanding of the group, as well as learning to think more with a Group perspective. As mentioned in the literature review, we can consider knowledge and learning as an antecedent to innovation. In this case, an innovative approach for the TRATON GROUP came to be through the knowledge sharing generated by the balanced decision making model. The conflicts which were had at the beginning of the project when choosing the provider contributed to the initial solution (the Strata method used by VW) to be rejected in favor of a better option. This contributes to showing how balanced decision making can be leveraged for innovation.

When considering the issue of culture and identities within this project, two important elements were identified. The first was a question of habits and processes. Indeed some team members found is difficult to move away from the idea of using the VW systematic, because that is what they considered to be a good solution. Now this could be considered a cultural issue in the way that their framework for what is a good solution had to be changed from this view of the VW solution as the only one, towards a more broad understanding of the needs of the organization and the spectrum of possible solutions. On the other hand, one could also argue that this person is just stubborn and an isolated case. It will be interesting to see if this case occurs in other projects as well. Another issue regarding culture was the problem of the different national contexts in which the brands are located. This was a very practical calculation issue, as the Brazilian market fluctuates more than the European one, basing the grading on the revenue of the company for the previous year was not realistic from a Brazilian perspective. What is interesting in this issue is the role that one board member, with experience in Brazil, played facilitating the adaptation for the Brazilian colleagues. This shows the importance of boundary spanning, which we will address as a facilitating factor.

The next factor which we will consider is the question of boundary spanning. Here we have identified three factors within this category which supported the project. To start with, the importance of location and socialization was brought up. Meeting the people from the different brands and going to the different locations helped to bring more understanding and better communication within the group, to come to a solution better fitting for all brands. Secondly, as hinted previously, the role of the HR board member was important here, as his experience in Brazil helped to facilitate the adaption of the concept for Brazil. Here the board member has a boundary spanning role, supported by his experience of the Brazilian market and his current position, which allowed him to leverage said experience. This shows the importance of having people in high places with experience in multiple brands, hinting at the value of another project we have observed, the Global Assignment Toolbox. Finally, the moderating role of external consultants was also mentioned, they were able to bring the discussion back to the important topics and unblock some of the conflicts. Finally, we will discuss the boundary spanning skills which were required within this project. One skill that was noted as essential within this project was the ability to have a global perspective and open-mindedness. As has already been mentioned above, when team members became unable to move away from what they believed to be the best solution, they endangered the success of the project. Furthermore, the ability to take a step back and consider the Group perspective rather than the brand perspective was also an important factor. Furthermore, a consequence of this project was a decreased formality of the German counterpart, as observed by the Swedish colleagues. This is an interesting point, as it could provide evidence of socio-cultural integration between the brands.

4.1.3 Pluralism & Inclusion Cooperation

To start with, this section will give an overview of the Pluralism and Inclusion project, describing the goal and the results of the project.

The topic of diversity was first raised within the TRATON holding, launched by the Truck Board, and it was suggested that this was a topic with synergistic potential. One interviewee suggested that pressure from the mother company, VW may have also played a role in the launch of this project. The holding team member created a meeting with all the representatives of the topic from the brands. She set up a meeting where all the brands shared their current status, their ongoing activities and their main focus. After sharing this information, it was decided within the project group that the concept owned by Scania would be developed and rolled out within the whole TRATON GROUP. This concept is called Skill Capture and here the topic of diversity is addressed as a business issue, with the idea that being more diverse allows the company to deal with the upcoming talent shortage and contributes to more ideas and better decision making. This concept takes the form of workshops performed within teams where they identify potential improvements regarding this topic.

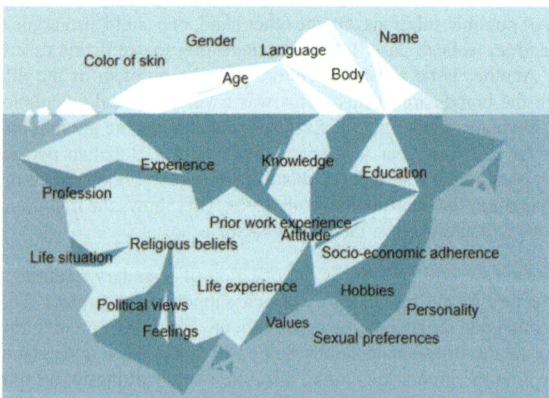

Figure 11: Visible and non-visible diversity (internal Scania document, 2018)

Overall, when asked, most of the interviewees are quite positive about the success of the project. They have managed to come to an agreement on how to move forwards together, implementing Skill Capture on a Group level and would be presenting the concept at the Truck Board meeting. However at the time of the discussion, the project was still in its infancy, the output only this decision to implement Skill Capture, which then had to be presented and approved by the Truck

Board and one of the respondents in fact considered this to be a more problematic project. Today, at the end of this research project, time has passed and unfortunately the status of this project remains the same, with the roll-out of Skill Capture now planned for 2020, two years after the first decision was taken.

4.1.3.1 Mechanisms of Control and Coordination

This next section will analyze the matrix organization issues and topics identified within this Pluralism ad Inclusion project by the interviewees, once again based on the analysis grid, starting with the mechanisms of control and coordination.

To start with, we will look at the role of the holding within this project. Here, the role of the holding was exacerbated and could be seen clearly due to the use of the concept of lead brand. The lead brand was in charge of the coordination of the project and responsible for generating results in alignment with group interests. However, this did not mean that the holding did not play a role, as can be seen above, in the case that the lead brand would not act according to group interests, the holding function could intervene to defend them.

Furthermore within this project there was an interface to Volkswagen AG. Indeed, TRATON has a reporting duty to Volkswagen regarding this topic, for example regarding the number of women in management. Here the holding played the role of the single point of contact and the link between the TRATON brands and the Volkswagen Group. This is a change noted by the interviewees, where before the brands would report their information directly to VW, whereas now this is done through the holding function.

> *It's more now centered around Truck & Bus, which from my perspective is very good (Int. 6)*

As explained in the section describing the governance structure, there is a two level structure, starting with the HRMC, made up of top HR managers and the CHRO meeting, the HR board members. This structure is used as a forum for feedback and gives the final approval. One interviewee described this as an escalation stair, where the team would come up with potential solutions which would then be brought to the HRMC for approval and potential modifications before being further escalated to the CHROs for final approval. She noted that within this process there were a lot of iterations, back and forth before being able to come to a good enough presentation of the solution. She explained that the difficulty here was obtaining a short presentation which allowed the top managers to understand the issue and be able to make a decision.

However, it seems that regarding the conflicts within this project, the interviewees described the issues as being too small to be worth escalating and here the governance structure was not used. Indeed, the conflicts were seen as too small or petty for escalation at this very high group level. This meant that the individual team members would go to their managers to obtain feedback before coming back within the project group to work on the solution again. This lead to slower decision making process in order to reach a consensus on the solution which could then be escalated within the official governance channel. In order to facilitate this process, one interviewee stated that it needed to be clear from the brand management what was expected of the team members within the working group in order to accelerate this process.

> *It needs to be more clear what's expected and it needs to be reinforced by their managers then. (Int. 14)*

Some respondents expressed the desire for a decision for the top to avoid this issue of slow decision making. However, one disadvantage of taking this approach was also noted, that being that the commitment from the brands could be lost. This lack of commitment to the idea, if the team members and subsequently their brands do not understand why the decision was made and are not fully convinced could lead to less effort within the implementation phase.

> *It's very easy to lose the commitment of everyone in this process (Int. 14)*

4.1.3.2 Decisions and Conflict

This is an interesting project to look into, as here it is not lead by the holding, like in the grading project we described previously, but rather one brand, Scania, was chosen to be the lead. During the discussions it became clear that there was more experience within Scania on this topic, who had developed this companywide workshop and action plan system to encourage diversity on all levels of the organization. Moreover the team member from Scania was relatively senior and experienced regarding this topic and had developed the system within the company. It was therefore decided that Scania would be the lead on this topic and that the system available at Scania would be adapted and launched company wide.

Having this concept of lead brand has been shown to lead to some issues. An interviewee described an instance where the lead brand did not want to ask the board members to nominate participants during the presentation of the project. This was due to the fact that is did not make sense for the lead brand (who had already launched the concept), it would however be value-adding to the other companies in the group. So from a group perspective it was important to ask the board members to nominate people. Indeed, board involvement gives the concept more power. By having the board nominate participants this would guarantee involvement from the organizations on the lower levels, which was important for the brands for who this was a new concept.

> *When the Board stand completely behind this project behind this project, idea of diversity then it «austrahlen » it's a signal for the whole organization. This is a very important thing for us. (Int. 13)*

This brings up the issue of the balance when there is a lead brand. Indeed, although the lead brand should theoretically focus on Group interests, the manager of the person has a natural focus on brand issues, therefore there is no escalation possibility or hierarchy above the lead brand. Furthermore, if and when the holding intervenes to safeguard group interests, it makes knowing who is in charge complicated. In this case, the holding had to intervene and explain the position of the other brands, why they would benefit from it and that it would be possible to minimize any kind of consequence for the lead brand. In the end the parties all came to an agreement, and it was decided that the board members would nominate participants but that it would be made clear that Scania would not be involved. It was also noted that it was quite a tense situation as it was important for the project from a Group side that the board nominate participants, ensuring the launch of the project within the brands. However, if the holding team members had been unable to convince the lead brand, the next steps would have been unclear. Indeed, this kind of issue is too small to escalate, and it would be seen as petty to bring such an issue to the board. Furthermore, there is the danger of losing the commitment from the brands if the holding comes in too hard and imposes decisions.

Since it's anyway a quite tight situation and we have to be quite quick, every of this discussions is quite nerve racking and leads to the fact that they are less willing to be committed to it. The more you discuss, the more you lose their commitment (Int. 14)

Another issue reported by the interviewees within this project, is the decision on how to implement the concept, basically how to launch the first workshops within the company. There were two options for this, either have a "pull" concept, where the initiative would come from the teams or a cascading concept, where the workshops would start at the top and then be rolled out further into the organization. From Scania's perspective a top down roll out would be the best option, but the TRATON team member felt that too many topics were already being dealt with this way, so they preferred to have a pull or first mover approach. In the end a compromise was reached through consensus and discussion, where the Truck Board would do the workshop first as the first step to show the example and would then volunteer some of their team members. This is the step described above. Here a simple compromise was reached using consensus decision making.

We had a lot of discussion with the brands. At the end the brands say why not we mix it a little bit, now we have a mixed principle. (int. 11)

This cross-brand environment is more complex, leading to the need to align with more parties. The alignment required is much wider, as much more people and different brands need to be involved. Interestingly, one interviewee mentioned that this might be a question of trust, and that within their own organization they would just let the project go ahead and not be so regarding, but within a cross-brand project the perspectives are different and the people are not yet used to working together so it takes more time. Furthermore, some explained that because of this matrix set-up, it seems that no one has real decision making rights and therefore a decision can only be made if there is a consensus. Obtaining this consensus obviously also leads to longer decision making processes. Dealing with this kind of decision making in this complex environment was also noted to be more stressful, as more meetings are required in order to be able to obtain an alignment than in the usual single brand setting.

You probably just say I've prepared this and the person just says "I know you I trust you" (Int. 14)

4.1.3.3 Learning, Knowledge and Innovation

Within this project one interviewee mentioned that at the beginning, the team members did not necessarily want to share everything within the project group. However, at the time of the interview she stated that the situation was better and that after some workshops and skype meetings, the communication channels were more open.

It seems that there may have been a lack of clarity or at least a lack of information regarding the goals, the structure and the financing of this project. One interviewee noted that it was unclear to them what the timeline on this project was, who was taking the decisions and what the budget and who should be financing this project. Another point where the Scania colleague reported that there was still a learning curve to be made, was a lack of understanding reported for the different environments and the fact that they were not familiar with the German processes.

I can also feel that it's a bit problematic when we try to explain that this is done in another way and sometimes a bit of lacking of understanding and it's like, "Yeah but you just fill this in!" it's like, Well, we don't, we can't ! (Int. 8)

Through the cross-brand project and if Skill Capture is implemented within the whole group, one could consider this to be a very innovative approach to dealing with the question of diversity within a company. Indeed this way of working does not focus only on one particular group of people, such as women as is often the case, but rather all aspects of diversity, both visible (such as ethnicity or gender) and non-visible.

However one barrier to being able to use this innovative approach is the context in which the companies are embedded. Indeed, in Sweden it is possible to take a step back from specific KPIs such as gender quotas, but in Germany for example, there is a regulation requiring companies to set goals for quotas of women in management, therefore making it harder to implement. Today, the situation is still open at TRATON on this issue, so we cannot say how this was solved.

The use of the consensus way of working has its benefits. Indeed, one could consider that thanks to all the input from the different brands and conflicting ideas, the final product is better, as was noted by some interviewees. The conflicting or diverse opinions of the team members allowed the teams to better evaluate the options and come to a more satisfying and innovative solution.

It's like actually using diversity in the creation process. Capturing what is good from all the places and coming into this (Int. 6)

4.1.3.4 Culture and Identities

As we alluded to when talking about the issue of innovation, the institutional differences the brands are embedded have led to some issues within this project.

Firstly, the companies had different starting points regarding the topic of Pluralism and inclusion. The MAN interviewee explained that they felt they were behind Scania in terms of implementing and living diversity within the company. Furthermore, it was noted that the Scandinavian culture in general was different to the central European culture regarding this topic. For example a Scania interviewee noted that it is quite normal for men to be on parental leave, whereas this may be less the case in Germany.

I felt that that was really strange from a German perspective, having a manager being on parental. (Int. 6)

These issues were also made more visible due to the reporting demands imposed by VW. In comparison to MAN, Scania found it difficult to respond to the criteria and report the figures required by Volkswagen, which is also German. For example, when asked to report on the presence of childcare options or special training for women on maternity leave offered by the company, Scania had to explain that this is something that is taken care of by the Swedish government or another body outside of the organization, and that there is therefore no need for it internally.

This number doesn't apply to Scania because we are the special snowflake (Int. 8)

Furthermore as mentioned previously, the German law requires targets and reporting regarding women in management, whereas this is not the case in Sweden. Therefore VW requires that these targets for the upcoming years, which leads to discussion for Scania, as they are not required to do it by law, but it is nonetheless imposed on them through VW.

Another institutional difference noted is that co-determination plays a prominent role at MAN, whereas at Scania the role of the co-determination partners is less pronounced. Where MAN will need the approval of the works council for many things and they will be involved in an active role, at Scania this is not the case. A defining feature of Germany is its system of industrial relations, collective bargaining and "mitbestimmung" or "co-determination" play an important role in Germany's business system (Lane, 2000), some may even say that is a determining factor of its management model. The works council plays an essential role within the company and has considerable power in Germany, much more so than any other country in Europe (Barmeyer & Davoine, 2008). This is further influenced by the fact that MAN has a particularly strong works council, with a very high rate of Union adhesion. Where the German works council has decisional power, the Swedish representatives need only to be informed. So although the desk research showed co-determination to also play a role in Sweden, this role is less active. One impact of this is on the speed of the implementation of decisions, because in Sweden once the management has approved the implementation the project can go ahead whereas in Germany there is a need to take certain things to the works council first.

One of the challenges also noted was the difference in the company organizational culture. Where Scania has a rather flat organization with a matrix-like structure, MAN is reported to be more hierarchical. According to one interviewee this leads to the fact that top management support is more important at MAN in order to bring a project to fruition than at Scania. Linked to this, the interviewees note that the decision making styles within the two companies are also different. Where MAN (and VW) are said to have a rather top-down approach, Scania tends to be more democratic. Furthermore, Scania has the need to pilot a concept before implementing it to be able to legitimize it, whereas at MAN it can be implemented immediately.

> *I think in the VW organization, as I have experienced it, it's more like you will be given an order, and then you just execute. (Int. 8)*

4.1.3.5 Boundary Spanning

Within this project, the interviewees stressed the importance of face to face meetings. In the international context it is not something that can be done all the time, but they noted that it is important especially at the beginning of the project. Furthermore, it seems that the participants would engage in more discussions between the brands, rather than just between the holding and the brand. So instead of two way communication there is more horizontal communication too.

One boundary spanning activity which was also mentioned by an interviewee was the need to build trust between the team members. Here however, according to this respondent, it has not yet been attained within this project, and it would require more time in order to build it. This time is not necessarily available to them, as they also have to invest their time into the daily operations of their respective departments.

> *We have a lot, both of Scania and my department, we are a small department, and we have very much daily work, and therefore, there's some sort question of time (Int. 13)*

It was explained that it is challenging to work within this project, as the workload is high and for some colleagues it was a new experience working in such a context. This context involves working in a different language than they are used to, with different cultures and having this group function which brings the brands together which is a new way of working which can be difficult to deal with. Furthermore, this cross-brand project which requires a lot of time, comes on top of already existing daily work, making it additional workload.

One interviewee stressed a potential facilitating factor which had yet to be implemented, that being shared IT systems to allow for more knowledge sharing on the topic.

> *I think I would find the platform earlier, to have an exchange on the topic, it would have been easier to have a channel to share documents to share everything (Int. 11)*

Within this project, multiple interviewees also mentioned the opportunity for learning, in this case it was best practices. Some mentioned learning from the Swedish, with of course the Skill capture concept, while other also mentioned a good example from Brazil and how they worked with deaf people.

> *We have got a lot of ideas from Brazil, from MAN, how they worked with deaf people (int. 8).*

It seems that the brands have also brought back some learning from this project. For example one interviewee mentioned that working within this project had improved the way they steer and have processes a little, as well as improved their English. Another interviewee from Scania anticipated further changes coming from this, in particular due to the reporting requirements coming from VW, and that Scania will potentially adapt to this, by becoming better at reporting.

> *In VW there is a lot of follow-up and so on. I think this is something that will be changed, and I think that will be good for Scania as well. (Int. 8)*

The interviewees expressed that at the time of their interviews they felt they have come together and have a "common spirit". Although at the beginning they did not feel this, now after time spent working together they have overcome their disagreements and are now able to have "one voice" (int. 13). Furthermore, through this project, the project team members have created a network, the interviews noted that now that they knew each other there would be no issue picking up the phone to ask questions for example. Some also have appreciated the opportunity to work with competent counterparts from other brands, and mentioned that they appreciated the expertize brought in by the colleagues.

> *It's become a tighter group. The interactions have become more frequent and as we now progress in knowing each other and understanding each other, I think I feel more and more at home in this construction (Int. 6)*

4.1.3.6 Key Findings

In this next section we will summarize our findings briefly in order to provide an overview of the important points found within this section.

To start with, this project brought to light the role that the holding has to play in the matrix organization, especially in the case of the lead brand concept being in use. Firstly, in this case the holding acted as a counter power to the lead brand in case of the Group perspective was lost. Furthermore, the holding also acts as a single point of contact towards VW. Within this project we were also further able to understand how the governance structure within HR is actually used. Here the HRMC and CHRO bodies were used for approval and feedback but were not used for escalation, as the issues were deemed too small to escalate to such a body. Finally, the question of top-down decision making was also raised within this project. This was not actually done but rather a wish from a respondent in order to deal with the issues within the project. However, it was also noted that the danger behind that would be the loss of commitment from the brands.

This project is an interesting one as it is led by Scania, rather than being led by the holding. The reasons behind the choice of Scania as a lead brand is that they have the most experience regarding the topic. This "lead brand" concept however did bring about some issues within this topic, as the lead brand was not always able to have a neutral position within this project. This situation helps us further understand the potential role of the holding in this matrix organization, since even with the lead brand, the holding had to intervene in order to protect Group interests. Another point which was raised within this project is the "classic" matrix organization issue of slow decision making, due to the need for increased alignment within the brands as well as the consensus (balanced) decision making style used. Finally, the issue of trust was raised by one interviewee, as a potential reason for this slower decision making. Indeed, she pointed out that within brand projects, as they know the people and how they work they would have a tendency to be less regarding and trust the work done by the other party, which would not be the case within this cross-brand project.

For our next category of analysis, knowledge, learning and innovation, this project also brought some interesting points to life. To start with, it was mentioned that there was a reticence to share information at the beginning of the project. This is an important point as it also brings about the importance of socialization as a facilitating factor, as the interviewee mentioned that meetings and workshops are what led to people being more open about sharing information. Another point raised as a barrier to cooperation were unclear goals and understanding of role and responsibilities as well as the financing issues. This slowed the development of the project. Furthermore, in terms of understanding, which we classify as knowledge, there was a reported lack of comprehension or willingness to accept the different brand environments, in this case regarding VW processes, which led to complications. Linked to these organizational differences are also the institutional differences noted within this case. The reason we also classify these difficulties here is that the innovative approach taken by Scania (of considering diversity more broadly and not focusing on the gender quota) is made impossible in Germany by the German law, requiring targets for gender within organizations. Finally, it was noted that the consensus decision making, which they called using a diversity of perspectives was beneficial to the project. This is once again one of the main advantages of this type of decision making within a matrix organization.

Now going into the question of culture and identities which has already been hinted at, we have found some elements which further contribute to our understanding of the challenges brought about by culture within a matrix. To start with, going back to the point mentioned previously, the issue of institutional differences was raised as being a barrier to successful cooperation, with different starting points in Germany and Sweden on the topic as well as the aforementioned question of the gender quota. Furthermore, here the cooperation with Volkswagen was raised. This is an important point as the embeddedness of the TRATON GROUP within the Volkswagen Group could also be a potentially determining factor. In this case, the question which was raised were the reporting requirements which were harder to fulfill for Scania than for MAN due to the different institutional contexts. The last two points found within this case are question of organizational culture, embedded in national culture. To start with, one point which was already found within the desk research is the role of co-determination which is much stronger in Germany than in Sweden. This is particularly true at MAN, as it has a very strong Works Council. Finally, the differences in decision making and hierarchy were notes, with a more hierarchical and top-down approach at MAN against a flatter hierarchies and bottom-up at Scania. On top of that, it seems that Scania likes to pilot projects and then adapt them whereas at MAN they like to launch a final product. These elements are important as they give us an insight into the culture and identities of two brands, and how they work, as well as where the differences potentially create issues.

Next looking onto the findings on boundary spanning within this case, we have started by noting the importance of face to face time between the project members in order to build trust. Not only the physical meetings, but also the time invested in these meetings is important, however it was also noted that the cross-brand work tends to come on top of the daily business, making investing this time a challenge. Linked to this, an interesting point was made regarding the type of discussions which are had on Skype, which tend to be bilateral, whereas in person there is a broader exchange. Finally, the question of a potential shared IT system as a facilitating factor was raised. These last two points lead us to consider these IT tool as potential boundary spanning object, an idea which we will further explore in the contributions section. This project was found to be a good opportunity for best practice sharing, as mentioned within the previous point on innovation. Furthermore, there was once again the idea that the learning made within this cross-brand project would potentially be brought back into the brands. The example used was that the interviewee claimed working in this project made them better at English, which is a rather small change, but further opportunities for transfer were noted. Finally, within this project there was a clear creation of a network between the team members, and they reported improved cooperation.

4.1.4 Management Dialogue

To start with this section will explain the goals and the output of the project, before going on to describe the findings of this project based on the framework for analysis.

This project concerns the implementation of a management dialogue on a group wide level, in order to create a joint standard for evaluation. It was decided during an HRMC meeting that there should be a common management dialogue for all brands in order to have a joint standard for annual performance appraisal for every manager including performance feedback, target agreements and development recommendations. This would allow for comparable performance evaluation within brands, once again supporting other HR processes along the way. The interviewees explained that this allowed for a similar standard to measure the quality of management and also led to management receiving constant and regular feedback, as well as being useful input for personal development planning. For example, if there is an open positon for a rotation across brands someone who has been recommended for a horizontal job change or experience abroad could be a good candidate. However this is not central performance management, as the information would remain in the brands. Rather, if there is a need to have performance indicators on the TRATON level, for example when selecting someone for a Group development program, or for a rotation, this information would be available. For the highest level of management the information is also available to the holding. As has been the case in the previous cross-brand projects too, the process was designed within the cross-brand team, with a core team made up of one representative per brand.

In the end, the project can be considered a success, as there is now a harmonized management dialogue in place within all brands. This was however only achieved one year later, since MAN used another system for one year. This will be further explained in the section on matrix organization issues.

4.1.4.1 Mechanisms of Control and Coordination

In this project, the role of the holding was rather clear. To start with the holding was able to mobilize the power of processes. Indeed, by including the Board member, which they were able to do, thanks to their access through the already implemented meeting structure (CHRO meeting), they were able to ask him for a decision from the top on the issues. Secondly, the power of meaning was also mobilized. Indeed, the holding places itself as the group interest champion, and by showing that MAN was not aligned with this, going in another direction, they were further able to convince the board member.

> *We presented an aligned chart from this cross brand team that stated that for most of the things we are similar but for two things the colleagues from that specific brand have deviations from the standard process (int. 14)*

Within this project, the value of consensus decision making is very much highlighted. Indeed, this allowed each party to include the elements which were important to them in order to reach a good compromise on the management dialogue format. Furthermore this allowed the brands to reach a solution which did not disrupt their corporate culture, but rather as one interviewee described it, it was an evolution which led to a good group versus brand balance.

4.1.4.2 Decisions and Conflict

In order to come to a decision regarding the format of the management dialogue, criteria were defined as to the format the template for this management dialogue should take, for example the team decided that it should fit on one page and have the same elements for each brand in order to allow for comparability. However it was agreed that adaptation would be possible to adapt to brand specific issues. The working group then had to agree on the characteristics for this template. For example an issue was brought up regarding the scale for performance within the performance evaluation. Indeed within the German logic, 1 would be the best and 5 the worst whereas in most of the rest of the world, this would be the other way around. The team also had to agree on how many targets and what the template would actually look like. Another scale issue came from how each brand classified and documented promotion potential. Where Scania had an ABCDE scale (with each letter corresponding to a status) whereas MAN was using "vertical" "horizontal" and "remain", depending on how it was estimated the person should evolve in the next year. The Scania interviewee explained that in their opinion, the Scania scale worked well for people who would not be promoted but was not the best for any other situation. Therefore they agreed to use the MAN scale of "remain" "vertical" and "horizontal". Scania's scale also included the timeline for promotion, with the option to look at the potential evolution in the coming year or in 3 years. In the final product a compromise was reached, using elements from both brands. Managers would therefore be categorized in "vertical" "horizontal" and "remain" and this would be qualified base on a 1 or 3 year outlook. The debate on the scale was reportedly quite easily solved with the team members discussing the value of each scale and reaching a compromise by using the best parts of each system.

There was another issue regarding decision making which was that the brand strategy was changed and the brand adapted their performance evaluation to it without considering the ongoing group project. By the time this was communicated to the team, it was too late and the new performance management system had already been set up within this brand. The TRATON holding therefore had to intervene with this brand by leveraging the "two-hat" position of the HR board member (who is the HR board member both for the TRATON GROUP and for MAN) and managed to obtain agreement that all the brands would have the same management dialogue the following year. This example highlights a key difficulty of working in this context of independently operating brands. Although the decision has been made centrally and there is agreement from all parties, commitment to this decision is not always guaranteed.

So basically we had to force them to take a decision. (Int. 14)

Furthermore, the timeline for the project was reported to be rather ambitious, and the process was also very time consuming according to the interviewees.

One holding interviewee mentioned that the communication on the fact that the Group perspective needed to be taken was not always done well enough, the reason behind this is that it could sometimes clash with brand objectives. Furthermore, since there are no real consequences, in this interviewee opinion, for not taking a Group perspective over a brand perspective, this was difficult to enforce.

We need to follow this principle and always follow what's best for the group, not necessarily for every brand individually and this is not communicated very well. And it's also that there isn't any consequence it's not followed (Int. 14)

4.1.4.3 Learning, Knowledge and Innovation

On the one hand it seems that the team members gladly learnt from each other and adapted the template based on learning from each other's necessary conditions in a flexible way, making learning and knowledge not an issue in this project. However, there was a lack of communication regarding the issue relating to the change in strategy which then delayed the implementation of the common solution in one brand, which could have been managed better if this information had been shared.

An interesting output happened on the Scania side. Indeed Scania not only benefitted from the harmonized group concept, but also gained a harmonized brand concept, which they did not have beforehand. This could therefore also facilitate Brand processes, like movements within Scania for example.

At least at Scania, we had different templates, etcetera, and this is a condensed material, you can have a broader discussion, on very concrete aspects and that has a value for an individual. And when you move within Scania on this level, you will also see the same template (int. 7)

When looking at the issue of innovation in this project, there is not really much to say. The interviewees did not describe the process as particularly innovative, as it is quite a classic HR process. In a way, one could mention the "innovative" scale which was developed by the team members as innovative, as it is different to what both brands had beforehand. By coming together in this team it allowed the brands to use the best both worlds, by each compromising on their previously used scale to come up with a new system which included the advantages from both systems. There were no issues regarding this the interviewees reported that discussion went rather smoothly.

4.1.4.4 Culture and Identities

Scania and MAN had two rather different starting points. Indeed, MAN had been using a management dialogue within the whole company for a rather long time now, whereas although Scania did have some form of performance evaluation within some areas, it was not applicable within the whole company, due to the decentralized nature of the organization. This is why it was decided that Scania would start by piloting the project with their top executives for the first year, in fact a year early. They did this on the executive board level in order to make sure they are aware of the tool and prepare them to work with it in the future. This is a way of getting buy in from top management, according to the Scania interviewee. After this year, the template was once again adapted based on the feedback from the pilot, for example including their leadership principles. Then it was launched for all the managers within Scania.

Another issue within this project was regarding the brand specific leadership criteria. At Scania, they have very strong leadership principles, which they wished to integrate into this concept. Indeed, due to cultural differences, these criteria could not be harmonized. It was very important for Scania to safeguard their culture. Therefore, the team had to be able to make the tool flexible enough so that they could include them within the template, without having harmonized leadership principles. Here there was understanding from the other team members both within he holding and the other brands, and the template was simply adapted to include brand specific leadership principles. This shows how the teams need to be able to design flexible processes and policies in order to foster integration without destroying brand identity.

> So we want our leadership principles in our document when it comes to that part in the evolution. And it was totally accepted. They understood that this is the brand culture and that should be safeguarded. (int. 7)

The interviewees also noted certain other organizational culture differences which had an impact on this project. For example, the decentralization of HR processes and policies, meant that there were different definitions of managers within Scania itself. Indeed because, as explained in the section describing the HR function at TRATON, each division has their own HR, the HR standards are different. This also means that the definition of management, and in particular who is a manager and who is not differs between Scania and MAN. This serves to validate the need for the grading project, as this allows for a common definition of management (on the top levels). Furthermore, the concept of promotion is different at Scania and at MAN. Whereas at MAN there is a personal grade associated to each person which can evolve independently of the position, at Scania a promotion is associated to a job change.

Moreover, the companies are reported to have different decision making styles and their leadership is therefore also different. Where the interviewees describe MAN as having a "tell" form of leadership Scania very much insists on involving all parties in the decision making. This had a very operational impact on the project, as mentioned above, for Scania it was very important to integrate their leadership principles into the performance assessment of their managers, and as they differ quite starkly from the MAN leadership it would not have been advisable to unify them.

> Definitely at Scania we are more encouraging that everyone contribute with ideas and so on. Even if you are a superior, you listen to your employees. Let's bring the best ideas on the table. I would say that the hierarchical up that is more common and definitely

*exist in Germany that you have a "tell" management style. Management tell you what
to do, what to choose. (int. 7)*

4.1.4.5 Boundary Spanning

When looking into the question of boundary spanning, within this project there is not much to
add. We can however note the importance of the understanding of the brand team members for
their performance evaluation systems and capacity for self-reflection on the quality of the
processes, for example when adapting the scale.

Through this project, an interviewee reported learning and further understanding of the context
for the other brand, which could be an interesting factor when looking into the development of
boundary spanning skills. In particular the case here was that MAN has gone through a lot of
changes in the past years, as they were pushed into the VW system, and then they now had to
change again. Whereas from the Scania side, they did not have as many changes, therefore they
understood why the other brand was fighting for their positon.

4.1.4.6 Key Findings

We will now briefly summarize the findings within this project, while attempting to focus on
the key elements which will be interesting for our analysis.

Within this project we have already started to find some similarities with the previous projects.
Indeed, once again the two-hat role of the HR board member was leveraged in order to deal
with the aforementioned issue of the change in strategy at MAN. Secondly, the value of
consensus decision making was noted for two reasons. The first, as already mentioned was the
opportunity to include the best elements from each brand, one again one of the known strengths
of this type of decision making, the capacity to explore the alternatives broadly. Where is was
also mentioned as a strength within this project was as a tool to make sure to preserve brand
culture. This is interesting as it also brings the symbolic meaning of using this type of decision
making to light.

When looking into the decision processes within this project, the decisions were once again
based on pre-defined criteria by the cross-brand team. There were conflicts reported, such as
the issues of the scale, but these were reportedly easily resolved as they seemed to be
complementary. One bigger issue which was noted, the issue of the change of strategy at MAN
is particularly interesting as it raises the question of the legitimacy of the decisions taken within
these cross-brand project. Once again this project had an ambitious timeline set from above,
which we will address in our contributions section in the form of a boundary spanning object
and a potential success factor. On top of that, within this project Scania required a pilot project
in order to legitimize the process before launching it to their whole organization. This matches
up to our findings from our previous project, where we found an organizational particularity of
Scania in comparison to MAN, to be this launch of non-final products. Finally one more
overarching issue which was raised was the question of the communication of the Group
perspective as being a priority which would benefit from being further explained in the brands.

Now looking into the question of knowledge, learning and innovation within this project we
found two points to make. The first is that the issue of the change in MAN strategy created a
rather big issue, which could have been avoided if the information had been shared earlier. This
would have been the case if the knowledge sharing had been done more systematically. On top
of that, the sharing which was done contributed to the creation of a new scale for the

management dialogue, which could be considered innovative. Furthermore, when looking into the learnings obtained, the most important point made within this project was an opportunity felt by Scania. Indeed, through the implementation of this group-wide concept, they naturally also gained a brand wide process, which they in fact did not have beforehand. In a way by harmonizing on a Group level, they were able to skip the brand level harmonizing step completely.

Looking into the findings within this project regarding culture and identified we can already start to see a pattern emerge. Indeed the question of the different starting points of the two brands was once again raised, with MAN having more experience with the process than Scania. On top of that the difference leadership styles were once again described, and this also has a more practical impact on the project here. Indeed, it was very important for MAN to include their leadership principles into the template. This is an important point, as these leadership principles, and the fact that they are very important to the Scania organization as the strong identification with these principles raises the question of identity within the Scania organization. Finally a point also raised which also brings us back to the question of the HR processes as a matrix supporting package, was the difficulties raised due to different definitions of promotion and management, which would potentially be facilitated by the successful implementation of the grading project.

4.1.5 Group Development Programs

The idea of this project was to develop a portfolio of development programs for top talents within the TRATON GROUP. These programs are specifically designed to develop cross-brand cooperation skills. There are multiple development programs on all the levels of the organization, from the trainee program at an entry level to the executive program for top managers. These programs are complementary to the already existing development programs within the brands, adding or completing the current offer rather than replacing it. These programs are international and all take place in at least two countries, and are in English.

As explained by the interviewees, the drive came from the top of the organization based on the fact that the brands needed to get to know each other and cooperate better, and these programs would create opportunities for people to meet. By bringing these people together within these programs, the goal is to create a network, and promote the understanding for different cultures. Furthermore, the goal was to add value through the content of these programs.

> *I think it's much much easier to pick up the phone and call a colleague when you know him or her. So I think this bringing people together; is a red thread going through everything we are trying to achieve (int. 3)*

Through these programs, brand employees learn about the other brands, and meet people from the whole Group, potentially becoming ambassadors for the Group. For example, one interviewee mentioned that the Trainees, who participate in the TRATON graduate program become TRATON employees (rather than Brand employees), as they have this knowledge of how to work together they have spent time in different brands, and are aware of the challenges and advantages of this Group. For this project, like all the previous ones, there were members representing each brand.

> *The main task is to develop global champions and ambassadors. (Int. 18)*

Overall, the interviewees were happy with how the project went and a program has now been developed on all levels. This is illustrated in the pyramid figure. Here the levels of the employees within the organization are pictured on the pyramid and the corresponding program is indicated, from the Trainee Program to the Executive Elite program at the top of the organization.

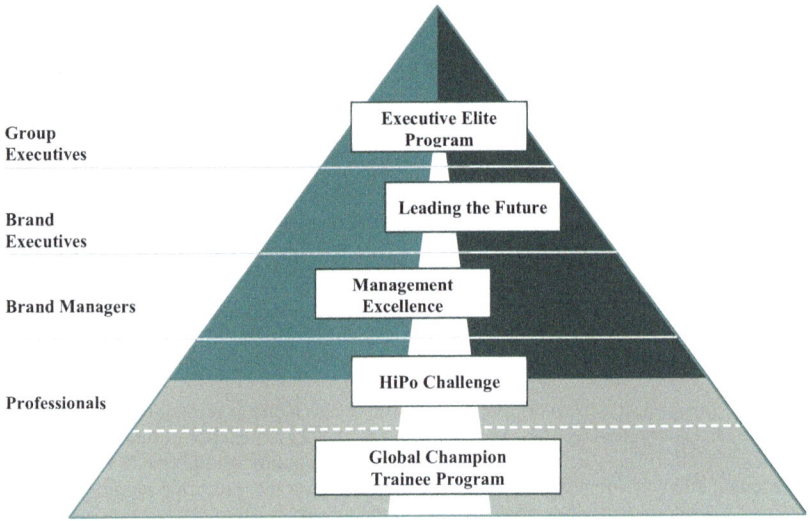

Figure 12: The Group Development programs on all levels (internal TRATON document. 2018)

The following figure is an illustration of how the Group programs serve as a complementary offer to the already existing opportunities within the brands, as they have already existing development programs. This further enforces the focus of the Group Programs on this creation of ambassadors and the development of cross-brand skills, or as they are dealt with within this research, boundary spanning skills. Furthermore, the participants of the programs were reportedly satisfied with their experience.

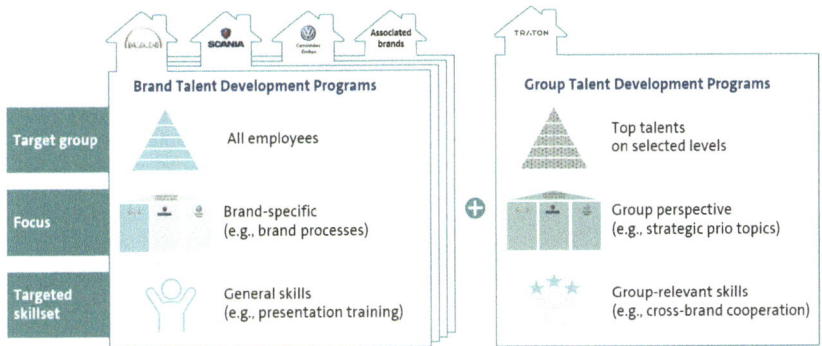

Figure 13: Group programs complementing brand offer (internal TRATON document, 2018)

4.1.5.1 Mechanisms of Control and Coordination

During this project, the governance structure played the usual role, which is to approve the concept developed by the working team. They also gave the general direction of the project as well as made some demands regarding what the project should do, such as have one program for each target group. Furthermore, one interviewee mentioned that this governance structure was sometimes used to legitimize a decision or an idea. If there was a decision made in one of the governance bodies, such as the HRMC or the Truck Board, then the holding could impose this decision.

> *So from time to time we had to say, this is a decision taken from the Truck Board or HRMC or whatever and say "this is the way we should do it". (Int. 3)*

Although the interviewees were aware of the potential for escalation, it was not used within this project. One interviewee explained that it was better to come to the solution within the project group, as they had all the information and that escalating an issue could lead to a solution which did not satisfy any of the parties.

> *If we need to point at someone or need a decision we can go to [HR Board member], because he's the HR head for the VWTB group. But for now we have always come up with a joint common proposal. (Int. 3)*

> *"(Who had the final say?) The working team and if they couldn't agree then it was the HRMC, they had the final but I cannot recall that any difficult questions were actually raised to the committee (Int. 2)*

Here the consensus decision making style used within the team was valuable. It enabled the brand to counter the initial idea of having an entirely new trainee program and voice their concerns. The holding team members had to be flexible and able to alter the initially set course. Furthermore, it was explained that the final solution was better thanks to the discussions and negotiations had within this cross-brand team, and the expertize brought by the different team members.

I think the solutions that we have found now and develop that's the result of the discussions and negotiations that we have had cross brands. (Int. 3)

One point that was also made within these interviews was that it was easier to work together when developing something new rather than adapting an already existing concept. One interviewee explained that there was less friction in this case as there was less heritage, and in the case of development programs it offered an additional opportunity for their employees so it was a benefit for the brands.

4.1.5.2 Decisions and Conflict

In order to develop this portfolio, the group started at the bottom, by developing the trainee program. Then the top program was developed for group Executives, "Executive Elite". Here the responsibilities were split up for each program in the portfolio, with in some cases the holding taking the lead (like for Executive Elite) or in other cases one brand taking the lead, like VWCO for "Leading the Future", for example. According to the interviews, the lead brand system was used here for multiple reasons. To start with, in terms of resources, it would not have been possible for one person from within the holding to drive all the programs. Furthermore, the expertise and knowledge lays within the brands. But as with the Pluralism and Inclusion topic, it was explained that the other team members were still involved in the development, the decision making and the delivery of the solution.

We have said don't take too many activities within TB because you don't have the resources, you don't have the time, is better that most is done by the brand themselves. (Int. 2)

However, not all programs were led by the brands. In particular, the Executive Elite program was very much steered and designed by the holding. The holding interviewee actually noted that this made the situation a little more difficult because the brands were not as involved from the start of the design process. This made explaining the program and especially why it was important and interesting for the brands to nominate people to participate more challenging, especially since the brands also have to pay for the program, and that it is a very expensive program.

One of the main issues within this project was that the goals did not seem clear at the beginning. Indeed, based on this general idea of developing cross-brand development programs, the team started to work. The pyramid which can be seen in the figure was only developed at a later stage. Therefore the team had to agree on what they were aiming for, what kind of programs they would be, how many and on what level? On top of that the team had to define why these programs would be developed, effectively designing programs which would benefit all brands and the group as a whole.

There was no clear assignment. Just more like a broader task (Int. 19)

This made the cooperation more difficult. Indeed, linked to this unclear goal, there was a reported lack of understanding at the beginning for the value of developing this portfolio. One interviewee explained that in his opinion this was linked to mistrust because of this lack of understanding why there was a need for additional training programs on top of already existing brand portfolios. If the brands do not understand why this program is developed there is a risk that they will not participate or participate begrudgingly. For example, one interviewee mentioned that a brand could threaten to not send any participants if a program went in a direction they were not happy with. In this case it would theoretically be possible to force a brand to send participants, but the interviewee noted that it would be much better to get the buy-in from the brand, and have them see the added value and want to send participants voluntarily.

Looking at one program in particular, the part of the project which focused on developing the Trainee program, took off in the wrong direction. Initially the idea was to cancel the brand trainee programs and create a new central TRATON program. However, it quickly came to light that it was very important for each brand to keep their own trainee program, as it was important that the trainees understand and live their brand culture first. So the initial idea from the holding was adapted after analyzing the needs of the brands and identifying how the Group program could add value to the already existing brand programs. Therefore it was decided to harmonize certain aspects and have a special TRATON module added on at the end. The team came up with a framework to harmonize the programs to a certain extent, like the starting time and duration of the program, as well as a common on-boarding event and a cross-brand rotation. This allowed the brands to keep their trainee programs, and instead added on the TRATON module and cross-brand rotation which benefitted the program and improved the offer. So in the end, after this these adaptations, the development of the trainee program was a success.

> *The trainee program, at the beginning it was a proposal that no one wanted to have but now we have developed all the group programs and created a framework for the whole group so that was really a success (int. 3)*

Once again, it was noted that this project was both time consuming and on a tight schedule. Furthermore, one interviewee noted that there may be a lack of understanding within the organization that these cooperations take time. They once again noted the value of meeting face to face and travelling to see each other, as well as the benefit of pending more time together when they do travel in order to get more out of the trips.

> *But I think the way we do it creates the frustration that everything has to be very pressured for time (Int.5)*

4.1.5.3 Learning, Knowledge & Innovation

Within this project one interviewee noted the lack of trust at the beginning of the project, which was linked to the lack of understanding for the goal behind the development of these programs. He stated the importance of knowing why certain information needed to be shared. This could be perceived as a lack of willingness to share information at the beginning of the project.

At the beginning, on the Scania side, it seemed that the cooperation with MAN did not have much value. Indeed, one interviewee explained they have a very well developed portfolio of programs, and did not feel they could benefit from the cooperation. However, according to the Scania interviewee, MAN had less programs, therefore there was more potential added value for them. Once the programs were developed and it was decided that the programs would be on top and complementary to existing ones, it was explained that the barriers have been overcome in that respect and that the brands see the opportunities offered by this.

> *I mean that's also my responsibility to say no, but it's quite difficult for one brand to say no. Because even though I think we would like to say no, I think what signal does that send, even one plays ball except Scania because they say no (Int. 5)*

Within this project and the development of these different programs, there was opportunity for innovation. Indeed, the idea was to use the expertize, knowledge and experience already present within the brands and develop something new and better. From the holding perspective it was explained that this was very much the idea, to obtain both synergies (as developing these programs allowed for resource synergies compared to developing them separately), and developing innovative programs by leveraging the different experiences within the brands.

Let's use the strength of all the resources and expertise in different brands (Int. 3)

4.1.5.4 Culture and Identities

Within this project, the interviewees also noted the issues related to the different cultures and identities within the brands. One interviewee from Scania explained that in Germany, decisions are made based on a pre-prepared PowerPoint presentations, where the team members are asked to discuss the content. One person would prepare the slides and then the team members would be asked to give their opinion on them. Then based on this the decision would be made. In Sweden, according to him, it is normal to start discussing and develop the concept together from a blank piece of paper. They would then discuss and brainstorm together until they have a common picture.

> *What we (Scania) do is that we discuss, discuss and discuss or we always talk with a blank piece of paper and we discuss together, so we develop something together and then there's a lot of discussion. Nothing happens, but we keep on discussing and feel we all share the same picture and then it happens. (Int.5)*

It seems that the MAN colleagues also need more details and prefer to have a set plan, while the Scania people would rather test a concept and then adapt it afterwards. The interviewees explained that at Scania, the decision can be taken on a "gut-feeling", without having all the details, but then adapt it afterwards. Whereas it seems that at MAN, the concept needs to be developed in more detail before it can be launched. Once the solution is implemented however, it is then not as easy to change the direction at MAN.

> *In Germany you don't feel good if you don't have all the numbers and you can take decisions on facts (Int.2)*

Furthermore, one person identified a different relationship with timelines and deadlines between the brands. Although they did not name any names, they explained that some would take deadlines as more fixed and important than other brands. On top of that it was also explained that the brands took decisions more or less as fixed. In some cases the brand would come back with some changes to the solution agreed, as they have discussed it further within their own brand, which led to a lot of back and forth to come to a final solution.

The leadership and hierarchy was also reported to be different at Scania and MAN. Where the Swedish organization is described as rather flat, the German one is described as more hierarchical. An interviewee explained that at Scania, there was no issue working and talking with whoever from the lowest to the highest ranking people in the organization. Another interesting example that was given was when during the onboarding week, the trainees were asked what they expected from their manager. According to this respondent, the Swedish answered that they expected the manager to motivate them, set up challenges, listen and discuss, the German and Polish trainees (from VW) said that they expected their manager to take decisions.

> *Many times when we want to discuss something "let's have a skype meeting" "I'm going to ask my manager and maybe my manager can ask your manager" "no but let's talk about this" (Int.4)*

Finally, it was also explained that employees from Scania tended to question and ask what the value added is when a decision comes top down and that this was not the case at MAN.

> *Why should we do this, what will this bring? What is the value added, if we are doing this? This is something that the culture here in MAN is not so typical for. (Int.19)*

4.1.5.5 Boundary Spanning

At the beginning it seems that neither the holding team members not the brand team members were entirely sure of the direction this project was supposed to take, according to the interviewees. Here the holding had to bring meaning to the project, which they did by for example developing the two charts included in this part. By clearly outlining that these projects were add-ons, and would not replace existing activities, and that there would be a program for each level within the organization, this helped to clarify the issue.

The importance of meeting face to face was once again stressed by the interviewees. The decision making processes were sometimes slow, attributed by some interviewees, to the fact that people do not meet enough.

> *The disadvantage for sure is the slowness of things. We're trying to coordinate, but at the same time we are not sitting together, we don't meet regular enough (Int. 5)*

> *There's always a risk of course that the people in the matrix, decision takers if they don't meet and have a common agenda it will take more time (Int. 2)*

It seems that decision making is different when meeting face to face rather than using Skype. Most agreed that by meeting face to face, trust is built and conversations tend to be more fruitful, leading to faster decisions. The interviewees insisted on the value of building a relationship in order to be able to build trust to overcome the challenges presented by the different views and opinions.

> *That is as well for me a key element is the personal, the relationships between the people (Int. 19)*

Within this project one interviewee noted the difficulties stemming from working in a second language and that although people understand each other in English, they may interpret things differently. This makes communication more difficult, so this goes in line with the importance of language and cultural skills as an essential boundary spanning skills.

Furthermore, the team members also reported learning more about the group while working on this portfolio. On top of that, it also allowed them to reflect on their own brand and get understanding from an external perspective, as well as furthered their understanding of the other brands.

> *I think I've learned quite a lot. We are very different. I think we (Scania) are the odds ones out, weird people (Int. 5)*

An interviewee also noted that there is now a good basis within this working group and that people are very cooperative and supportive with each other. Using this cross-brand matrix approach was appreciated, one interviewee mentioned for that example that it was a good opportunity to tell the Scania story and that the discussions were open. People within the team were not stuck in their ways and were listening to each other.

> *Every day it gets better working together because now we know each other, we know how we are and the way we work and our group, it's very aligned at the moment. The connection is better. (Int. 18)*

On top of that, sense making was shown to be important during this project. Indeed, there was a reported lack of understanding or the goal and the added value of these programs at the beginning, therefore it was important that the team members create this understanding. They did this through the co-creation of objectives and participative decision making.

Finally, there was further evidence that this project impacted the organization on a broader level. Indeed, multiple interviewees noted the fact that now that this network has been created within this group and HR in general, that it is used when a brand starts a new project to gather best practices for example and this is thanks to the relationship that has been built which allows them to pick up the phone and contact their counterpart in the other brands or the holding.

> *For me it's just opened doors, for example now that I am starting this little new group as I said, I really, one of the things that I am going to do is definitely talk to Truck & Bus and see how they are working in this area (Int. 4)*

4.1.5.6 Key Findings

We will now summarize the findings from within this project. Due to the fact that many interviewees worked on this project, the amount of data gathered is rather rich.

To start with, we will summarize the section on mechanisms of control and coordination found within this project. The committees (HRMC, Truck Board) played two roles within this project. The first was to approve decisions made within the cross-brand team and the second was to legitimize decisions within the working group, in a way stopping the possibility for debate. Although the interviewees were aware of the potential for escalation offered by the committees, they were not used as such. Furthermore, when looking at the processes, the decision making process, which was to use balanced decision making, was report to be appropriate and a good way of ensuring brand adaptation and a quality product

When looking at the decision making within this project we can make multiple conclusions. Interestingly within this project, for some of the programs a lead brand was assigned. The reason behind this is twofold. To start with the holding did not have sufficient resources to run this project for all programs. Furthermore, there was on opportunity to capitalize on the knowledge, which is help by the brands. Indeed, once again the brands held the necessary information and knowledge on the topic to be able to develop a value-adding product. Of course the input from all brands was still required, but one brand held the coordination role. It seems that the lead brand system was rather successful here. It was even explained that the one program where the holding was in the lead it was difficult to obtain the buy-in from the brands. This is interesting as this lead brand way of working is a way of creating rule-based decision making. However, this is only to a certain extent, as within the project itself, it is still expected that the team find consensus. However, the lead brand is responsible for making sure the team comes to a decision.

On top of this question of lead brand there were some issues regarding the question of decision making within this project. It seems that the goal of the project was unclear, and that some interviewees had a lack of understanding of the value of the project at the beginning, which potentially led to a lack of trust. This is particularly relevant as it brings about the role of the holding team member, which is be able to explain and sell this added value to the brand team members at the beginning of the project. As it was also explained within this project, this sense-making is also adapted and co-created in a way by the whole cross-brand team. The other issues reported were regarding the question of time. On the one hand it was noted that this project was time consuming and on a tight schedule and on the other hand, it was reported that there was a lack of understanding from within the organization that this cross-brand work takes time, one of the oft cited disadvantages of matrix work.

This project showed three clear points regarding knowledge, learning and innovation. To start with, at the beginning of the project, a lack of trust reportedly due to the unclear goals, led to a reticence to share information. However, once the goals were clarified and it was made obvious that the cross-brand projects would not replace the brand offer, information was shared more freely. This once again shows the importance of having clear goals and sharing an understanding of the value of the project. This project also shows a good example of how this matrix set-up and the balanced decision making style within the projects allowed for innovation. Indeed thanks to the knowledge sharing, the programs developed were supposedly better, with a concrete example to be find within the trainee program.

Within this project, issues due to cultural differences were also present. To start with, the style of decision making was reportedly different for MAN and Scania. Where MAN required higher levels of detail, Scania was prepared to launch a project earlier, and adapt it later, whereas at MAN once a decision was made, and a product launched, changing it was more difficult. Furthermore, within the team itself, the different styles of working were noted. It was explained that the MAN colleagues would prepare a presentation in order to get an approval or disapproval on it, whereas at Scania they preferred to start together with a blank page. Finally, the different styles of leadership and hierarchy, with Scania having flatter hierarchies and MAN taller ones, as well as the fact that it was reported that Scania employees were more likely to question things coming from the top than MAN employees.

When it comes to boundary spanning within this project, two points were raised. The first is the role of sense-making which, as already noted was an important issue at the beginning of the project. This is a boundary spanning activity which was performed by the holding team member, as well as partly done by the project team, for example in the case of the trainee program. Furthermore, the importance of socialization was also noted, as well as the difference in quality of the cooperation when using Skype versus when meeting face to face. This once again points out the importance of generating occasions to meet, a role also played by the holding team members or by the lead brand. The boundary spanning skills which are required and developed within this projects were described. To start with, language skills, in particular English, were noted here, as well as the potential issues with interpretation. Once again the ability to clarify the goals can be insisted upon in this section too. The interviewees also noted that from this cross-brand work they learned a lot, about the TRATON GROUP, the other brands, and were able to reflect on their own brand too. Finally, an important point which was noted was that this network created through this cross-brand project could be used in other cases too.

4.1.6   Global Assignment Toolbox

This project, the global assignment toolbox, was launched in 2017 with the goal of adding more mobility options to the current brand offers in order to promote more cross-brand mobility. This included both having more assignments between the brands as well as enlarging the target group for mobility, potentially to people that had not been considered before.

The general idea was to be able to have more cross-brand exchange without a high cost increase. The forms of assignment in use tend to be very costly and therefore only used for a small amount of strategic positions. Developing the mobility opportunities also as the benefit of making the TRATON GROUP a more attractive employer, as well as increasing the talent pool. The initial working group started from this idea to enlarge the global mobility offer, and the brands shared their own experience and the current mobility policies that they had. Based on this, three focus areas were identified, the cafeteria model, allowing for more flexibility in the conditions related to an expatriation contract, a focus on young professionals and the self-initiated assignment, or "SIA". These concepts were worked on in sub-groups and it was concluded that having a cafeteria model would not be manageable and would not fit to the legal requirements. The concept for the young professionals was also dropped in favor of focusing on SIA.

SIA is a slimmed down and simplified assignment type, where employees choose to go abroad within the Group, on positions which are not particularly strategic, therefore going for personal reasons. The company offers a basic package supporting this. One interviewee explained that having more assignments will help with the integration within the brands. Furthermore, the idea is that not only people who are pre-identified or nominated get the opportunity to develop their skills, but the employees themselves can also make sure to have the right competencies. She explained that managers tend to give opportunities to people who are like themselves, so having this self-determined rotation option also leads to a broader and diverse talent pool.

> *This gives power back to the employees and someone else might consider them talent or potential and then we have a bigger pool. (Int. 10)*

Overall it seems that this project was successful. Today the SIA policy has been approved and is ready to be piloted.

4.1.6.1 Mechanisms of Control and Coordination

Here there was no project lead, but rather the holding was leading this project. The holding team member sets the meetings, reminds the team members of expected contributions and follows up on work done. The holding team member is also the one that nominates topics for the HRMC meeting, therefore putting them on top management's agenda. This does not mean that everything comes from the holding team members, the brand team members can also influence the project by adding topics to the agenda.

> *If one of the colleagues reached out to me saying, "Oh maybe we should discuss this and that" I made sure we put it on the agenda. (int. 15)*

Here the HRMC was also used as a governance body, so the project team had to make a proposal for a solution which was then approved by the management committee. Consensus was always reached on a team level before being presented to the governing body and one interviewee noted that so far the HRMC had always agreed with the solutions proposed and their recommendations.

So far they have move forward with our recommendation they haven't really questioned us (Int. 10)

However as in the other projects, it was not used for escalation but rather as a decision approval body. Indeed, once again it seems that the HRMC would not be appropriate as an escalation possibility, but that the group needs to find its own solution, with the holding team member acting as the moderator. The holding team member explained that if the team had not managed to come to a solution, she would have suggested another face to face meeting in order to find "the least painful solution for all" (int. 15) in order to be able to make a proposal to the governance body.

4.1.6.2 Decisions and Conflict

Within this project, the idea was rather broad, the goal was to have more rotations between the brands and in order to do this, the cross-brand project started by analyzing what the current status within the brands was and where there were gaps which could be filled and there could be added-value for the Group. As explained above, they came up with three focus areas, one being the SIA, which we will go into more detail later. The other two focus areas were the cafeteria model and an option for young professionals. The cafeteria principle considered the fact that not all expatriates have the same needs, for example looking at the housing budget, or home leave. So the expatriates would be able to select the options that interested them the most. However, after analysis, the interviewees explained that legally this would not be easy to attain and overall the idea was too complicated to implement. Therefore they did not recommend proceeding with this idea. As the SIA model was developed, the Young Professionals idea was deemed redundant, as the young professionals were also included in the SIA model. Therefore the HR Management committee decided to focus solely on the SIA model.

At the beginning if the project, a lack of clear goals was reported. It seems that the fact that the drive for this project came from TRATON made it unclear in the minds of the brand. They themselves did not see the value yet. One interviewee mentioned that it would have been appreciated to have a little more guidance on what the goal of this project was. This could theoretically have been dealt with by using the HRMC. Instead, the team itself defined its goals and proposed the result to the committee which approved. Once the team had managed to define their goals more clearly, they could start being productive.

I think I it was needed these types of first initial meetings but is was also quite frustrating, what are we doing here? What are we trying to achieve? But once we got out of that and started to be productive it was good. (int. 10)

The interviewees raised the issue that things tend to take time, including information gathering and decision making. This is due to the complexity of the environment and the number of people involved. For example, it could take longer to get information from within Scania if they have to confer with another department. On top of that it was reported that the departments within the brands are of course very busy, so the holding team member had to keep the brands focused on this topic, as well as manage the expectations on how much work is distributed an can be achieved.

Within Scania, it can take very long, surprisingly if it then turns our "yeah we need to ask the tax department". "And how long will that take until Tax gets back to you?" "I don't know". But if they would have to ask their own manager it is extremely fast. (Int. 15)

Another issue that was brought to life during this project was the lack of follow through on agreed deliverables. Even though the decision was made in the HR Management committee and it was agreed that work would be done, when coming back to the brand slater and asking for an update nothing had been done. This shows the importance of following up on decisions and reminding the participants.

> *Everyone, agreed: we want to proceed, we are doing this and that. And if you go back to them and after three months and ask then, what has happened: nothing. (Int. 15)*

Another challenge related to this project is the alignment with Volkswagen. Indeed, Volkswagen remains the mother company of the TRATON GROUP and the SIA policy is a new type of assignment, not available in the Volkswagen portfolio of assignment policies. According to an interviewee this was one of the biggest constraints, and in order to get the approval, it was declared that SIA is a pilot project which could also potentially be used within VW if it turns out well.

Furthermore, the different processes within the companies are reportedly different, and this affects the speed of the project. At MAN, there are more internal processes, and therefore approval rounds to get through in order to launch a project. This therefore affects how fast the project can be started.

> *Scania they want to proceed as soon as possible, but they have different internal processes, they're not as strict as we have here in Germany (Int. 20)*

4.1.6.3 Learning, Knowledge and Innovation

Like in the previous projects, the team members started by sharing their experience and explaining their status regarding global assignments, thanks to this information sharing a gap was identified. There seem to have been few issues, or in any case they were not mentioned by our interviewees.

Within this project, the cross-brand team once again developed a new concept for a process within HR. Here the diversity of legal and institutional settings was a barrier to innovation. Indeed, the cafeteria model, which would have been a new way of managing expatriate benefits could not move forwards due to this complexity. Furthermore, the challenge of aligning with the mother-company VW was also highlighted here. As this assignment type, SIA, was different, new, this required negotiation to get it approved. If VW had not approved, I could have been possible that SIA not see the light.

4.1.6.4 Culture and Identities

The interviewees noted some cultural differences which also affected the project. It seems that on the MAN side, there was a more analytical and risk averse attitude. One Swedish interviewee gave the example of anticipating potential consequences of choosing a host or home approach. MAN had worries that their employees would be reticent to go with the host company conditions or that too many Scania employees would come to Germany for example.

The interviewees also noted that from Scania's side, the top down direction was not enough to have people work on a topic. There is a need for understanding the reasoning behind the project. They need to understand the reason behind a direction in order to follow it, which according to the interviewees is not the case at MAN.

There was a debate between having a host country approach or a home country approach. With a host country approach, the working conditions for the expatriate are based on the ones within the host country, whereas in a home company approach, the conditions are based on the situation within the employee's home entity. Here Scania and MAN were using these two different approaches. One interviewee explained that Scania used a host country approach, because the salaries are lower therefore it would be a disadvantage for the expatriates to have a home country system, and for MAN the opposite is true, the salaries are higher at MAN. Furthermore it would seem that what is important for the German MAN employees may be different to what Scania employees attach importance to. Here it seems that for potential assignees from MAN, the pension is an important factor, whereas at Scania it seems to be less of a concern. One interviewee explained that German employees have to have safety first, and that they would never go into a country where they earned less. This further explains the attachment to the home company approach. Therefore, both organizations wanted to keep their approach as it benefitted their employees. The Scania interviewee explained that she had to convince the MAN team member to go for a host approach within SIA. This was difficult as MAN was used to doing it in another way. In the end by discussion and talking and spending time on this, they were able to agree on the host approach. This agreement was made and it was made transparent that depending on the host and home country, some situations are more advantageous than the other. However, this was already the case in other assignment types, so this was not a very big issue.

> *Whereas Scania said the pension payment isn't that important for us especially if we aim for the younger generations, they're not yet as far as thinking on what is going to happen in-40-50 years. (Int. 20)*

What made the situation more complicated was that each brand also had different terms, or the same terms with different meanings, like for example the "local plus" concept. This led to some confusion as although both brands were using the same term, local plus, but the meaning of it is different within each organization.

4.1.6.5 Boundary Spanning

This project highlighted the role of the holding related to temporal boundary spanning activities. Indeed, the team member had to make sure that the brands spent time on this project, by sending out reminders, or setting meetings with objectives for example.

Furthermore the role of the holding was also in moderating issues and making sure that the discussions stayed on track and kept moving forwards. For example, one interviewee explained that she would make a proposal in order to get the discussion started on a solution.

> *I could have made a proposal to say, "Okay guys, let's go for this in a first step, present it like this. And that to support them to find a way at least to proceed, not get stuck in this. Okay, we don't know what to do because we have different approaches. (Int. 15)*

One issue that was brought up within this project was the problem of language. Here the issue was that the team members were using the same term for different things. The brands reached this solution by clarifying the language and the definitions that each brand had for their different policies, as well as simply calculating and comparing the conditions related to each option. This stresses the importance of communication and language as a boundary spanning skill.

I think they did a lot of calculations actually cost calculation and really walked through some concrete cases to find out what would be the consequences to a plus and minus and then just comparing them and discussing within our group and then in the end, having the feeling that we all agree on going in direction A instead of B. (int. 15)

Once again within this project the participants insisted on the importance of face to face contact, through meetings or workshops. They gave an example of a meeting where the Scania team members went to Munich and had a one day workshop with the team, and this day was reportedly very productive and a lot of the work was done then, with a lot of the policy developed within that day. Furthermore an interviewee noted that MAN was maybe not very used to using Skype, as they have only had the system for half a year and they used to only use the phone. Finally, one interviewee mentioned that participating was an issue for VWCO as they are much further away. She explained that giving them more travel budget would be very helpful.

From the team members' point of view, participating in this project has been beneficial. Although it was frustrating at the beginning, due to the fact that the goal of the project was unclear, the interviewees appreciated the opportunity to learn from each other.

It's really nice, as we can compare ourselves, and discuss business models and try to compare ourselves with other companies. This is nice, I'm really happy to join. (int. 20)

I think I it was needed these types of first initial meetings but is was also quite frustrating, what are we doing here? What are we trying to achieve? But once we got out of that and started to be productive it was good. (Int. 10)

Furthermore, there were some "side-benefits" from this project. For example, as process used within Scania, E-signatures, using a software called "Scrive" has now been implemented at MAN. This adds value not only to the Group, making signing cross-brand documents simpler, but also MAN itself, as based on the experience at Scania, it could implement this software.

What we worked on at Scania for example is e-signature of our global assignment contracts and now this is also going to be introduced at MAN, as a part of this project so that it going to be a huge added value, not only for them but when we have a company cross company transfers because that has been a very slow process to get all those documents signed, it could take months, and now we can really have a lot of efficiency by having the e-signing. And I think we wouldn't have this in place so fast if it wasn't for this project. (Int. 10)

4.1.6.6 Key Findings

The findings for this final HR project will now be summarized, before moving on to the description the of the R&D function.

Now, looking into the facilitating factors for this project the findings regarding process design, organization and role distribution are similar to those within the previous projects. Here there is no lead brand, but the holding plays the coordination role, with the brands bringing in knowledge and input. Furthermore, the HRMC is used to approve decisions. Once again, this body is not used to escalate issues.

When looking at decisions and the issues related to decision-making in this project, an issue that has already been mentioned in other projects was the issue of the lack of clear goals. It was explained that the fact that the drive came from the holding led to the brands not seeing the value of the project at the beginning, once again pointing out the importance of sense-making in these projects. Furthermore, slow-decision making was also reported, with another reason brought to light. Here the issue was found in the case of cross-functional information required. On top of that, interviewees mentioned an issue related to a lack of follow through on the deliverable agreed upon in this project. This is interesting as it shows an important role of the holding, making sure deliverables are worked upon in the brands. Moreover, it seems that the brand decision making processes are different, leading to the organizations running at different speeds. This raised the point of temporal boundary spanning. Finally, one issue that was mentioned was the need for alignment not only within the TRATON GROUP, but also with the mother company, Volkswagen. Although within this research we focus mostly on the internal Traton issues, Volkswagen plays an important role within Traton HR, as it imposes certain standards.

The point just mentioned about the alignment with VW also could have been a barrier to innovation, since if VW had not approved the concept, Traton would not have been able to move forwards with it. On top of that, some innovative ideas had to be benched because of the complex environment and diverse institutional contexts which made the implementation too difficult.

When looking at culture and identities within this project, many issues arose. To start with, Scania and Man reportedly have a different attitude regarding risk, where Scania is more prepared to take risks than MAN. This is in line with Hofstede's findings on uncertainty avoidance in Sweden and Germany. Once again it was noted that decision making tends to be more top down at MAN than at Scania. Another issue that arose within this project was that employee needs and expectations were reportedly different, so when developing a Global Assignment model, it was challenging to deal with these diverging expectations. Finally, the issue of language was raised, as the team members were using the same words, but actually with different meanings, leading to some confusion which needed to be cleared up.

The holding has a particular boundary spanning role here, as mentioned above, where the holding team member must perform temporal boundary spanning in order to ensure both follow up align the different tempos within the brands. On top of that, the moderating role of the holding team member was noted here. When looking into boundary spanning skills we can note once again the point which was raised regarding the importance of socialization and meeting face to face, as well as the lack of experience in using digital communication. On top of that, a by-product of this project was noted, once again bringing up the fact that the benefits of these cross-brand projects can sometimes leak out and affect elements beyond the boundaries of the project itself.

4.1.7 Summary and Analysis of Key Findings within HR Projects

In this next section, we will summarize the results found within the HR projects. This section will be divided into 5 parts, focusing first on the governance and the power capabilities of the holding. Then, we will discuss the classic matrix issues identified within these projects before going on to the question of knowledge sharing and the value of balanced deciaion making in the matrix. Furthermore we summarize the findings related to organizational culture differences and finally we will discuss a key success factor, boundary spanning.

4.1.7.1 Governance and the Power Capabilities of the Holding

Within the matrix, the governance structure plays an essential role, as the committees are made up of the top executives from all brands, they effectively have the authority to decide. By having these committees take or commit to the suggested decisions, also give the decision legitimacy within the brands. The role of the committees was to oversee the projects and they would authorize the decisions as the project went along.

Within the HR organization, the brands hold most of the power of resources within their organizations. Financial resources as well as knowledge and expertise remains within the brands. Indeed the holding employees have a coordination role and the knowledge and expertise comes from the brand members However, essential resources which the holding can leverage are its employees. Indeed, the holding employees are fully focused on cross-brand projects, unlike most of the people within the brands, in a way the holding has the power of "time" where the holding employees have time to focus on cross-brand projects. Because TRATON has little power of resources, the power of processes which they possess is very important. Furthermore the boundary spanning skills of the holding team members become all the more important as these informal mechanism of cooperation allow TRATON to drive decisions.

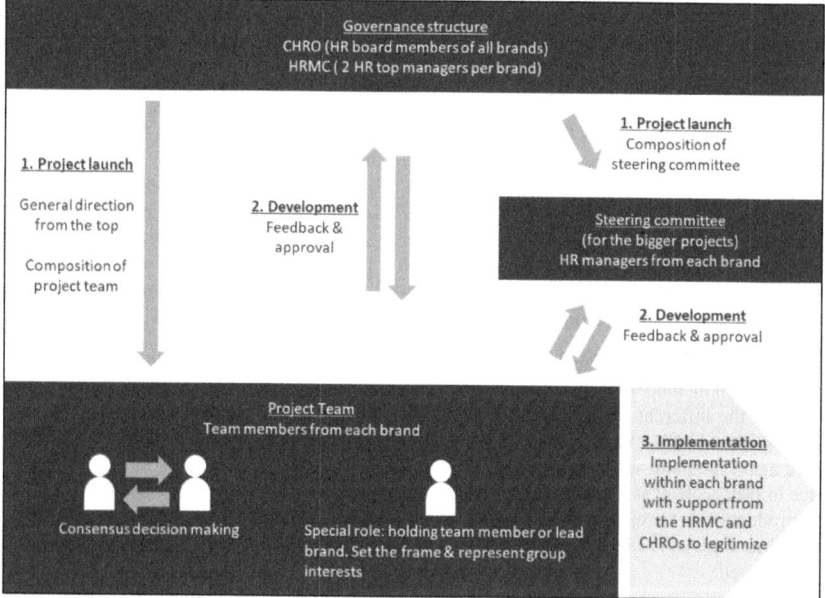

Figure 14: The HR governance structure in practice (own elaboration)

One actor in particular emerged as particularly important in the decision making processes of this holding matrix organization. This "actor" is top management and the particular role they play within this matrix organization. To start with, top management can have a strong influence by giving a specific and precise goal (or not) to the topic. Furthermore, the escalation process, which also rests on the top management involvement, is not used as a conflict resolution tool.

However, the committees and governing bodies, namely the HRMC and CHRO meeting, which are made up of these top managers play an important role in the legitimization of the activities of the cross-brand teams. Another role that was highlighted, was the rather unique "two-hat" role of the HR board member, who occupies both a position within the brand organization and within the Group board. Here, his position was able to be leveraged as a conflict resolution mechanism. On top of that the interviewees also spoke a lot about expectations. These expectations come from above, and are related to two things. The first is the expectations regarding timelines of the project. Some noted that the top managers had a tendency to underestimate how long this type of cooperative work took. Furthermore, one could consider that they are the ones responsible for these ambitious deadlines that we have mentioned previously. On top of that, by giving attention to a topic, they also give more power to the project team to implement their product.

4.1.7.2 Classic Matrix Issues with Contemporary Complexities

Within our research framework we identified decision making as a key matrix issue, highlighting in particular the theory of Wolf and Egelhoff regarding rule based and balanced decision making as well as the classic issues related to decision making in a matrix organization, the speed of decision making and the issues related to conflict around decision making power in the matrix.

Within nearly all of the projects studied, the issue of slow decision making was brought up. As mentioned, this is one of the classic criticisms of the matrix organization (Davis & Lawrence, 1977, Goold & Campbell, 2003; Galbraith, 2008; Wang et al., 2012; Wolf & Egelhoff, 2017). The interviewees within these projects tend to attribute the slow decision making to multiple factors. The first factor is the complexity of the matrix, which therefore requires more alignment and internal rounds than the simpler (to an extent) brand organizations. To start with, as reported in most research on matrix decision making, the process is more complex in such a structure due to the multiple parties involved. One interesting point made was the potential additional alignment required in a matrix due to the lack of trust between the dimensions. This brings up the issue of trust building as an important potential facilitating factor, as it could support the acceleration decision making in the matrix, effectively countering one of the classic matrix organization issues. Furthermore, as mentioned within some of the projects, this matrix work tends to be done as an additional project to the usual brand work. This leads to very busy team members with conflicting priorities within their brands and within the matrix environment. On top of that, it has been highlighted that gathering the necessary information and alignment within the brands can be a lengthy process, also slowing down decision making. There is therefore an important role to be played by the cross-brand team members in two ways here. To start with, the holding team member or lead brand has to ensure that the project remains a priority. Secondly, team members must be able to gather information and alignment from within their brands, which supposes a certain network and standing within their own organizations. Therefore, the boundary spanning activities and capabilities of these team members are particularly important. Finally, one further reason used to explain the slow decision making of the matrix organization is the conflict involved in this process. Indeed, in some cases, conflict would take a long time to resolve, usually because of a lack of communication between the parties. This is linked to the question of trust between the two organizations. Furthermore, it seems that the process of escalation was either not used at all, or used with no actual results. In general, although there is a governance structure which could potentially be used as an escalation possibility, the conflicts reported in the HR projects were not escalated. The reason behind this is that the conflicts were thought to be too small to be escalated to such a high level. Sometimes, if needed, the direct managers of the cross-brand team members were used as an escalation mode. However, this proved to be difficult, as the managers only have authority over their respective brands and not the cross-brand project itself. This has two effects. The first is that it potentially slows down the conflict resolution, as taking these issues up with one of these committees could be a way of solving the conflict. On the other hand it allows for the decisions to be discussed and agreed upon on a lower level, developing and solving the conflict in a consensus kind of way, potentially coming to a better solution, however slower.

Interestingly though, the question of speed of deciaion making is even more complex. The two organizations tend to run at two different paces. Where MAN would start faster than Scania and then have gather all the authorizations and alignment once the project was started, Scania will be slower at the beginning, making sure every party agrees before even thinking of taking a decision. In particular, at MAN the works council has a stronger role to play, and their approval and support must be gathered. Furthermore, Scania would also be inclined to run a pilot project which would then be adapted, rather than immediately using a final product. This makes it potentially possible to launch a project faster, but then requires adaptation. This is a clear example of the issues illustrated within the research on temporal boundary spanning. Here the idiosyncratic time of both organizations, embedded in their processes, is different, leading to issues of synchronization within the team including both brands. Therefore this underlines the importance of temporal boundary spanning as a potential facilitating factor and will be addressed in the section dedicated to these factors. We have illustrated this in the figure. It must be noted that this figure does not claim to understand which organization would be faster, and is not trying to make a judgment on the exact speed or duration of each phase, it is for illustration purposes only.

A second classic matrix organization issue, which has been pressed a lot in the literature and is often cited as one of the reasons for matrix abandon in the past is the issue of conflict in the matrix organization. We have not looked into the quantity of conflict per se, as was often done, but have chosen to further understand the causes for conflict and their consequences in the contemporary matrix organization. Our finding, is that, as mentioned by Wolf and Egelhoff (2017b), it seems that the most common type of conflict within the matrix is task conflict. In particular, although there was some mention of authority conflict, goal conflict is the most present within our findings. Indeed, in general, the issue of goals plays a very important role within these cross-brand projects. To start with, the conflicting dimensions of the matrix, in this case the brands, report having issues within their projects due to conflicting goals. Interestingly however, some reported triggering these conflicts as a way to move the project forwards. This is a point worth mentioning as it highlights one of the important characteristics of balanced decision making. Another issue often reported is the question of unclear goals. The consequence of these unclear goals partly responsible for slowing down the project, as the teams had to align on the objectives of the project. Another reason cited for the lack of understanding of the goals is if these were to come directly from the holding, therefore not issuing from an identified need within the brands, making the understanding for this goal more difficult for the team members. On top of that, it was also mentioned that the lack of clearness of the goals could lead to mistrust within the brands, as they would not understand the reasoning behind the work they were doing. This raises once again the issue of trust, and also allows us to add the idea of sense-making, understanding the "why", as a potential facilitating factor. Furthermore, it was noted that the definition of the goals by the cross-brand teams led to further commitment than if these objectives were already set. This is a relevant point as it leads us to the issue of balanced versus rule based decision making.

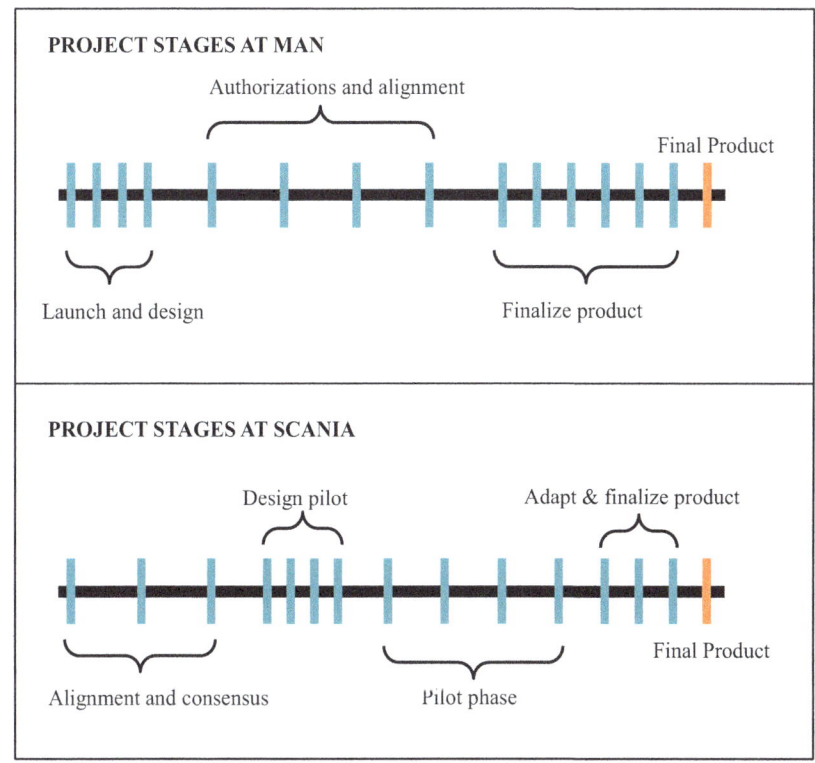

Figure 15: Idiosyncratic project timelines at Scania and MAN (own elaboration)

Indeed, in a matrix project where the decision making is balanced, the idea is the parties will attempt to reach a consensus in order to come to a decision. This would potentially include the definition of the goals and objectives for the project, as the idea is to reconcile different viewpoints in order to come to a common solution. Although Egelhoff and Wolf (2017) posit that the balanced matrix may no longer be the desired state for a matrix in the contemporary MNC and that many of their respondents in their research expressed the desire for more rule-based decision making, the fact that the decision making is balanced in this case is important. It plays multiple roles. To start with, within all these HR matrix projects, the goal was to find a common (to a certain extent) solution for all the brands. Therefore, having the information processing capacities of balanced decision making is value adding here. Furthermore it plays an important role in the creation of a common culture for the team. On top of that, this type of decision making plays a symbolic role. Indeed, the importance of preserving the brands has been made clear, with the desire to keep the brand identity, expressed for example through the "Scania way". Therefore in having balanced decision making, both brands are able to enter the project on somewhat equal footing. However, there have been counterexamples for the value of this decision making type. To start with, it seems that in certain cases, the conflicting goals of the brands overshadows the consensus reached within the cross brand teams. Indeed, we have seen examples within our projects of brands changing course even after a certain decision had been taken on and agreed upon, like for example within the management dialogue project. It is important to also consider rule-based decision making as it could potentially help avoid issues occurring within balanced decision making. The way rule based decision making is formally done in our case is through the concept of the lead brand. The lead brand concept was used a little within HR. Looking into the functioning of the lead brand in the HR organization, there are three ways the lead brand seems to be selected. The first is experience and knowledge about the topic. Another reason behind the choice of the lead brand is fairness and division of labor. Therefore, it seems that there may also be a symbolic value in the choice of lead brand, maintaining a form of balance. However, apart from taking responsibility for moderation and organization, the impact of the decision of a lead brand is rather low. Furthermore, the holding retains the right to balance power in the case that the lead brand is not protecting Group interests.

4.1.7.3 Knowledge Sharing and the Value of Balanced Decision Making for Innovation

Within our research framework we address the issue of innovation. We do not wish to dive deep into the concept of innovation itself and the innovative products, but rather want to empirically understand how a matrix could potentially contribute to the ambidexterity of a firm. In our case, it seems that the matrix organization does play the role as described in the "flexible matrix" by Egelhoff and Wolf. Indeed, the projects are targeted towards finding synergies or improving the offer of the company (which can be described as exploration), whereas the exploitation, business as usual, is left to the brands, within their hierarchical organizations. By having these two brands work together, the idea is that the value of the final product or process will be greater than something simply developed and implemented by one brand, or the headquarters. Oftentimes it does seem that this was the case within this organization. Now this is not exactly as described in the literature, as our case is quite particular, with the previously separate entities, but we do believe we can contribute further understanding to the concept of the ambidexterity of the flexible matrix. In order to do this we have identified some barriers to innovation within our research.

When looking at the benefit of balanced decision making for innovation, within these cases conflict acted as a lever for innovation. Through the discussion and the learning coming from them, the teams were able to gather the best of both worlds to create a better product, process or method. In general, our interviewees tended to agree that the solutions they came up with were better for having been done in cross-brand projects, with contributions from multiple brands, which leveraged more knowledge and expertise. Furthermore it seems that these projects, working in this balanced decision making mode, allows for learning in three different ways. To start with, by participating in a cross-brand projects, the participants were able to learn more about the Group and gain a more global view of the organization. Secondly, by working together with their counterparts from other brands allowed them to understand how the other brand worked as well as gain best practices. And finally, this interaction with the other brands also held up a mirror to their own brand, leading to potential self-reflection and to questioning of their own practices.

There were some issues regarding knowledge sharing in some of the projects. This was due to a reported lack of clear goals and understanding of the value of the projects. This led to a certain amount of reticence for active knowledge sharing, especially at the beginning of the projects.

This is interesting as it points out the importance of having an understanding for the goal of the projects. Some external factors were responsible for hindering the implementation of the new solutions found within the cross-brand teams, such as the institutional and legal differences where the different brands were embedded meant that although some ideas were good, they could not be applied everywhere. This brings us to our next point, the issue of culture and identities within the matrix organization.

4.1.7.4 Organizational Culture Differences

The varying institutional contexts were reported to be an issue within HR projects. The different rules, regulations and practices within the countries were noted to have an impact on the projects. This influences the HR projects heavily in their need for flexibility.

A topic related to organizational cultural differences which has been mentioned is the style of decision-making. According to interviewees, the Scania employees prefer a consensus style and joint decision making based on open discussions. The Scania employees are described (both by themselves and by the MAN employees) as taking a lot of time to discuss topics, attempting to reach a consensus. The MAN respondents on the other hand are more used to top-down decision making, with structured decisions. The way the MAN employees work is often described as structured, like in meetings where the agendas are fixed well in advance. The decision making at Scania is often reported as being slower, but with potentially fewer implementation issues, as all parties have agreed on the decision. The theory on this topic is that obtaining consensus would promote commitment therefore increasing the likeliness of implementation success (Dooley et al. 2000). Therefore theoretically, one could understand Scania as being slower in the decision making phase than MAN, but faster in the implementation. Interestingly, this consensus style of decision making (or balanced decision making) was then used in most of the cross-brand projects. It was often commented on that decisions would take a long time to make. Although one would expect decision making to be very much anchored within an organization, these findings do match what can be found within literature comparing the Germans and the Swedes. Overall, the Germans are more consequence-oriented whereas the Swedish as consensus oriented (Müller et. al., 2009). Therefore when coming together in multinational teams, there are initial struggles simply in the way of working and coming to a solution.

Another significant cultural difference which has affected the effectiveness of the cross-cultural teams is the risk-taking and the decision implementation style. Within some HR projects, it was noted that the Scania employees would rather start with a pilot. In doing this they like to implement the decision quicker, but with the idea that any issues or changes will then be found within the pilot phase. This obviously allows for faster implementation, but then requires changes to the initial product. Furthermore, the pilot is to legitimize the value of said product. The MAN employees however prefer to spend more time deciding, and making the product sounder, before immediately implementing it in its final form. This can lead to impatience and misunderstanding with the project teams. This also requires flexibility either of one or both sides as well regarding the product. Furthermore, at Scania it seems that they tend to not have an issue with changing a decision once it has been made and aligned, whereas at MAN once a decision is made and approved it is final. The decisions are perceived as less binding within Scania than at MAN. According to the interviewees, MAN is used to a top down decision making style, where directions from the top are followed to reach the goals set by the company. For the Scania however, the employees have to understand why this action needs to be taken, it is essential to obtain buy-in from the employees. This involves spending a lot of time in discussions.

The professional practices, embedded in the organizational culture also have an impact on the cross-brand projects. Indeed some HR practices are radically different. However in general it seems that the MAN professional practices tend to be closer to the VW ones, potentially due to two factors. The easy assumption would be that it is because they are a German company too and they therefore have the same institutional challenges. That is however not the only factor. The history of the companies will also play a role here, where MAN has been a part of VW for a longer time and has seemingly accepted the VW processes more than Scania has in the past.

We have summarized the cultural differences which impacted the projects and were mentioned by the interviewees within these HR projects in the table. We would however like to stress that this is the opinion of the few only, and has no claim to being a full picture of the organizational culture of these organizations.

Table 11: Perceived cultural differences within HR projects (own elaboration)

MAN described culture	Scania described culture
- Decision making top-down - Hierarchical - Risk averse - Detail oriented - Decision is final - Professional practices closer to VW professional practices	- Decision making consensus style - Flatter organization - Risk taking - Trial and error - Decisions can be changed and adapted based on new information - Used to working in a more complex environment

4.1.7.5 Boundary Spanning, a Key Success Factor

When looking at the boundary spanning activities of the members of these cross-brand teams, it makes sense to start with the activities performed by the holding team members. Interestingly, in setting up this matrix, the TRATON GROUP has effectively set up formal boundary spanners in the form of these holding team members. Indeed the core role they play within the company is to facilitate the cooperation between MAN and Scania. The role of the holding team members, include coordinating cooperation efforts, such as planning meetings, gathering and sending out materials. Furthermore, they are also responsible in regards to the governing committees for delivering results. Finally, they play the role of defending group interests above individual brand interests. The lead brand, when there is one will play this same role. They perform all the boundary spanning activities, as described by Barner-Rasmussen et al. (2014). One could also say that the holding team member also acts as 'cultural liaison ', as described by Carmel and Agarwal (2001), as they are resolving and mediating culture based conflict and effectively bridging cultures, therefore facilitating the flow of information between the parties. Furthermore, a boundary spanning activity performed which is essential to the success of these projects is the facilitation of communication between the parties. The team members need to understand the motivation of the different parties in order to be able to successfully cooperate with them.

We would like to point out the role of HR as a facilitator. In fact it seems that HR itself also has a boundary spanning role to play. Many of these HR projects described contribute to creating what Galbraith (2009) calls the "matrix supporting package". He states that these policies are essential to the successful matrix organization. For example by having a harmonized grading system and performance evaluation, this facilitates movements between the brands which in turn improve the socialization of the employees within the group. However, as has been seen within this case, having completely common processes would not be beneficial. There is a need for HR flexibility coming from the cultural and environmental differences. Another topic related to HR appeared within this study. We have had the chance to interview people who used to work within the brands and now also work within the matrix organization. It was mentioned that the cross-brand work is time consuming. Indeed, cooperation, as has been described within the projects, represents a high workload, and the brand employees received this on top of their previous jobs. However, it was pointed out that employees enjoyed working within this international context.

In order to perform the boundary spanning activities, the holding and brand employees need specific skills. These skills will be explained in the next section and then summarized in the table below. It is interesting to note that these skills are both needed to perform the cross-brand work, as well as developed by practicing these boundary spanning activities, effectively creating a virtuous circle.

The first, within this case is the ability to have a Group perspective. Indeed, each team member has their own brand focus, but to successfully be able to cooperate, they need to be able to see the value for the Group as a whole. However, an issue that was reported in most projects was the fact that the goal of the project itself seemed unclear at the beginning. Therefore, it is difficult to have a group perspective if the team members are not aware of what that is. It was explained that it is important in the first stage to make it clear for all the team members what the goal of the project is, and be able to set objectives. By creating common goals, defining together which elements were important, therefore moving away from the discussion about what was currently being done was helpful. The brand team members must be able to see the Group picture, while still making sure to defend their own brand interests. This requires a capacity to see the Group perspective, as well as flexibility in order to move back and forth from the brand perspective to the Group perspective. In fact, this skill is so important that some people who did not possess it were moved from projects. This skill is also especially important for holding team members. Indeed when the holding was first set up, the employees recruited to work in the holding often came from the brands. However, they needed to adapt and learn to not favor their "home" brand over the other and get this group perspective. Linked to this, a very present theme within this research as well as clear facilitating factor for cross brand work, was the ability to define the value of the project.

Another essential skill is the understanding of the different brand cultures. The team members not only need to understand the other brands culture, but also understand how their own is perceived. This also confirms the findings by Barner-Rasmussen et al. (2014), on the importance of intercultural skills for boundary spanning. Closely linked to the previous skill is the open-mindedness that is required. This ability to take a step back and consider all perspectives in order to contribute positively to the decision making also requires, empathy and flexibility. Indeed, the team members need to understand the other brand's perspective as well and be able to empathize with the conditions and environment from the other brand in order to develop a solution together which is the best for the whole Group.

Communication and negotiation skills are also essential within this setup. Indeed, with the decisions not so much coming from the top but rather being derived by the negotiations between the brands, it is essential to have this skill. On the one hand, as a brand team member it is important to be able to fight for their own brand interests in order to make sure they are protected. On the other hand from a holding point of view it is essential to be able to guide these negotiations, in fact more of a moderating role, in the right direction in order to protect group interests. This is also facilitated if the brand team members have the first skill mentioned, that is the ability to have a group perspective. Here, the role of trust was important, as it acts a conflict inhibitor. The interviewees within this case study see trust as essential to the cooperation and to keeping the conflicts functional and reducing the significance of the conflicts. The elements required, according to the interviewees was generally the opportunity to meet and socialize. Indeed, an important factor that was noted as a facilitator to the boundary spanning activities of the team members was the importance of creating a personal connection, this supported by meeting face to face. This was also noted as an important factor in building trust in order to hinder conflict. This is a facilitator because as the team members are working in a virtual organization it is not always easy to build this connection. However this obviously has a cost consequence as it is both expensive and time consuming for the parties to travel.

Moreover, an essential skill remarked upon was technical expertise in order to be able to explain company practices and defend them. Moreover, the knowledge required is not always simple knowledge of company policies and processes, but are rather deeper understanding of the meaning and interests behind them ('knowing why' more than ''knowing how'). This expertise is essential to the credibility of the person, which is necessary to be able to defend brand interests within the working group and afterwards to be able to promote the measure within the brand.

Table 12: Boundary spanning skills within cross-brand projects (own elaboration)

Boundary spanning skills required and developed within cross-brand projects	
Language	English as a requirement to work in cross-brand projects Some terms used in different ways, importance of realizing this
Group-brand flexibility	Ability to consider Group and Brand interests, as well as go back and forth between the two perspectives
Cultural openness and ability for self-reflection	Openness and understanding towards other brand culture, as well as awareness of the perception of own culture
Communication and negotiation skills	Be able to push the project, both within the working group, as well as within own brand. Ability to moderate these discussions from a holding perspective.
Developing trust	Need to obtain the trust of the other working group members, as well as be trustworthy within their own brand
Technical expertise & brand knowledge	Have a good understanding of their own brand

Another interesting point that was mentioned was the role of language in cross-brand projects. There is still a good level of English within the working groups and the fact that both parties are speaking a second language levels the playing field, with a potential slight advantage to the Swedish, who learn English from a very early age (Birkinshaw, 2002). It is therefore an essential boundary spanning skill to be able to work in English. This goes in line with Barner-Rasmussen et al. (2014) and their findings on the importance of language as a boundary spanning skill. Furthermore the different uses of language are important. Indeed there were instances where both parties were using the same terms to describe different things, making it essential to be able to critically deal with this and check that everyone is talking about the same thing, which is more difficult in a foreign language and even more so in this intercultural context.

It is important to note what we call the snowball effect of the cross-brand project. In fact setting up the structure and the governance of the matrix is not what had created the matrix in this case. In fact the participation in the cross brand projects has done the brunt of the work. Indeed, it was reported that the participation in cross-brand projects led to the creation of a network between the participants. As the people get to know each other, they create an informal bond, allowing for further socialization beyond the limits of the projects. This enable further knowledge sharing, for example gathering best practices for topics which are not dealt with cross-brand. Furthermore, this will act as a facilitating factor for the cross-brand work. On top of that, when issues are identified and solved within a cross-brand project, this sets a precedent. There have been examples of these projects leading to group wide policies being put into place although this was not the goal of the project in itself, such as the set-up of Scrive within MAN thanks to the Global Assignments project.

Now that we have finished summarizing the results found within the HR projects, we will move on to the analysis of the findings within R&D projects.

4.2 The Research and Development Project Processes

4.2.1   The R&D Function Governance and Chronology

At TRATON, each brand has its pre-existing R&D department. This department can be considered to be the heart of the business, as it is where the products which will then be sold, meaning trucks and buses and their components (amongst others, see the company description for more details on all the TRATON products) are developed. Behind the creation of the TRATON GROUP, the idea is to obtain synergies by jointly developing certain components. Indeed, both big brands, MAN and Scania, have a similar end product and customer. However these two brands remain competitors on the market, making this cooperation solely internal. The TRATON holding R&D, which according to the interviewees, has a coordination function which is currently focused on joint component development. Therefore from the market point of view the brands remain separate and competitors.

> *So the customers are expecting and are continuing to expect MAN trucks or Scania Trucks or VWCO trucks in Brazil, this will state the face to the market (Int. 8)*

The R&D function at MAN is organized in 7 main departments: Engineering Bus, Engineering Rolling Chassis, Engineering Electric/Electronic Systems, Engineering Karosserie (body), Engineering Powertrain, Engineering Vehicle, and Engineering Central. Due to data protection reasons, the organigram could unfortunately not be included in this thesis. The headcount for R&D at Scania is about 4300 employees, of which about 650 consultants and 3650 internal employees. The R&D function is organized into four purely R&D functions: Connected, autonomous and embedded systems, Powertrain development, Truck, cab and chassis development and vehicle definition. On top of that there is a so-called cooperation office, the Scania Way office, a controlling and a human resources department. As explained previously, the Human Resources within Scania are decentralized and therefore report directly into the functions. At Scania this is a Scania Way office, which is also decentralized. This function looks after the change and culture topics within the organization. In comparison to the R&D functions within the brands which are very big, the R&D function at TRATON is very small, counting around 30 people at the time of this research. As explained above, the holding does not actually do any development itself but rather has a focus on coordinating the activities of the brands. It is divided into four areas of focus, namely powertrain, chassis cabin axles, embedded systems and methods and processes.

Within the R&D function certain components or products have been selected as they have potential to create synergies through joint development. The holding has the role of coordinating this joint development. This is done by the CTO office of the TRATON Holding, which is based in Södertalje, Sweden. According to the interviewees, it has been found that most of the synergies can be found through common component development.

> *"Our business environment is rapidly changing and there is a pressure on us to act in order to stay competitive. The ambition is not only to face the challenges, but to achieve a position as global champion. A step towards this ambition is the Lead Engineering concept, which is an initiative designed to improve our strength as a group. Working together is how we can improve the time to market and be the benchmark in R&D efficiency. It is how we can free required R&D competences and resources to stay innovative even in a changing industry" Anders Nielsen, in the VWTB Collaboration Guide for Engineers.*

Based on the information provided by the "collaboration guide for engineers", which is a document addressed to the engineers working within the technical office of the TRATON holding, we were able to further understand the role of the holding within the R&D organization. The role of the CTO office and of the brands is described as follows by the Collaboration Guide for Engineers (TRATON internal document). The TRATON CTO Office drives the collaboration forward and make sure there is transparency in resources, roadmaps and competences of the brands to identify synergy potential. They are an integral part of, challenge, follow-up and approve the plans, budgets and resources (organization) made by the brands to ensure collaboration opportunities are realized and targets met. They also facilitate and approve the common technology roadmaps and act as a referee when road blocks occurs. The brands are responsible to decide on their own plans, budgets and resources (organization) and are jointly developing the common technology roadmaps together with the other brands and TRATON CTO Office.

In order to coordinate this development, a governance structure was put into place. The highest governance forum is the CVPSK (commercial vehicle product strategy committee). The CEOs of each brand, the CEO and CFO of TRATON, as well as the CTO of each brand are members of this committee. The next governance instance it the TBTC (Truck & Bus Technical Committee). All the CTOs from the brands, as well as their direct reports are members of this committee.

> *CVPSK that is a commercial vehicle product strategy committee. I just had a report to this forum yesterday, so this is consisting of Andreas Renschler and Christian Schulz so our CEO, our CFO, is consisting of the CEO of the brands, the CTOs of the brands. This is more or less the higher forum we are reporting to, and also frequently reporting to the forum of CTOs, the so-called TBTC, and then we have a number of other steering committees or steering groups, all of them consisting of management members of the brands (Int. 8)*

We have also been able to use the collaboration guide for engineers as a source to further understand the role of the TBTC and the CVPSK. These two committees are then further illustrated in the figure below.

Furthermore, in order to coordinate the activities of these R&D departments, the concept of lead engineering was developed. The idea is that for each joint development project, one brand or the other will be in the lead. As described by the collaboration guide for engineers, the brand in the lead is responsible within the topic, like for example Engine, Axle, or transmission, to:

- Be the Owner brand of all common projects in the specified area
- Own and develop technology roadmap(s)
- Do product follow-up, i.e. life-cycle management
- Allocate and control budget over the Lead Engineering area

However, within the projects it is noted that a job-share can be set up or that some parts of the projects or sub-projects can be done by another brand. This is decide on a case by case basis.

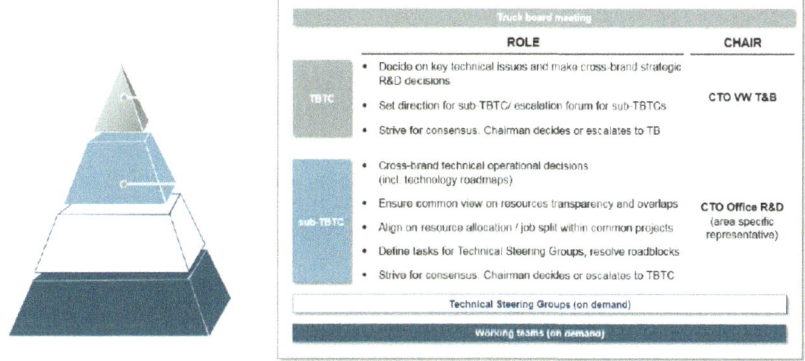

Figure 16: R&D governance (TRATON internal document, 2018)

The CTO office has also taken into account the balance of resources and competencies when looking into the lead brand concept and making decisions on lead brands.

> *"It is important to ensure balanced build-up of competences within the brands and at the same time ensure long term competence specialization to avoid duplication. The allocation of projects between brands also intends to allow for meaningful job-share, as well as aim for attractive development opportunities for the co-workers and for new employees" (Extract from the collaboration guide for engineers)*

Within these R&D projects there are different types of collaboration models. The three common types of project are either to have a shared purchased part (saving costs through a shared supplier), having an internal customer-supplier relationship, where one brand will develop a product and act as a supplier for the rest of the Group and finally a joint development project, where there will potentially be a lead brand, and a product will be developed jointly. Within our case, we have observed internal customer-supplier relationships and joint development projects.

The first project this research has studied it the so-called CHAMP project. This is a project to enable cross-brand R&D development, meaning that enables the R&D department within Scania to work the R&D department at MAN. This project also includes to a lesser extent VW CO and Navistar. The project is divided into nine sub projects called capabilities. A capability can be translated like an area or certain functionality for example, change management, CAD, test criteria and so on. The second project was a project which aimed to install an MAN engine in a Scania truck. This is a project that is currently on hold because it was not approved, as was estimated to not be cost effective. This project nonetheless presents interesting challenges. The third project concerns the development of a common rear axle. There were two R&D organizations developing axles, one at MAN and one at Scania. The project was started long before the creation of the TRATON GROUP, but at that time it failed. The project was relaunched, and the teams managed to find a solution which allowed them not to develop a complete common rear axle, but rather the components which it is made out of. Now the axle department has disappeared from Scania, but the different components for example, the axle gears and the housings and the integration to the complete vehicle has been distributed in other departments here. The last project this research will study is the Gearbox project. Here the goal was for MAN to take over the Scania gearbox, the G-set. Man was already outsourcing its gearbox to a supplier, Scania had a very good gearbox which is produced within the group, so MAN just basically changed suppliers, with Scania becoming an internal supplier. For Scania, this allowed them to almost double their volume of gearboxes. Now that this section has given a brief overview of the projects, they will be studied in more depth using the framework developed.

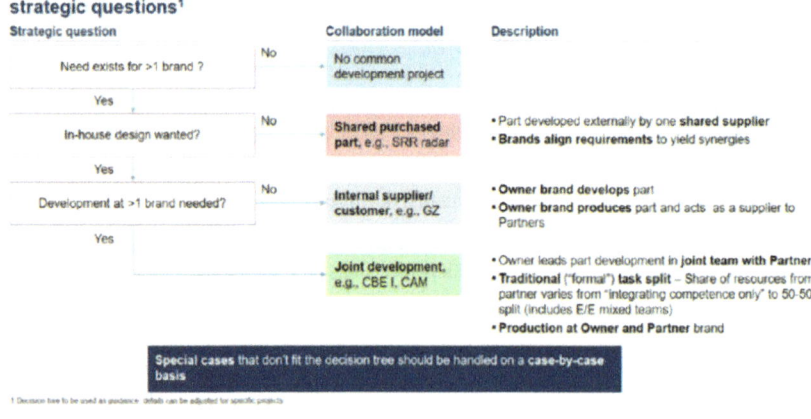

Figure 17: R&D collaboration model (TRATON internal document, 2018)

Table 13: R&D Project Overview

CHAMP project	
Goals	Enable cross-brand R&D development through IT system, methods and processes.
Members	100
Interviewees	4 MAN, 2 Scania, 1 TRATON
Timeline	2016 – ongoing
Phases	Project divided into 9 capabilities
Output	Ongoing
Perception of success	Successful collaboration
Engine project	
Goals	Develop and use a common engine
Members	10 people
Interviewees	1 MAN – 2 Scania
Timeline	2017 – on hold
Phases	First phase of concept development and cost calculation Project put on hold as it was not considered viable financially due to too many adaptations necessary
Output	Project put on hold
Perception of success	Project put on hold
Axle project	
Goals	Common axle (first project) Common axle parts (second project)
Members	Approx. 100 (including full time & part time)
Interviewees	2 TRATON – 2 Scania
Timeline	Launched long before the matrix, relaunched
Phases	Failure of first project (before the matrix), second project launched later.
Output	Adaptation of the project, focus on parts development rather than on the complete axle
Perception of success	Second wave successful
Gearbox project	
Goals	Install the Scania developed gearbox in MAN products, instead of MAN buying gearboxes externally
Members	20 to 30 within R&D
Interviewees	3 Scania, 1 MAN
Timeline	2013 – 2016, 2018
Phases	Gearbox in MAN vehicle

	Further ongoing project: Gearbox in Navistar vehicle
Issues	Branding Information sharing
Facilitating factors	Clear requirements
Output	Gearbox implemented in MAN truck
Perception of success	Positive customer feedback from new gearbox in MAN trucks

4.2.2   CHAMP Project

This is a project to enable cross-brand R&D development, meaning that enables the R&D department within Scania to work the R&D department at MAN. This project also includes to a lesser extent VW CO and Navistar. The project is divided into nine sub projects called capabilities. A capability can be translated as an area or certain functionality for example, change management, CAD, test criteria and so on.

The CHAMP project's goal is to enable the two big R&D departments of MAN and Scania to work together by providing processes, methods and IT tools. The project is still ongoing, since, as one interviewee explained, the problems related to cross-brand projects and subsequently the processes, methods and tools required are not yet all known. The goal is reportedly to build a bridge between the two organizations, without modifying them, by translating the information form one brand to the other. In order to do this the team members must investigate the needs of these two departments in terms of collaboration and analyze where there will be collaboration in the future in order to provide solutions for them. Therefore the team members must work with the organizations in order to find out where data is exchanged between the companies and facilitate it. The project focuses on identifying where in the product development process there will be a need for connection between MAN and Scania and providing the tools, methods and processes to facilitate this information exchange. Therefore, the team members need to analyze in which steps there needs to be connection within the brands, and what kind of information needs to be exchanged. Then this is broken down into IT tools, processes, programs, routines, whatever may be required to facilitate this exchange. This project is divided into 9 parts, called capabilities, including for example change management or test criteria.

This project has a steering group, the CHAMP Steering group for the overall project, which is made up of R&D and IT representatives from the brands, and then multiple technical steering groups. The Champ project team members also provide information in the TBTC and CVPSK. However the TBTC is a pure R&D committee, whereas CHAMP also involves IT as a major part of the project.

> It's a separate organization because the TBTC organization is an R&D organization. We are focused on R&D but we have also a major part of our project is IT and IT is not part of TBTC so we have our own steering committee consisting of our R&D representatives and IT representatives from both brands. (Int. 16)

4.2.2.1 Mechanisms of Control and Coordination

The role of TRATON was reported to be not present enough in some cases, and some of the interviewees would have liked to have a decision coming from the holding or from above in order to move the project forwards.

Sometimes it would be helpful to get more clear decisions from the TRATON GROUP. Today, it's very much the brand have to align and this is not always easy or possible. So sometimes it would be helpful to get really clear decisions. (Int. 16)

If I would have started as a TRATON manager being in charge I would ensure that I would have the last word. I mean in the market MAN and Scania are competitors. They are selling more or less the same truck to more or less the same customers, so of course there must be conflicts. (Int. 17)

The various steering groups also played a role within this project. To start with, the steering groups can be used as an opportunity to get further resources. One interviewee leveraged the short deadline in order to get more resources on the project, by explaining that either more resources would be needed or that the project would have to be delayed. Such as it is in this case, when bringing issues up to these steering groups, such as the technical steering committee, the team members need to already have alternatives or solutions, as it seems that if there is an issue that the team is not able to solve, the steering committee cannot make a decision. Therefore there needs to be at least a proposal of a potential solution. It was reported that there were a lot of discussions within these committees but it was not as decisive as would be desired by some of the interviewees.

4.2.2.2 Decisions and Conflict

Within one of the capabilities, an issue was reported. Here the goal was to set up a system called "Jira". The first issue related to this was that the two brands had different views on how they wanted to use the system. The debate was about how many details needed to be included within the system and what the purpose of the system would be. According to one interviewee, Scania wanted to have it as an overview system to control the project whereas MAN wanted to have more details within the system. There was also a lack of communication regarding this issue. It seems that from MAN an order came from the top which the team members were not able to question, therefore they had to fight for this view for the system. However they did not really communicate it in this way to the Scania colleagues, who could have potentially understood their problem if it had been explained. This debate cost the team a lot of time, spending over ten weeks discussing it, rather than the two days it would normally take within one brand to set it up. This was considered to be a waste of time by one interviewee. This once again shows the "traditional" matrix issue of slow decision making.

So it ends up in a 10 week discussion about how to set up an issue management system that for us usually ... It's a waste to spend more than one or two days to set it up as a support system, not more. It became a really big issue. (Int. 10)

Another factor which reportedly slowed down decision making was the debate that the team had on how to work together. The team has reportedly been discussing this issue for over a year on how to run their project. The two brands had different views on being more or less structured in the way they work together. This issue was raised up in the governance structure, but it seems that they were also unable to find a solution. One interviewee explained that in his opinion, a decision coming from above on which direction to take would be beneficial, instead of continuing with the discussions and not coming to a solution. This has reportedly been slowing down the project considerably.

I would have expected somebody to just say, "Okay, you try to get a common understanding. You didn't manage to do that, so just go that direction, and if you like it or not, please do it." But we're still stuck in discussions and that's really slowing us down heavily. (Int. 17)

Another challenge which this project faced is that big R&D projects had already started beforehand, which made delivering solutions for these projects in time a difficult task. Indeed, as we can see in other examples, such as the gearbox project, cooperation has been happening between the brands before the holding was even crated so there are naturally projects already running. This was reportedly one of the biggest challenges this project faced.

The big issue is really to deliver the solutions in time, because our customers, these are the cooperation projects, are already running (Int. 16)

One difficulty within this project was getting management to buy in to it. The work that that the CHAMP project is doing is not tangible, and does not involve developing a product, so selling the idea and getting the resources to do the work was a big challenge. According to one interviewee, the amount of effort and resources required to support the collaboration projects in order to obtain the synergies thanks to collaboration projects was underestimated from the top management side.

A lot of our managers are really good in developing really excellent trucks then we have the kind of challenge that they often tend to evaluate and give value to things related to the heaviness of the product, and if it smells like oil and metal. (Int. 10)

Potentially stemming from this, the interviewees reported having a lack of resources for this project. They needed people with specific MAN and Scania expertize, making it difficult to add external resources, meaning that the potential people who could work on this project was limited. Furthermore, one interviewee reported that although there was a consensus within management that this project was required, it took a certain amount of time to receive the budget, and subsequently the people for this project. This therefore also impacted how fast the project could move forwards.

We spent a lot of time with all that, bringing it to the board, asking for money, asking for people, explaining, so that process costed us like half a year or something. (Int. 17)

4.2.2.3 Learning, Knowledge and Innovation

The goal of this project is to facilitate the transfer of information between the brands. Its purpose is therefore to help knowledge flow from one organization to the other, by translating it. Once again the knowledge regarding the project was held by the brands. However there were no particular findings regarding the topic of learning, knowledge and innovation within this project.

4.2.2.4 Culture and Identities

One issue reported within this project is working across departments. Here the issue is related to working with the IT department in this kind of complex situation where the technical solution which needed to be found was very complex, and therefore the work with IT needed to be collaborative, rather than the IT department simply offering a solution to a problem. This makes the environment the project team works in more complex, as they not only need to work across brands but also across functions. One interviewee explained that the way the IT department functions is that they ask for requirements and build the solution based on them. However, within this projects, the requirements were not easy to explain and would actually be developed in a gradual way, and therefore the IT department would actually need to be part of the process of developing the requirements. It was reportedly a challenge to get the IT people on board, and working together with the team within this project. This brings to light another matrix organization issue, that in this set-up the brand functions are brought together, however, the cross-functional cooperation is not supported by this structure.

Another issue which could be considered an issue of culture and identities was the previously mentioned debate on how to work together within the cross-brand team. Where on MAN's side they wished to be more transparent and structured, Scania viewed this as excessive administration leading to debate on how to collaborate.

> *We, on the MAN side want to be really structured and transparent. What I feel is that Scania doesn't want to be that structured and transparent. They more or less see that as bureaucracy [...] it's completely different views on the same thing. And yeah, we are not able to find common ground there. (Int. 17)*

Furthermore another reported issue were the differences in how the two organizations consider hierarchy. In this case, it was reported that the MAN team members got an order from their managers regarding the Jira system which they were not able to question much, Therefore they were fighting for their solution, a more detailed use of the system, which Scania did not understand until it came to light that the reason they had to have it this way was because the order came from above.

> *So then the hierarchy comes in where the MAN colleagues basically agree on our colleague's approach, but, they had a different order from their managers which they are not allowed to question much. Then comes the transparency issue because they are not used to make the problems transparent. They are not saying that they have an order from their bosses to implement the system in that way. So, they start to argue about the set-up of the program and our people don't understand why they argue so hard to create something that we treat as totally waste. (Int. 10)*

One interviewee mentioned the danger that these conflicts on the task level also impacted the interpersonal relationships between the team members. However although he mentioned the danger of it, he did explain that overall within this project there were not many personal conflicts, considering the size of the project.

> *But then yeah, at some point we just have different understandings, and then of course that influences your personal interaction as well [...] I think we are working together good, so there are no real personal conflicts I would say, or just very few personal conflicts. If you see the size of the project I think the work is good (Int. 17)*

4.2.2.5 Boundary Spanning

In order to deal with these issues, certain factors were important. To start with, communication is an essential part. One issue explained within this project was the challenge of receiving management support, and therefore the team members had to obtain this support, and get management attention for the project. Furthermore, communication was also important within the project team, especially on order to understand each other's issue, like for example when the issue regarding the Jira system came up. On top of that it was also necessary to share knowledge regarding each other's environments, IT and infrastructure in order to come to a solution to create this bridge between them.

I think it's all about communication. It's about talking to people. It's about being curious. It's about respect. (Int. 8)

A factor which also facilitated the cooperation was focusing on the best technical solution. As one interviewee put it "physics are the same in Germany and Sweden". The interviewees explained that coming to the best technical solution was not the issue, as there were good engineers on both sides, and they could generally adapt, develop and create a technical solution once they were working together. However, in order to be able to come to this point, the people had to first led go of their brand focused mentalities and look at the group perspective in order to be able to focus on finding this best group solution.

What we need to overcome first is that we're not willing to change for another company because we still have these ... let me just use it like Trump says, MAN first or Scania first (Int. 18)

The essential boundary spanning skill which was reported within this project was the ability to explain the value of the project and showcase it. Indeed, it was explained that as these facilitating processes and tools are not as tangible as an actual project, it was necessary to be able to sell this project.

From my department the one of the biggest communication challenges we have is that it's really hard to describe the value added of what we are doing. I mean if you get the number of people and the number of money and 4 years and then you develop a new engine and then it's standing there that's quite impressive (Int. 10)

4.2.2.6 Key Findings

In this next section, we will summarize the findings from the CHAMP project. To start with, the governance bodies were used to leverage more resources. One of the team members was able to obtain more resources by negotiating based on the short timeline. This highlights both the skills required to work in this context, as well as one of the roles of the deadlines within these projects, as a facilitator. On top of that, it was mentioned by multiple interviewees that this project would have benefited from a more decisive role of the holding than was the case within this project.

When looking at decision making, the issue of slow decision making was once again raised by the interviewees within this project. There were two examples found for slow decision-making within this project. The first time mentioned was when it came to setting up a common IT system. Here the decisions making was slowed down as the two parties were unable to come to a decision regarding how it would be used. This was partly due to a lack of understanding as to why the MAN team members were pushing so hard one direction. This brings up multiple issues, the first being the fact that this information was not shared readily and fast enough, which could have accelerated the conflict. The second is the fact that the top down direction from MAN had to be followed, bringing a concrete example of the different attitude towards hierarchy in both brands. This once again brings about the importance of boundary spanning, where the team members need to be able to explain and share why they pushing for a certain decision. The other point regarding slow decision-making which was brought up was the fact that it took the team a long time to agree on how to work together. This issue was reportedly escalated, but to no avail. On top of this another issue which was explained by the interviewees was that as this project is supposed to support R&D projects, some of which had already started, creating a challenging environment. Moreover, one of the issues reported was the lack of management buy-in for this project as well as the lack of resources, partly linked to this.

Regarding the question of knowledge, leaning and innovation, there were not many findings within this project. CHAMP is however meant support and facilitate knowledge sharing. Furthermore, as we also saw within the HR projects, the brands were those who held the knowledge within this team, whereas the holding had a coordination role.

When talking about culture and identities, two elements were identified within this project. The first was the issue of cross-functional work. Indeed, it was noted that one of the challenges within this project was actually working with IT, as they were used to working in a different way (having an issues and solving it). Moreover, the different rapport to hierarchy was also noted, in the same way as within the HR projects, it was found that MAN was more hierarchical than Scania. On top of that, it was also mentioned that one of the difficulties that needed to be dealt with was not finding the best technical solution, but rather going beyond the Scania first or MAN first mentality, which is in fact an identity issue.

The boundary spanning activities of the team members were highlighted within this project. To start with, one of the big issues reported within this project was management buy-in, which meant it was very important that the team members sell the importance of the topic to top management. Furthermore, there needed to be an understanding gained for the environment and situation of the other brand. As mentioned previously, one of the challenges here was getting beyond the technical solution of each brand, which people tend to be attached to and trying to come to the best technical solution for the group. Finally, when looking at important boundary spanning skills, the importance of being able to sell and explain the value of the project towards top management was very important within this project.

4.2.3   Engine Project

The idea behind this project was to have a common engine for Scania and MAN vehicles. A new engine was already under development at MAN and therefore TRATON thought it could be a potential synergy opportunity both to have this engine at Scania and even potentially in the other brands. When looking into the engines, it was found that one of Scania's engines was quite old and could be replaced by the new MAN one. However, after working on it, it was estimated to not be cost effective at this time. The idea was to use the engine being developed at MAN within the Scania vehicle.

This project is currently on hold because it was not approved for financial reasons, therefore Scania will continue to use its current engine. The expectation of one of the interviewees is that there will be new legislation soon, which will be an opportunity to develop an engine together which fulfils the requirements of the new legislation.

4.2.3.1 Mechanisms of Control and Coordination

When looking at engines within the TRATON GROUP, the lead is assigned based on the size of the engine. One brand has the lead for a certain size and the other brand will have the lead for another size, because there are competencies within both brands. Within this project, MAN was in the lead. The value of the project here was to obtain financial synergies by sharing the costs of the development of the engine and getting more volume by using the same engine for different brands. Since the engine was already under development at MAN there would be less redevelopment to be done if Scania were to use this engine.

However regarding the question of mechanisms of control and coordination, we were not able to make many findings due to the fact that the project was described to us by few interviewees and that it was put on hold.

4.2.3.2 Decisions and Conflict

A general issue raised within this project was that the way Scania and MAN develop trucks is different. Scania has a modular way of working where they adapt and change different parts of the truck separately whereas at MAN they build a new model from scratch, making the requirements for a new engine different within both brands. At Scania when a new engine is developed it has to fit into the exiting model, the exiting vehicle, as well as future vehicles. Therefore it is rather complex to make sure the product is suitable for Scania products. At MAN on the other hand as the whole vehicle is developed at once, the engine needs to fit with the current model only, according to the interviewees.

According to an interviewee within this project, the engine that was planned to be included in the Scania vehicle was already under development at MAN. Apparently, MAN stated that they could not change anything regarding the MAN project, as the product was still under development. This meant that there would necessarily be changes which needed to be made to the engine for it to be able to fit in the Scania vehicles as this engine was solely developed for MAN. This would mean further financial investments for redevelopment. When the team members looked into the developments which needed to be made, there were a lot of changes required in order to adapt it, to fit it into another vehicle, as well as some different requirements regarding the performance of the product. This was not an optimal starting point for the project.

> *"It will have a bad starting position. That means that all the changes we may need to do to get this work in the other brands, we need to do the investments again, or some of the investments again. (Int. 11)*

These redevelopment costs which would be required were not immediately understood or expected from the project team. Therefore they worked on this project for two years, trying to understand what they would need to do and create a good business case for this engine. Because of these high redevelopment costs, this project was put on hold as the cost of the engine would be too high. The project and its funding was not approved.

> *This project is now on hold and can be started later for other requirements to come in the future. (Int. 11)*

However, as an interviewee explained, if this project is started again in the future, it won't be as simple as simply picking up where they left off. One interviewee explained that in his opinion the decision makers, who were not engineers but rather controllers or ex-consultants, did not understand that a development project could not simply be put on hold and restarted at another point in time.

> *A stop and go process, like any inner city traffic, is possible in development that is completely wrong. It is not possible, but those people don't know this (Int. 14)*

Another consequence of this decision was that a project which was strongly linked to this engine, the after treatment system, was also stopped as it made no sense to continue the development.

4.2.3.3 Learning, Knowledge and Innovation

An issue which occurred within this project was the question of information sharing. Apparently, the parties were unwilling at the beginning to share information. One of the respondents explained that there was some unwillingness to share data, which led to additional work as they needed to describe what data they needed and what they were planning using it for. One facilitating factor which was identified within this case was the rule created for information sharing, or the "gentleman's agreement" as it was addressed by the team. Agreeing to have it only on an engineer level and deciding together which information would be shared with management was important. In order to do this they had this "gentleman's agreement" that they would only share data on an engineering level, but would not use it to make presentations for management. If there was to be a presentation made for management they would first get approval from the team. Thanks to this agreement, the parties felt it was safe to share the information on an engineering level. This showcases the importance of creating rules for working together in order to generate trust and understanding between the parties.

They pointed out that this was the case especially at the beginning of the project. As the project went on, he explained that with increased trust the information sharing improved a little.

Making these rules how to work with information, and that really helped. (Int. 11)

4.2.3.4 Culture and Identities

Within this project, the engineers' attachment to their own work and way of doing things was also noted. One interviewee explained that for engineers, their technical solution is their "baby", making it difficult for them to accept another technical solution, and making them very critical of it. This led to evaluation conflict on which product or technical solution was better.

According to one respondent, this conflict actually developed into relationship conflict. It seems that there was some bad blood between the different engine development teams which led them to be overly critical of each other, harming the cooperation. He explained that when Scania was developing a previous engine, MAN had been very critical of it, as they also had a similar engine which they thought to be just as good. The respondent explained that this was echoed back in a way, that Scania potentially had this in mind and were therefore overly critical in this case, when MAN was the developing team.

There's cash back, and echo comes back every time (Int. 14)

4.2.3.5 Boundary Spanning

One element noted which could have helped in this project was to have more already established common processes on how to work cross-brand, which would then theoretically be a boundary object. Indeed, one interviewee explained that when they started the project, it was one of the first projects with MAN in the lead and it was unclear how to proceed. This issue could be considered validation of the importance of the CHAMP project, which is also described within this thesis.

There were some common milestones but they were not very clear, according to the respondent, so there were a lot of timing issues, which stresses the importance of temporal boundary spanning activities. In a way the main issue within this project could be considered to be timing, as the engine was already under development which meant that common development was off the table before the project even started, had the organizations been able to bridge this issue, the project could have potentially had a better outcome.

A lot of difficulties to know what do we need to do, to which timing? I think we need to have at least on some level, a common process how to work in the project. (Int. 11)

4.2.3.6 Key Findings

In order to summarize the findings of this project briefly, we will start with the issues found regarding decision making in this project. Because of the fact that this project was not completed, there are not that many elements to be described here. To start with, the main issue which led to the fact that the project was not successful was an issue of timing. Indeed, the engine was already under development at MAN, which meant that in order to adapt it for Scania, the costs would have been very high. That is why this project is now on hold. The interviewees shared that at the beginning of the project, there was also an unwillingness to share data. Issues of culture and identity were also found, in particular, the attachment of the team members to their own technical solution was noted. On top of that, the fact that there was some bad history between the brands around this project, reportedly led to some conflicts.

Some interesting points were made during this project. The importance of setting rules was noted, in particular regarding information sharing. Furthermore, potential boundary spanning activities could have supported this project, for example if the timing had been better managed, through temporal boundary spanning activities, this could have avoided the main issue. On top of that, it was mentioned that if there were already exiting processes rearing cross-brand projects, this could have also helped to make sure this project had a better outcome.

4.2.4 Axle Project

Today there are two R&D organizations developing axles, one at MAN and one at Scania. Both companies have been developing axles for a very long time and are good at it. But axles are overall not very different from one another, and the customer requirements could be considered to be the same. Therefore the idea for this project was to develop a common axle. Now the axle department has disappeared from Scania, but the different components for example, the axle gears and the housings and the integration to the complete vehicle has been distributed in other departments there. Today MAN has the lead in axles.

They have developed axles for 100 years each company and they are both very good at developing axles but more or less you could say that a rear axle are very similar. So our customer demands the same from us and the question is why should we develop two separate set of axles, why not make common axles. So what we are doing right now is looking into the possibilities of having a common development on the next generation of axels. (Int. 1)

This project was actually started before the holding even existed. However this project failed. The two brands worked on this for over two and a half years, and there was reportedly a lot of conflict, before the project was abandoned as the two parties failed to come to a solution. Apparently, the issue behind this was that the interfaces to the rear axle were different therefore making it impossible to develop it commonly.

Today, however this project was relaunched and can now be deemed a success, as the number of parts required for both brands has been reduced by 20%, while augmenting the customer offer by 80%.

> *So there were much more customer offers now by joining forces we could reduce the content by 20 percent but the customer offers became much bigger and that is a possibility then for our sales department to increase the sales and to be able to offer the customers better solutions (Int. 1)*

4.2.4.1 Mechanisms of Control and Coordination

Within this case it is very interesting to be able to see how a project which initially failed was turned around. Here one could considerer that the holding had an important role to play, as they for example renamed the project to move it away from the bad history related to the failure of the initial project. Furthermore, the holding also supported by designing and organizing a trust workshop for the teams to meet and develop a functional working relationship. This will further be discussed in the section on boundary spanning.

4.2.4.2 Decisions and Conflict

It seems that what the initial project was aiming for, developing a common axle, was in fact impossible in the current conditions. There were discussions on developing a modular axle toolbox for example, but as the axle is very dependent on the chassis geometry, and because the chassis for MAN and Scania trucks are very different, this made it technically impossible to have a common axle.

Initially in the first project, the idea came from the top to develop a common rear axle. The interviewees explained that the teams did not question this and attempted to develop it together and could not come to a common solution. Because of this top down approach, focusing on the whole axle the teams were not able to find a solution. Some interviewees explained that a bottom up approach would have allowed the axle team to work on this solution better and identify the smallest common part they could develop together, but as the word came from the top to have a whole common axle, they were unable to come to this solution.

> *I mean you can't fight gravity if something is not working then you can press or push as hard as you want from a political perspective you will never get it flying. I think it's important that you scope your project in a rational way. You shouldn't strive for something which is literally impossible (Int. 8)*

Today, this project has been redefined. Rather than developing the whole axle together, it is the parts that make up the axle which will be harmonized, such as the gears for example. Some parts are impossible to harmonize due to the interfaces to the rest of the vehicle being different, but some of the individual components could be developed together.

This redefinition of the project was an important step I being able to bring this idea to life. Although it is not a fully common axle, it is the closest technical solution to this issue. When relaunching the project, it was also renamed, in order to really separate it from the previous failed project regarding this topic.

> *Yeah but we have redefined it, we have renamed the project to get away from all this bad history. (Int. 2)*

Another type of conflict present within this R&D project is authority conflict. Here the source of this conflict is that the team and managers would agree on a decision within the project team, but as the decision went up the ranks, some decisions could be modified by managers without checking with their brand counterpart. Since managers are used to being able to decide on their own, or just within their brands, they may not realize the importance of aligning with their counterpart in the other brand.

> *But when you are in a matrix like this you cannot change the decision without talking to the other guy and that's on all levels. And these are things that are complicating it. And then when you come to these decision meetings people are really really upset, "but you told us, (I told them) that the team has agreed "(Int. 1)*

4.2.4.3 Learning, Knowledge & Innovation

Within the initial project, there was a clear issue with the lack of communication and information being shared. One interviewee explained that as the teams did not trust each other, they were not communicating enough, therefore they could not share enough information to reach an alignment. Because of the lack of trust and communication the teams were not able to reach the solution which was found in the next project. However in the second project, this trust was built, allowing for better information sharing.

> *They were discussing technical concept and did not have trust for each other so they could not align it. So a lack of trust and different technical solution could not be aligned because of that. (Int. 1)*

4.2.4.4 Culture and Identities

Within this project, the issue of the attachment to technical solutions was found. As both organizations already had axle departments, which both developed successful axles, led to conflict on finding the right solution for both organizations.

> *I think that you should design the rear axle like this but you think like this but my solution is better than yours. Different opinions on how to solve a technical problem, very much going back to the history and how axle development has been done previously in the different brands (Int. 1)*

4.2.4.5 Boundary Spanning

One countermeasure which was used within this project was building trust. Indeed, in the previous project, it had been found that the teams did not trust each other enough to be able to have open communication which ultimately led to a solution not being found,. Furthermore, by building this trust in the second round of this project allowed the team members to move away from their own technical solutions and find common ground. Within this project, the managers and team members actually had a trust workshop, in order to teach them how to cooperate and take into account the other brand. This workshop was developed in cooperation with TRATON HR, in order to build the relationship between the two teams and develop their understanding on how to work together.

> *So we actually held a two day trust workshop with the managers to get them to understand the importance of not just listening to what's happening and make their own conclusions but also to check with their counterpart on the other side. (Int. 1)*

Another factor which was important within this project was to make sure that the team members and managers knew each other and ensuring that they met face to face was reported to be important in building this trust. One interviewee explained that having these meetings on Skype would not be as good, as there is a risk of misunderstandings. Of course this then requires effort and resources, as time needs to be invested as well as money for travel. Both brands shared the travelling, alternating between coming to Munich, for Scania, and coming to Södertalje, for MAN, in order to share this burden. When the team did have Skype meetings, it was reported that it was run with a strict agenda and there were not many discussions as the fact that the teams could not see each other's reactions could potentially need to further misunderstandings and mistrust.

> *So I would say that one week the Scania guys flew down to Munich and then the next ... I think every other week they were flying back and forth to Munich and Sodertalje so they split the burden of travelling but every other week they travelled. (Int. 1)*

Furthermore, the redefinition of the project was an important step and could be considered a boundary spanning object. By redefining the goal of the project, from a complete axle to finding common components which could be developed jointly, this allowed the team to find a solution to a previously thought to be technically impossible mission. It was important that the people working on this project came to this solution rather than a top down direction, as they were therefore able to have a full technical solution.

Another point which was mentioned which could help with the cross-brand project was having more methods and processes in place for cross-brand cooperation. This helps to underline the importance of the CHAMP projects described above. In fact thanks to this project, it was reported that it enabled the teams to develop processes and methods which can then be used within other projects.

> *I mean one thing that would have been really really nice if you want to dream how would be the perfect way it would be how we developed some more processes and governance before we started this (Int. 1)*

Within this project some essential boundary spanning skills can be identified. To start with, it seems that the importance of being able to build the trust between the brands was an essential role which was played by the holding, In order to do this though, the project team members also had to be able to let go of their own technical solution, and be adaptive.

Furthermore by participating in this project, the interviewees explained that they had learnt how to cooperate with each other, and that this would hopefully support them within their next cross-brand project.

4.2.4.6 Key Findings

We will start the summary of the findings related to the Axle project with the issues found related to decision making. To start with, one of the issues which led to the project failing at first was the fact that the team members did not question the top-down direction, and therefore were unable to come to a solution. Furthermore, this project also illustrated an authority conflict within the matrix organization, where the decision would be made on the team level, but as it went up in the ranks it was modified until coming to the top with different decisions. When looking at the question of knowledge, there was a lack of sharing at the beginning of the project, as has been found within other projects, which was attributed to a lack of trust. For the question of culture and identities, there was once again a problem related to the fact that the team members were attached to their own technical solutions.

Now for the facilitating factors, many interesting elements were also identified within this project. To start with, the role of the holding was brought to light, as the holding team members had a decisive role when relaunching the project, by renaming it, redefining it and starting with a trust workshop. The redefinition of the goals of the project was a key success factor, and could be considered to be a boundary spanning activity. On top of that, essential boundary spanning activities were identified, the first being building trust, notable through this workshop. On top of that, the importance of meeting face to face was once again noted. It was also mentioned that this project would have potentially been facilitated by processes and methods for cross-brand work, had they already existed. This was unfortunately not the case but it was mentioned that a by-product of this project was that it was precedent setting, because the methods and processes which were developed could then be used in further projects. Finally, when looking at the essential skills required, the ability to support the team in building trust was very important here. Furthermore, it was noted that the skills acquired during this project would potentially be used in further projects.

4.2.5   Gearbox Project

Within this project, the goal was for MAN to take over the Scania gearbox, the G-set. MAN was already outsourcing its gearbox to a supplier and Scania had a very good gearbox which is produced within the group, so MAN just basically changed suppliers, with Scania becoming an internal supplier. For Scania, this allowed them to almost double their volume of gearboxes. Interestingly this project actually started before the matrix was even set up, as both companies already belonged to the VW Group. This project therefore doesn't have any holding team members. It is a supplier – customer relationship project rather than a common development project, it does however still present interesting challenges.

In order to do this, the two brands worked in a kind of customer – supplier relationship, in the same way that MAN was doing with their previous gearbox supplier. MAN established a book of requirements for their product, as they usually do with external customers. Then engineers from both sides sat together in order to discuss this book of requirements and had engineers sitting together and doing testing together and help with the installation. One interviewee explained that by working together with Scania, MAN was able to adapt the product to their specific requirements, overall making it a better product than they could have obtained from an external supplier. Indeed by working together this way, MAN was able to adapt the software as they wanted, with the help of Scania, which offered more functionalities than they could with an external supplier where they would simply buy the operating system with the gearbox.

By having MAN use the Scania gearbox, instead of using an external provider, the money spent on the product stays within the TRATON GROUP instead of going to another company, and it also gives Scania a big customer, almost doubling the volume of gearboxes that they produce. In the future, this will also be beneficial for MAN, as they will be able to participate in the development of the next generation of gearboxes.

> *Because now we are developed the next generation and then they are part of the development and they can influence each and every detail from the start that you can never do when you buy a gearbox (Int. 2)*

One interviewee explained that today, now that the gearbox is installed in the MAN trucks, it has been said to be a good product. Furthermore, from a customer point of view it is not a Scania gearbox, but rather the new MAN gearbox. This is in line with the idea behind this R&D cooperation, which allow for common component development but safeguard the brand image in the mind of the customers.

> *Because I see how much money the group saves on it also when I read test in the magazines about MAN trucks with the new gearbox which the customer appreciates very much. We have succeeded. They don't think of it as a Scania gearbox obviously, because it's as MAN now but it's the new MAN gearbox. (Int. 2)*

4.2.5.1 Mechanisms of Control and Coordination

This project once again brought to light the importance of having rules in place for information sharing, as well as processes and tools for cooperation. Indeed, as this project happened even before the holding was created, none of the cooperation processes were in place. However, in a way this project was aided by the fact that it was in its nature a change of supplier rather than a common development project.

> *Without all these processes and tools and information, nothing happens. (Int. 10)*

4.2.5.2 Decisions and Conflict

This project was more complex than expected. Indeed, although for MAN it was just a change of supplier, the product developed by Scania still needed to be adapted. According to one interviewee, the expectations for top management were that this project would be rather simple, and only required minimal adaptation. In reality however it seems that the project was more complex.

> *We had on the higher management now I'm kidding to be clear, they have more or less the idea that it's all about the gearbox and then we put a sticker on it with the address in Munich and then we bring into the postal office and then it that's it (int. 10)*

There were in fact many technical questions of how to adapt the gearbox and to what extent, in order to make it fit into the MAN vehicle. As little as possible needed to be changed in order to keep the cost down, but as much as necessary to fit the gearbox into the MAN vehicle, while providing a product with equivalent quality to the one previously used. Furthermore, these adaptations meant that one brand or another would potentially have a disadvantage, and the interviewees noted the importance of having a group perspective on this.

Another issue the project group faced was the branding of the gearbox. The Scania gearbox obviously has a Scania logo, and since the brands are still competitors on the market it is not possible to have a Scania logo in an MAN truck. Since there was no process in place as to how to deal with such branding issues, this caused a conflict.

4.2.5.3 Learning, Knowledge & Innovation

After this project, the next step that the TRATON GROUP is currently working on is implementing this gearbox at Navistar. Here, there seem to be some information sharing issues, where Scania does not wish to or cannot share its software. The gearbox is not only hardware, but also software and this software is what allows the gearbox to work with the engine. The standard software comes from Scania whereas the engine software comes from MAN. In order to be able to put the Scania gearbox and MAN engine into a Navistar vehicle, it is MAN's job to adapt the software of both these devices in order to fit them into a Navistar truck. Therefore, according to this interviewee, MAN needed the software from Scania, and they have never managed to receive it.

In terms of innovation this project brings an interesting concept to light. Indeed, thanks to the issues within this project, a process was developed regarding branding when working with common components within the TRATON GROUP. This showcases the value of conflict as a precedent setting process, as well as a trigger for innovation.

> *The gearbox had a Scania logo on it and you can understand not so funny in an MAN vehicle. And then the question is how much should we take away, what is the cost for that and now we have a common standard, how to do it. That was not in place then and that was a tough negotiation of course. (Int. 2)*

4.2.5.4 Culture and Identities

Within this project, the brands had to learn to work together in a customer-supplier relationship. It seem that this was in fact rather successful, and one could attribute it to the experience on the MAN side working with suppliers. Indeed, in this context MAN had already been working with an external supplier for their gearboxes and were therefore good a defining their requirements. Furthermore, Scania also has considerable experience developing gearboxes, and although becoming a supplier was new for them, one interviewee considered that thanks to the experience on the MAN side, this functioned well. This could be an explanation of the lack of reported cultural and identity issue, as in this case each brand had a very separate role, one being the supplier and one being the customer.

> *There it was more natural and I think there the cooperation has worked really well. Because MAN was good at putting requirement to do specification and Scania had the experience of developing and producing gear boxes (Int. 3)*

4.2.5.5 Boundary Spanning

In this project, the business case for it was clearly outlined. Indeed, by changing from an external to an internal supplier, there were clear financial synergies to be made. This synergistic potential could therefore be considered a boundary object, as both parties could clearly see the benefits, both on a brand side and a group perspective. Indeed for Scania this allowed them to have more volume for their gearbox, a clear financial advantage and for MAN they were able to influence the product more, especially regarding software, than they could with an external supplier. On the group perspective the added volume and the fact that the money to buy this product stayed within the group allowed for clear financial synergies.

> *Because I see how much money the group saves on it also when I read test in the magazines about MAN trucks with the new gearbox which the customer appreciates very much. (Int. 2)*

Interestingly, when dealing with external or cooperation partners, one interviewee mentioned being a "bottleneck". Effectively here it is a "translation" (Barner-Rasmussen et al., 2014) boundary spanning activity. In the way that this person will centralize the information and distribute it accordingly.

Finally when looking at the boundary spanning skills within this project, the capacity of the two brands to create rules for cooperation was essential. Indeed due to the lack of a holding function at the time, as it was before the creation of the TRATON holding and its participation in the coordination of such projects, this had to be done by the team itself. Today however, one could consider that this would rather be the role of the holding, or at least the holding would be able to facilitate this.

4.2.5.6 Key Findings

To summarize this project it is of course important to start with the fact that this project stands out from the others due to the fact that it was run before the holding was used to coordinate. However, we believe that the issues here are still relevant, and it was interesting to see what issues occurred and how the existence of the holding could have potentially facilitated this. To start with, one issue noted was that the complexity of this project was initially underestimated within the organization, and in particular by top management. Furthermore it was noted that the fact that there was no process in place regarding branding led to challenges. However, thanks to this and the conflict had regarding this issue of branding, a process was then created, which can be used for the next project of this kind. In terms of issues, the question of knowledge sharing was once again brought up, but this time regarding an "external" partner. Furthermore, the importance of rules regarding information sharing was once again highlighted. On top of that, it was noted that the clear added value for both parties facilitated the project. This highlights a finding already made in previous projects about the importance of sense-making. An interesting boundary activity when dealing with Navistar was also pointed out, where the holding team member had a bottleneck function. Finally, the ability to create cooperation rules was found to be an important boundary spanning skill in this project.

4.2.6 Summary and Analysis of Key Findings within R&D Projects

4.2.6.1 Lead brand and the Role of the Holding

Within our study of the R&D projects, we found that the concept of lead brand was what could theoretically be considered rule-based decision making where each brand is given responsibility for the decision making based on the project, as recommended by Egelhoff & Wolf (2017). However, one could note that this is done on a high level, with one brand being assigned the lead for the development of a specific product, however within the teams there is still a consensus style of decision making (like in a balanced matrix) in order to get the benefit of having these two (and occasionally more) brands working together. However, this can lead to some projects getting slowed down or stuck due to the fact that nobody is able to make a decision if a consensus cannot be found. When using this balanced style of decision making within the working groups, the parties need to be able to compromise in order to reach a common solution. Here the boundary spanning skills of the team members will be important. If they are too rigid, the team will not be able to reach a solution and the result of the project will be impacted.

It was noted within some of these projects that they would have benefited from a stronger position coming from the holding. This was explained in the case of conflicts which would slow down the project too much, where an executive decision coming from the holding would have been beneficial. Furthermore the role of the holding was highlighted in the process of building trust between parties, illustrated here through the development of a trust workshop. Finally, the role of the holding was also noted when they helped redefine the scope of the project and symbolically renamed it.

Furthermore, the importance of creating rules for cooperation was noted, in particular as a facilitating factor for information sharing. One team set up a "gentleman's agreement" for example, where they decided together which information would be shared and with whom.

The importance of investing in this cooperation must be noted. For example within this R&D function, the CHAMP project was set up in order to facilitate the cooperation, effectively creating the boundary spanning objects essential to the cooperation. This requires a lot of manpower, with 100 people just working within the CHAMP project. Furthermore, one could consider the cost of travelling, the example of a trust workshop which was developed and other such elements which require time and resources to be invested, but which are essential to the success of the cooperation.

4.2.6.2 Slow Decision Making and Conflict

As mentioned in the literature and confirmed by our findings, it seems that matrix work does tend to lead to slower decision making. Within R&D we found a particularly strong example of where this slow decision making was harmful to the organization within the CHAMP project. Indeed, the issue was due to a lack of communication on the reasons behind a conflict. This is interesting as it points out the importance of communication, and in particular the communication of goals, and the reasons why one party or another takes a position. This will bring us to an important boundary spanning skill, the ability to know and explain why a certain decision is desired. Another reason cited was the fact that the team could not decide on how to work together. This was linked to the different working styles present in each organization, where MAN wanted to operate with more reporting and transparency, Scania viewed this as unnecessary bureaucracy, which points out the impact of organizational culture differences on these matrix projects.

Overall conflicts which were not able to be solved were also held responsible for slowing down the projects within R&D. When talking about conflict the potential for escalation is of course a factor. In this case, some conflicts were said to be reported to the respective committees, however the results of this escalation were seemingly not decisive and it seems that the results of this escalation and the solution provided did always help solve the conflict or issue. Here a desire was expressed for more top-down input and decisions, as well as a more decisive role of the holding. One interesting point however, in a way counteracting the previous idea of more top down decision making, is that one reason given for the failure of one of the projects is the fact that a top down decision was made and unquestioned. However led to failure as these goals should have been adapted to fit the technical environment.

Another issues noted within these R&D projects was the problem of timing. Indeed, there were multiple occurrences when the project was led to difficulties due to the fact that another project had already started, or due to the fact that one brand was ahead of another in the development process. This will lead us to the importance of temporal boundary spanning as a facilitating factor.

We also noted the important role of top management within these cross-brand projects. Their attention on a topic is an important success factor to a topic and the expectations of top management also play an important role. It seems that there were some occurrences of top management underestimating the complexity of certain processes, which had an impact on the project, as these expectations would then not be met. On top of that, by giving attention to a topic, they also give more power to the project team to implement their product. This was a point particularly noted within the CHAMP project for example, where it was a challenge to get management impact on this topic.

Finally, there was a mention of relationship conflict occurring within one of the R&D project, and the potential danger of the occurrence of relationship conflict was also noted. The example found here was that there was bad history between the parties based on a previous project, which seemed to leak over into the next project.

4.2.6.3 Knowledge Sharing and the use of Conflict as a Lever for Innovation

To start with, in R&D, the project's basis is often to find synergies between the brands. Therefore the information sharing which happens in this balanced decision making offers the opportunity for understanding of both sides and the common development of a solution appropriate for the group as a whole. This is in line with the benefits expressed in the literature for balanced decision making, as well as the idea that this type of decision making is more suited for exploration (here of the potential synergies) than exploitation.

One of the theoretical principles of decision making in the matrix organization is that balanced decision making would be more conductive to innovation, because of the more exhaustive information processing and the increased conflict in balanced decision making. Therefore if we start by considering the question of information processing, we can address it through the issue of knowledge sharing which was raised a lot within the R&D projects. In the projects here, the knowledge is held by the brands, the brand team members have the expertise and the knowledge required in a technical sense. Where this expertize comes into play, is regarding brand specific knowledge. Indeed, this is the important factor for the knowledge of the conditions and environments that the brands evolve in, as well as knowledge of the technical requirements of brand products. Here the role of the cross-brand project is highlighted, as it brings this brand specific knowledge together in order to create a product which can be used Group wide, or in order to adapt a product to another brand. There were reported cases of issues with information sharing and this seemed to occur especially at the beginning of projects. Moderating factors for this have been identified, in particular the creation of trust within the team as well as the creation of rules regarding the information shared and how it would be put to use. Furthermore, one of the goals of the CHAMP project is to support with knowledge sharing.

Finally there was also an occurrence within these R&D projects of conflict acting as a lever for innovation. Indeed, thanks to the matrix project and the conflict which occurred within the brands, a solution was found and a new process was created regarding the branding of products from one brand to another. This is particularly important, as we can see here that the impact of this conflict and subsequent innovation goes beyond the limits of this one matrix project and is in fact a precedent setting situation. In the future there will be no need for this conflict as the solution is already clear.

4.2.6.4 Cultural Differences and Identity Threats

The interviewees noted the difference in leadership styles between the two brands. At MAN, the manager is expected to push topics and drive the team whereas from a Scania perspective the drive comes more from the bottom, where the manager will consult the employee in order to know what the decision to be made should be, whereas it is the opposite at MAN. On top of that, it seems that the hierarchy plays a more important role at MAN than it does at Scania. Where the decision lies with the experts at Scania, where they try to push the decision as low as possible down into the organization, at MAN the managers are the ones who are the important players in the decision making. This was noted both by the Scania and MAN interviewees. This difference in the hierarchy has a consequence on the cross-brand projects. Indeed, since the experts within Scania are able to take the decision, when sitting at the table with the MAN engineers, there is an unbalance, as the MAN engineers would need to involve their manager.

Within this study we also found a mention of the challenge related to cross-functional work, as opposed to cross-brand work. Here in this case it was work between the R&D and IT department which was noted to be difficult. This is interesting as it once again points out the complexity of this matrix work, which in reality not only occurs cross-brands but also has, as with any other project, many other interested parties and actors who have a stake in the project, with matrix works simply an added level of complexity. It is also interesting that this was mentioned as an issue, as this could potentially show the difficulties related to professional culture and how this impacts the organization, and maybe even more than national or organizational differences.

Finally, we have found some evidence that there have been identity threats felt within the organization. In fact this is one of the strongest patterns which we have found within R&D projects. Indeed, a cause for conflict which has been illustrated in the projects, is the initial difficulty for team members to move away from the current status of their product within their companies. The engineers who work within the cross-brand projects are attached to their technical solution that they developed within their brand and find it difficult to consider an alternative.

Finally, one point we would like to mention is the fact that there were no cultural issues found or mentioned within the gearbox project. The reason behind this could simply be that these issues were not found, or it could be because of the nature of the project. Indeed, the gearbox project was a customer-supplier relationship project. As a reminder, the "collaboration guide for engineers" from the technical office of TRATON identified three types of relationship for cross-brand project. The first is the shared purchased part, the second is an internal customer-supplier relationship like in this gearbox project and the third is joint development. However, we must note that the Engine also had a form of customer supplier relationship where culture and identity issues did occur. But in this case, both brands developed engines whereas in the gearbox project only Scania developed gearboxes internally whereas MAN would purchase them externally. We cannot conclude much from this point, but it would be an interesting avenue for further research, to study the impact of these relationship dynamics on potential culture and identity issues.

4.2.6.5 Boundary Spanning Activities and the Required Skills

An essential boundary spanning activity reported, which has already been mentioned above, was the ability for the teams to decide how to work together. Effectively, they needed to design the rules of the game. This was reported to both support with information sharing issues as well as counteract cultural differences, as it helps to build trust within the cross-brand team. There were mentions of the fact that there were no existing established processes on how to work cross-brands, and that this would have supported the projects greatly. However, within some projects processes and methods for cooperation were developed, which could then be applied to other projects. The question then needs to be how the organization ensures that these processes and methods are effectively shared in order to be used throughout the organization.

Within this case study, the interviewees see trust as important to the collaboration. In particular, the importance of socialization and meeting face to face was also noted as a potential facilitator to trust building. Indeed, according to the interviewees, the opportunity to meet and socialize was an important point. On top of that, one team even co-designed a trust workshop with HR in order to support the launch of their new project.

Within these R&D projects, redefining the goal around having the best offer for the customer allowed people to move away from the debate on whose solution is the best (evaluation conflict) and focus on creating the best product based on the customers' requirements, using the best parts of each product. In some cases the value was clear to see, for example if financial synergies could be identified through common development. In other cases however, the team members had to understand and define how their product would bring value. Here we once again see the importance of having clearly defined goals, which also make sense to the team members. The fact that these goals are understood is important as it helps the team members move away from their attached to the product that they often spent years developing within their own brand.

The importance of having common platforms and IT systems was also noted. We would consider this to be an important boundary spanning object. Some of these boundary spanning objects are still in development by the CHAMP project team members such as IT systems allowing for the sharing of complex technical data (such as CAD models) which is not possible simply through email for example.

Within the issues it was noted that the role of top management and obtaining their buy-in was an important factor for project success. This leads us to an important boundary spanning activity which must be performed by the team members, which is selling their project and its importance to top management, in order to potentially obtain further resources or support.

Finally, we would like to once again note the importance of temporal boundary spanning. Here we have multiple of examples of issues due to these organizations moving at different paces. For example, we saw within the CHAMP project that a big challenge stemmed from the fact that many big R&D processes had already been started and required the offer that the CHAMP project had to give, but had not yet developed. In another case, the cross-brand project was started when the engine was already developed, leading to adaptation being too expensive.

Now we will look into the findings regarding boundary spanning skills within these R&D projects. One of the boundary spanning skill that was reported within these cross-brand projects was the importance of being able to have a Group perspective. This is particularly important for the lead brand as they need to move further away from brand interests and defend Group interests. They therefore not only need to see and defend the Group perspective within the team, but also with their manager who lies within the brand. In order to be able to do this, it is important that the Group view be seen not only by the top managers but also the people working in the teams, in order to resolve the goal conflicts. This was not always the case. It can be hard for the brand who is performing better within a certain topic, to have to slow down and support the other brands in order to bring them up to speed on the topic.

Looking at the advantages of this matrix organization, the interviewees can see a competence advantage. Indeed, by having common process, product or policy development, the idea is that certain resources will be freed up, and be able to focus on important future oriented topics. Furthermore, there is a lot of learning potential, especially in this technical department. This leads to the products becoming more competitive as each brand can learn from each other and get the best out of both brands products. Furthermore, the snowball effect of participating in cross-brand projects was also noted, where the skills obtained within one project could then be integrated and used within the next project. This is especially important as the transportation market is currently facing a technological shift, and keeping up with this change is essential to the Groups survival. Another skill that is essential and which has been hinted at throughout this section is the ability to create and design cooperation rules. Indeed, we found within these R&D projects that creating rules for cooperation and information sharing were a clear facilitating factor. Therefore the team members and in particular the lead brand must be aware of the importance of this factor and must be able to support the team members in creating these rules, however formal or informal. Finally, we would like to once again note the importance of being able to explain and sell the value of the project. This is an important boundary spanning skill, as it will be needed both within the cross-brand team and towards top management as has been explained above.

4.3 Summary of Empirical Analysis

Now that we have given an overview of the projects as well as the issues and facilitators for these projects both in HR and in R&D, this section will now summarize the results found, by using the same framework as was used for analysis. The goal here will be to offer a comprehensive overview of the results, as well as point out any stark differences or similarities between the findings within the HR projects and the results found in the R&D projects. It must be noted that our findings from R&D are somewhat less rich than those within HR. Indeed, the research process was more complicated within R&D for multiple reasons. The first is that the contact people were not as easy to obtain as within the HR department, where the embeddedness of the researcher helped to create a network of potential interviewees. Furthermore, the HR results were particularly good due to the fact that the group of people working within cross-brand HR projects is relatively small, meaning that creating an overall picture based off of our interviews was possible. Finally, the R&D projects are very technical and within very different fields, making them very difficult to understand from an external perspective. However, we feel that we have managed to extract valuable data nonetheless, as the interviewees were for the most part very competent in using layman's terms and explaining the stakes of the projects they were involved in.

4.3.1 Governance and Leveraged Power Capabilities

When we look into the concept of the lead brand, this is how rule-based decision making has been operationalized and formalized within our case. However, we would like to note that this rule is actually more complex than just having one brand be in charge of the project. Indeed, even if the one brand is in charge, the holding will still play a role, serving as a potential ambassador for Group interests. This was observed within HR. Furthermore, it seems that we have observed within our two departments the idea of the flexible matrix, but not exactly as described by Egelhoff and Wolf (2017). Indeed, they see the flexibility in changing the decision making style based on the situation, therefore sequentially. In our case, we have observed this based on the different levels. Within the working teams, even if one brand is in the lead, the teams tend to have a consensus style decision making, in order to explore all the alternatives and fully understand the issues which could occur, before suggesting a decision.

Furthermore, we have also found that the committees, both within HR and R&D, play an important role as a facilitating factor. Indeed, they are the body which serves to legitimize the actions and decisions of the cross-brand teams. Because they are made up of the top management from each brand, their approval and support is important. However, we have noted that their role, to this day, does not extend to escalation. This was noted within HR, where the issues were deemed too small to be escalated, as well as within R&D where either the issues were not escalated or a solution was not found. This poses the interesting question of the value of escalation. Indeed, by forcing the teams to come to a decision themselves, through balanced decision making, the chances are that the decision will obtain more buy in and will have considered most of the alternatives. On the other hand, this does lead to the aforementioned issue of slowing decision making down.

In order to play their role, the holding can leverage their power capabilities which will act as a lever and support the implementation of the projects (Ferner, 2000). The power capability leveraged the most by the holding function is the power of processes. In setting up the governance structure, they could greatly influence how the organization functioned. Furthermore, by setting the agenda for this committees, the holding function can also push the projects which are important to them, making sure decisions are followed through upon for example. Furthermore there have been cases as described within our empirical findings where the membership of the teams has been greatly influenced by the holding. By changing the composition of the team, the holding is able to mobilize the power of processes to influence the decision making. Within the project group itself, the power of processes also sits with the holding and in the case of a lead brand part of the "process" power capabilities goes to the lead brand. This comes for example from setting the meetings or the "rules of the game".

The power of meaning is also essential for the holding the leverage. Indeed, in order get the project successfully implemented, the buy-in of the brands must be obtained. The power of meaning which the holding can also leverage is that Group interests are the bigger picture whereas the brand interests are pieces of the whole. On the other hand, the brands can leverage their individuality and local environments as being conditional to their success, and therefore that of the group.

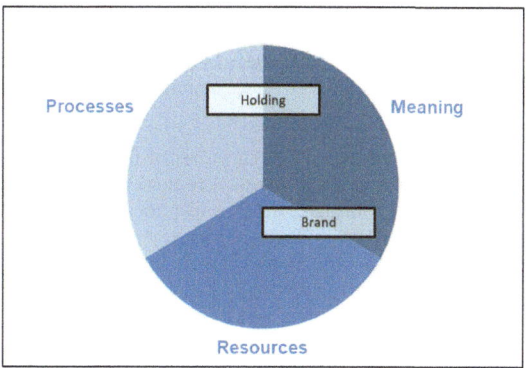

Figure 18: Power capabilities leveraged by the brands and the holding (own elaboration)

Overall, we have noted the financial investment required in order to make this cooperation work. Within R&D, we found that there was a big project focused on facilitating cooperation and many of HR projects aim to create the matrix supporting package. Furthermore all the employees within the holding are also fully focused on this cooperation. Another resource that the Group has needed to invest is time. Indeed, the cooperation has evolved slowly, which has been essential to make sure all the parties buy-in and the brands identities are preserved. Furthermore financial investment is necessary to create the boundary spanning objects necessary to the collaboration, as well as to ensure that the team members meet face to face, incurring travel costs.

4.3.2 Issues and Actors in Decision Making

Both in R&D and in HR the "classic" matrix issue of slow decision making came up. This is not surprising and has been brought up a lot in matrix literature (Davis & Lawrence, 1977, Goold & Campbell, 2003; Galbraith, 2008; Wang et al., 2012; Wolf & Egelhoff, 2017). However what is interesting is that we have been able to further our understanding of the reasons behind the slower decision making in the matrix organization. The first reason, which is also present within matrix literature is the question of complexity. Indeed, by adding a dimension to the structure, there are more parties involved therefore making the environment more complex. It was also mentioned that gathering the necessary information and alignment within the brands can be a lengthy process, therefore slowing down decision making. On top of that, the question of lack of resources was brought up, both in terms of workload and financial and technical resources. Finally, the issue of conflict not being resolved in a timely manner led to slowing down the decision making. In general these conflicts were task related and mostly due to conflicting interests or different views of the same problem, therefore goal or evaluation conflict. When looking into the issue of goal conflict, we not only found conflicting brand goals, but also unclear goals within the project itself, highlighting the essential boundary spanning role of defining and clarifying aligned project goals.

Overall, the role of top management has emerged as an important factor within decision making. This is not a surprising finding, however, our research is rather interesting in this regard, as it involves people from all levels, as opposed to much of the past research which has mostly focused on interviewing managers. This is why we are able to highlight the role of the managers in a matrix in a different way than has previously been done. The role of top management was operationalized here through the creation and use of committees for project legitimization. These committees were not used to a great extent as an escalation means, but rather as an approving and supporting body. We described these committees in part two and part four of this chapter.

Furthermore, we found both within HR and R&D issues of timing which would potentially require temporal boundary spanning. These issues were however different. Where we found that the organization had their own idiosyncratic time and ran their projects at different paces due to different stakeholders within HR, within R&D the issues mentioned were generally due to ongoing projects having already been started within one brand but not within another, therefore making common development difficult, or simply the processes and methods being developed by the CHAMP project which were meant for projects which are already running.

Moreover, we found trust to be an important factor both within HR and R&D. Trust was found to play an important role to hinder dysfunctional conflict (Jenn & Mannix, 2001), in this case conflict which lasts too long and slows down decision making considerably. On top of that, trust was said to support knowledge sharing, where the parties needed to build trust at the beginning of the project to allow for better knowledge sharing. Overall, the trust building tool that was mentioned within both departments was socialization.

We must note two important points related to the concept of the lead brand observed in this case. To start with, although it is used both within HR and R&D, it fulfills a different role within these two departments. In HR, this is done in order to save resources, as there is not enough capacity to have all the projects led by the holding. Furthermore, there is symbolic value to be drawn from is, as in one example each brand was able to be the lead for one topic. However, although there were some noted difficulties, notably the issue of having one brand in a two-hat role, which sometimes required holding intervention in order to ensure that group interests are preserved, the consequences of having one brand or another in the lead tend to be rather minimal. Within R&D however, this is completely different, as has been explained previously as the consequences of one brand getting the lead over another, can lead to entire departments being shut down. Within these big R&D projects, having consensus based decision making like in the HR projects would have potentially been much harder, since these projects involve many more people and parties than within HR. Therefore, we must consider these very different stakes and consequences when looking into the concept of lead brand.

One final point that we noted both within HR and R&D was the fact that the involvement of other functions also led to issues and especially slower decision making. This is interesting to point out as our matrix, in comparison to a product X function matrix for example, generally only involves actors from the same function in the project itself.

We would like to note that we have gone into more theoretical detail regarding the question of rule based and balanced decision making within the contributions chapter.

4.3.3 Knowledge Sharing and the Barriers to Innovation

When we started this research, we had in mind the idea elaborated by Egelhoff and Wolf (2017), that a flexible matrix organization, which is able to change its decision making mode to either fit an exploration or exploitation goal would support ambidexterity in the MNC. This is why we choose to look into the question of knowledge, learning and innovation in the matrix organization in order to further understand how this theoretical concept could potentially work in practice.

In general within our case study, both within HR and R&D, the projects could be considered to be exploration projects, as opposed to exploitation which is left to the brands. Indeed, the brands run their operations independently, meaning that the daily business, exploitation is fully done within the brands. The matrix projects then tend to be more focused on exploration, in the wide sense of the term, looking into improving and harmonizing processes and finding synergies.

Now if we look into the question of knowledge, which we consider to be an antecedent of innovation, we must first note that for both HR and R&D, knowledge tends to be, for the most part, held by the brands. Indeed, the expertize regarding the technical elements such as product or process knowledge, as well as environmental knowledge as well as the understanding of how the brand functions and its specific challenges lies within the brands. Therefore in this sense, the matrix organization is used to facilitate knowledge sharing between the brands, by bringing this brand-specific knowledge together within one team.

There were, in both departments, issues noted regarding knowledge sharing, and this seemed to happen especially at the beginning of the projects. Some interviewees noted that this could be because of a lack of trust, which would also explain why this knowledge sharing issue improved as the team members got to know each other better and built trust. In order to deal with this issue it was mentioned within R&D that creating rules for knowledge sharing helped minimize the issue. This was however not noted within HR. We would suppose that in HR these "rules" were more informal, and presented themselves rather as an unspoken understanding that information would not be shared inappropriately, something which is possible thanks to the small number of people within the organization. Another element which was noted as important to facilitate knowledge sharing was having a clear understanding of the goals, understanding why the information needed.

Within HR a factor which had the potential to hinder innovation was found, which was the different institutional and legal environments which the brands evolve in, as well as the VW Group context, which also had the potential to stop a new idea in its tracks. This is an issue which was specific to HR, and which we did not observe in that was within R&D. However, in a technical sense, these differences also affected the R&D projects, for example the fact that Scania has a modular system, whereas MAN builds a truck from scratch also creates barriers as it makes the compatibility of the developed product difficult.

Finally, within both HR and R&D, we found instances where conflict acted as a lever for innovation. The conflict created by the conflicting ideas and opinions of the brands led to finding a solution which was both innovative, the best of both worlds, and precedent setting. This shows how the matrix can create an environment for exploitation, by creating the necessary arena for these conflicts to occur.

4.3.4   Organizational Culture Differences and Identity Threats

At the beginning of this research, the expectation was that cultural challenges would be an issue on the HR side, but not as much for the R&D department, as the solutions and common ground which needed to be found were purely technical. In fact, cultural issues were still very present within the R&D department.

When looking into the literature on Swedish and German cultures, one could think that the cultures are very close, however, there have been significant barriers reported regarding national cultural differences as well different organizational practices (embedded in national culture). As we have seen in the desk research, it is very difficult to actually separate national, organizational and other levels of culture, as each one will influence the other. Although this is an international environment, we must remember that the national cultures may not be the source of cultural differences here but rather a combination of the national culture and the organizational culture, as well as other sub-cultures which are tightly interlinked as seen in the literature review (Leung et al., 2005). These cultural differences are a potential source of friction and conflict. We would however be able to compare our findings to the already known elements about the Swedish and German culture. Furthermore, we would assume that there is a potential identity threat to be found for the brands, when joining the TRATON GROUP. We will see how this was illustrated within the projects. It must be taken into account that the cultural issues may be perceived as greater than they actually are, as they can be used as scapegoats for "everyday" organizational issues (Kanter & Corn, 1994). It is interesting to look into these cultural differences as one could consider them to be responsible for most evaluation conflict which happened within these projects. Although some did acknowledge the fact that theoretically, German and Swedish cultures are very close, the issues were still present.

When looking into the organizational cultural differences, although we were able to draw more conclusions from the HR findings, we found a consensus within the two departments that MAN tends to be more hierarchical and has a more top-down leadership style than Scania has. This led to issues within decision making, as the actors within the cross-brand project, although working on the same level, did not have the same decision making power.

We also found some elements that we were only able to identify within HR, but this does not exclude this being the case for R&D too. The first is the question of risk taking where MAN was found to be more risk averse than Scania, as well as more detail oriented. Furthermore, the finality of the decisions was also interpreted differently within MAN and Scania, where Scania liked to change and adapt decisions based on new factors or information, whereas for MAN the decisions tend to be more final. This is of course then linked to the idea of risk taking.

We found a strong tendency towards identity issues within the R&D projects, which came in the form of attachment to the brand product or technical solution. However this was also noted within HR, but to a lesser extent, as the attachment is potentially less emotional. However, it seems that these incidents rather happened at the beginning of the project, and as the team worked together, got to know each other and the different perspectives these issues no longer occurred.

Overall, and this is not an absolute fact, it seems that the Scania employees were more talkative about how they perceive themselves and their colleagues from MAN. Now this could mean that they have stronger identification with Scania, than the MAN employees do. This is plausible theory, since as was mentioned, MAN has been through many changes and is therefore missing some stability, potentially not contributing to the "enduring" factor of their identity. Furthermore, as they have generally accepted the direction coming from VW more readily, this could also have contributed to a less strong MAN focused identification. On top of that, it must be said that the Scania values play a very strong role within the organization, potentially contributing to a stronger culture and therefore stronger identification with this culture.

4.3.5   The Snowball Effect of Boundary Spanning and Associated Skills

As a reminder, the four categories of boundary spanning activities are described by Barner-Rasmussen et al. (2010) as the following: exchanging (gathering or delivering information), linking (creating links between disconnected actors or groups), facilitating (assisting in cross-border interactions of others by acting as channel, interpreting information, explaining behaviors and so on) and intervening (resolving misunderstandings, managing conflict and building inter-group trust). These boundary spanning activities increase in complexity, with exchanging being the simplest and intervening the most complex.

To start with, there is no question that the exchanging activity must be performed by all actors within the matrix projects. Indeed, gathering and sharing information is the basis for these cross-brand projects and is performed by all the actors involved. Within our research, we have identified the importance of boundary spanning as a key facilitator to matrix work. We have found that the matrix organization formalizes these matrix boundary spanning activities through the matrix project structure. Indeed, the matrix brings the unlinked parties within the brands together within a project, effectively linking them together through the project goal. Therefore, the matrix organization actually has a linking role, where it provides the opportunity for the disconnected brand parties to meet. On top of that, we also found HR processes to have a linking role, by providing arenas for people to meet, with for example development programs, and making exchanges easier by harmonizing the grading systems and management evaluations and creating assignment tools.

Next, when looking into the boundary spanning activities of the actors within the cross-brand projects, we have also identified some facilitating activities. To start with, it was noted with R&D that it was important to create cooperation rules to facilitate knowledge sharing within the teams. On top of that, the importance of clarifying goals, and sense making, for example by focusing on customer requirements or technical needs, was found both within HR and R&D. On top of that, the desire for common IT systems could be considered as a boundary object, which would then play a facilitating role, as it would act as a communication channel and would also support in translating technical information from one brand to another. Finally, we also noted, both within HR and R&D the importance of temporal boundary spanning. We would classify this here as a facilitating activity, as we this is done for example through flexible timelines which differ from each other before converging later.

Furthermore, we have noted the importance of trust consistently within our research. Trust has been said to support conflict resolution or hinder conflict, it has also facilitated communication and information sharing. We found that building trust is especially important at the beginning of a project, as it helps deal within the issues related to knowledge sharing, which were mostly noted within R&D. In particular, we found that this is done through the socialization of actors. We have also noted the importance of HR processes in facilitating building trust. On top of that, we have found that it is important that the actors be able to obtain management buy-in and leverage top management influence when necessary. Therefore, the actors within the cross-brand project must also perform the most complex boundary spanning activity, which is intervening.

Within our case study we identified boundary spanning as being a clear facilitating factor to the success of the matrix organization. Therefore we also examined the necessary boundary spanning skills required.

To start with, we noted within both the observed departments that the skills required were also developed through cross-brand work. Indeed, by participating in a cross-brand project, team members are able to obtain cross-brand skills as well as build a cross-brand network. Furthermore, within HR we were able to identify learning on three levels, not only were the team members able to learn about other brands and understand the Group strategy better but is also allowed for self-reflection on their own brand's activities and processes. A competence advantage was also noted within R&D, with the opportunity to learn from other brands, as well as the potential for freeing up resources for other projects and endeavors thanks to the matrix organization. We are calling this the snowball effect of cross-brand project participation, where the more people participate the more boundary spanning skills they obtain. We would like to note that a further snowball effect was noted within HR, where the participation in one cross-brand project made the person a good candidate for the next project. This is potentially linked to the first point of increased boundary spanning skills.

Furthermore, we have also noted that the benefits of cross-brand projects also "leaked" beyond the project itself. This was observed in different ways. To start with it was explained that the network gained though participation in a cross-brand project would potentially be used afterwards, for sharing best practices for example, even when having a brand specific project. Second, some of the processes and methods developed for one cross-brand project can also be used for other cross-brand projects. Finally, one could imagine that the skills gained would also be beneficial on a personal level.

Now that we have given a quick overview of the snowball effect associated to boundary spanning, we will now look into the boundary spanning skills in more detail. Within our summary of findings both in HR and R&D we gave an overview of the skills required for matrix boundary spanning. We would now like to classify them into three categories, namely know-how, know-who and know-why.

Within our research, in both departments, we found an important skill required of the team members was know-how. This includes technical competencies and expertizes as well as a sound understanding of their own brand processes and environment. This is important as this knowledge is the added value they bring into the cross-brand project. On top of having this brand understanding they must also be aware of Group interests and be able to consider them too. Moreover, not only must they consider them, but they must defend these Group interests, or at least the cross-brand projects interest within their own brand too. In this way, they will be acting as a Trojan Horse, as described by Tempel et al. (2006), when considering the transfer of practices in MNCs. On top of that we have also noted the importance of speaking English and of being open minded, which we will classify as language and intercultural skills, in line with Barner-Rasmussen et al. (2014).

Second, an important capability which we identified is the network required for successful cross-brand work. This is the "know-who" required. In particular, the team members must have a network within their own brand, which will allow them to successfully bring in the right knowledge for the project and implement the decisions made within the project. Furthermore, the cross-brand network is also value adding, but as mentioned before, the participation in the cross-brand projects also supports the creation of this network. On top of that, this network and the relationships within this network must be trust-based, as the team member must have the trust and legitimacy within their own brand as well as have the capacity to build trust within the cross-brand team.

Finally, the last capacity which we have identified, is "know-why". This is a key capacity for multiple reasons. To start with, by making sure that all the cross-brand team members understand the goal of the project allows for buy-in. This capacity must therefore be held by the lead brand or the holding team member. We have also noted that the co-creation of the objectives of the project allow for stronger buy in from the parties involved. Furthermore, it is important for the brand team members to be able to sell the project within their own brand and towards top management, making a clear understanding of the importance and added-value of the project important. This is linked to the ability to have a Group perspective and brand perspective as well as go back and forth between the two perspectives which was explained above. We noted that this capacity was able to hinder trust issues, as if the objectives of the Group and the brands are communicated and understood, then the information sharing is improved.

5 Contributions and Conclusions

Now that the findings of the empirical analysis have been summarized, these results will be analyzed through a more theoretical lens, in order to contribute to the literature on matrix organizations, including the mechanisms of control and coordination, decision making, ambidexterity, conflict, the role of culture and identities and finally the question of boundary spanning. We will start each section by a reminder of the literature gaps that we wished to investigate, before elaborating on the contributions of this research. We will use our conclusions from the empirical findings and based on this, we will show how our research contributes to the existing knowledge on the topic.

5.1 Main Contributions

5.1.1 A Matrix Organization Supporting Lateral Coordination

We started our research framework based on the literature on MNCs. From this, we built an understanding of the contemporary MNC, notably the evolution of the role of the HQ towards a softer, bottom up role, where the role of the subsidiaries has become more prominent. We noted that the literature evolved from looking into formal control and coordination mechanisms towards informal ones (Martinez & Jarillo, 1989), and that today it is important to understand how MNCs can combine these two types of mechanisms. Furthermore, it is necessary to further research how informal mechanisms and power resources are leveraged to support formal mechanisms (Ferner, 2000). Finally, the question of leveraging subsidiary knowledge, since it was noted that the management of knowledge flows could be one of the most important sources of competitive advantage in the MNC (Bartlett et al., 2004; Doz et al., 2001; Gupta & Govindarajan, 2000), was raised within this first section of our research.

We have studied the TRATON organization, and found the role of HQ in this organization to be a middle ground between the two options which were described in the literature. One option would have been to simply have the brands keep operating as they do, as separate entities. The down side to this very simply being that there would be little cooperation between the brands, making synergistic potential low, and effectively not having any added value from having multiple truck and bus companies within the Volkswagen Group. Another option would be to have this same holding systematic as is presented within the case, but instead of having this matrix organization, to simply have the holding play the role of a classic HQ, with decisions being developed at the top and implemented in the brands. Here, as noted by some interviewees, the issue would be that the decisions would not necessarily be well informed of the realities of each brand, potentially making decisions which would be destructive or at least not the most productive for one brand or another. Therefore this set-up aims to counteract these potential downfalls, by attempting to gain synergies while preserving the brands uniqueness. It can be associated to the concept of partnering (Kale et al., 2009) found in M&A literature, where operational autonomy is left to the subsidiaries and key synergies are focused on, here in the form of cross-brand projects. As can be seen in the empirical findings, it is not without issues, but as has been noted by the reported improvement of cross-brand work, does seem to be on the right path.

This case presents the holding matrix organization as a potential coordination mechanism to deal with the issue of the balance between central control and local autonomy. Indeed, this

© Springer Fachmedien Wiesbaden GmbH, part of Springer Nature 2020
J. Shahani, *Limits and Opportunities of a Matrix Organization*, Auto
Uni – Schriftenreihe 149, https://doi.org/10.1007/978-3-658-32261-8_5

matrix set-up allows for very strong brand autonomy, as they operate as independent companies. This supports the requirements described by Bartlett and Ghoshal (1989) for global efficiency, obtained here through synergies on a group level, and local responsiveness which is done through the independent work of the brands. This is also aligned with the view Geppert and Dorrenbächer (2011) have of the MNC today, as a dispersed structure of power, where the HQ neither can, nor desires, to exert full control on its subsidiaries. We can see here how the holding has a "referee" role between the subsidiaries, as described by Birkinshaw (200) and Birkinshaw and Hagstrom (2000), using this holding matrix structure to formalize the role. Therefore this case study serves to show empirical evidence of how the HQ can both lead the firm and assume a more facilitative role, by using the holding matrix organization.

In order to deal with the danger of having a control gap (Prahalad & Doz, 1981), the matrix organization serves to identify the areas where global integration would benefit the MNC. However, it is also clear within this case that there is a desire to preserve brand autonomy, which is important to allow them to keep generating skills and knowledge (Harzing and Noordhaven). Coordination is done through the cross-brand projects, within areas which have been identified as potentially value adding. By using these cross-brand projects, the HQ is able to leverage the knowledge from the subsidiaries, an effect amplified by the balanced form of decision making which allows for exploration of the alternatives and an overall better platform for knowledge sharing. Therefore this research provides evidence of how HQ can capitalize on subsidiary knowledge through the use of a holding company matrix. Indeed, our case dealt with brands, which can be considered to be "global innovator" subsidiaries (Taylor et.al, 1996). As noted in the literature, managing such subsidiaries in order to ensure the balance between autonomy and control is a subtle and complex task (Bartlett & Ghoshal, 1986). We have shown how this can potentially be managed by using a matrix organization, as well as pointed out the issues and facilitating factors.

Our case study also provided further evidence of how HQ can support lateral coordination between subsidiaries, answering to the need for more cross-border learning (Bartlett and Ghoshal, 1989). In particular, how headquarters can deliberately support the creation of networks, which is a research gap identified by Egelhoff and Wolf within their article on the role of HQ in the contemporary MNC. In particular, we have been able to provide evidence of the role that HR can play in this regard. Indeed, we have found further evidence of what Galbraith (2009) called "the matrix supporting package". In particular, we have found the role of HR to be particularly strong in the development of boundary spanning capabilities of people, especially when it comes to supporting in building networks. We have seen this through the various projects we have described and how HR contributes to facilitating movement within the company and how it helps develop the boundary spanning skills of the actors within the matrix.

Another factor which is important in the facilitation of lateral coordination are the digital internal communication tools. This is important because it is one of the reasons why the matrix today is different to the matrix in the 70s-90s. The IT landscape of the MNC is very different, allowing for spatial boundaries to be more easily bridged. Based on this we would propose to use the contingency theory which was developed by Egelhoff and Wolf (2017) for the decision making styles within the matrix organization, and adapting it to the use of digital versus face-to-face communication modes. For three of the factors presented by Egelhoff and Wolf we have found clear evidence within our research of the most appropriate form of communication. Indeed, when it comes to economizing on human and monetary costs during decision-making, then using digital communication tools is a clear advantage. However, when it comes to the novelty and innovativeness of alternatives generated, as well as the thoroughness with which alternatives are evaluated, face to face meetings and communication are the stronger alternative. However, there needs to be more research, focusing on the use of digital communication within the matrix in order to understand the other two criteria better, namely the question of accountability as well as the question of the speed of decision making. Indeed, we did not find any clear evidence as to whether the question of accountability is affected by the use of one communication mode or another. We would assume that this is better supported in a face to face context, but this would need to be investigated. For the question of the speed of decision making, which as we have seen throughout this research, tends to be a central topic when studying matrix organizations, the question is more complex. Although there is less travelling involved, which would therefore imply that decision making was faster, the amount of information processed tends to be lower, leading to a longer time to come to a consensus within the team. Furthermore, face to face conversations were very much associated with trust building by our interviewees, a factor also potentially affecting the speed of decision making as we have seen in our empirical findings. We would therefore leave this criteria open, stating that further understanding of the role of internal digital communication and the role that it could potentially play in a matrix organizations still could be further studied.

Finally, we would like to note that most of the coordination mechanisms we have observed within our case study tend to be social ones. Within this research we have attempted to further understand these mechanisms using the theoretical concept of boundary spanning, and through this we were able to illustrate how the social mechanisms of control are used in combination with the formal ones, such as the governance structures, as well as their limitations in this context. In order to deal with some of these limitations, and in particular when formal mechanisms were not adopted, such as in the cases where the decisions agreed upon were not implemented, the holding used their power capabilities to enforce these decisions, as described by Ferner (2000).

In terms of contributions for this section, we have provided an illustration of a contemporary HQ and its role in supporting lateral coordination between subsidiaries. Furthermore, we could supply an example of how a matrix organization could potentially be used to deal with the control gap, by leveraging global integration in key strategic areas, while allowing for subsidiary autonomy. However, it must be noted that we only interviewed people from the different HQs, within the holding and within the brand HQs. There could be potential for further understanding of local issues and the effectiveness of the matrix organization by interviewing deeper into the organization and seeing how the brand HQs and their subsidiaries operate and are affected by the TRATON GROUP. Furthermore, it would be interesting to further research these questions within the finance function, as the setting of financial objectives could potentially be a key power capability which can be leveraged by the holding.

5.1.2 Decision Making Contingency Theory and the Role of Conflict

Within a matrix organization, the actors have different goals expectations, practices and power resources, it is a contested terrain (Morgan, 2001), where, as such, conflict and negotiations occur. In our literature review we found decision making to be a key factor of the past research on matrix organizations. The nature of the matrix changes the way decisions are taken in an MNC, naturally leading to certain consequences. The very often cited issue within a matrix is the speed of decision making, which is reportedly slower and potentially also less effective (Davis & Lawrence, 1977, Goold & Campbell, 2003; Galbraith, 2008; Sy & Cote, 2004; Wolf & Egelhoff, 2017). Wolf and Egelhoff elaborated on this past research and found that the decision-making studied in matrix organizations was mostly balanced decision-making and they found that in fact rule-based decision making within a matrix organization was desired by the leaders of the companies they studied. They therefore developed a contingency theory describing when to use balanced versus rule-based decision making. Within our research we have been able to further understand the issue of the speed of decision making and empirically study the idea of rule-based and balanced decision making in a matrix. Closely related to decision making, the issue of conflict in the matrix is often reported on in the literature. When looking into the question of conflict in the matrix organization, we found that the existing literature on conflict is very wide, but that there was still opportunity for further research when considering conflict in the context of a matrix organization. Indeed, although excessive conflict is often cited as a cause for matrix abandon, more recently evidence has been found that a matrix does not necessarily have more conflict than an elementary structure. Furthermore, it seems that conflict may even be natural in a matrix. Linked to the idea of conflict, the question of power in the MNC has more recently been in focus for authors such as Blazejewski and Becker-Ritterspach. They found that there is a need for further research on the topic of conflict and power, which we have attempted to contribute to in the context of a matrix organization. We will now present our findings on the closely linked concepts of power and conflict in the matrix organization, based on the research questions. We will start this section by reviewing our findings related to decision making, before diving into the reported conflicts and their consequences.

To start this discussion on the contributions of our research towards the academic understanding of decision making in contemporary matrix organizations, it is important to remember that the case study that we did is not what can be described as a classic matrix organization. Indeed, this holding acts more like an HQ than a matrix dimension, with the dimensions being represented by the brands. We find it important to state this reminder, as when we talk about rule based decision making and balanced decision making, the role of the holding will play an important role. Furthermore, due to this set-up with very independent brands, the quantity of decisions taken within the matrix organization is actually comparably low, on the scale of the group. However, these are key decisions with Group wide implications, meaning that we have been able to study some very strategic decisions.

We would like to summarize our findings regarding decision making within this matrix organization in order to compare them to our expectations based on the desk research. In particular, we have focused on further understanding the research made by Wolf and Egelhoff regarding rule based and balanced decision making, as well as observed some "classic" matrix issues. Within our case we have seen evidence of balanced and rule based decision making to a certain extent. However, most of the decision processes which were described to us were balanced in nature. The reason behind this probably stems from the strategy behind the matrix organization within our case. Indeed, the brands already work independently on their products, meaning that their activities related to exploitation are performed within their brands themselves and not on a group level. The projects we studied required the new implementation or development of a new process or product, an activity which is more related to exploration, which Egelhoff and Wolf claim is more suited to balanced decision-making.

Looking into the question of the speed of decision making, it does seem that the findings regarding the issue of slow decision making within the matrix organization have also been replicated here. One of the reasons most cited was indeed the issue of conflict or inability to align and find a consensus. Indeed, it was found within this case that more alignment was required between all parties slowing down the decision making processes. Although these findings are not new, we were able to find some facilitating factors which could further the understanding of the topic. In particular, the importance of trust building through socialization and the role of boundary spanners was highlighted in our research as potentially counteracting the issue of slow decision making.

Now very practically looking at the antecedents and consequences of rule-based decision making as it was used in this case, we have some findings which could potentially further contribute to our understanding of this new form of decision making within a matrix organization. As a reminder, the most visible "rule" which was found within our case was the concept of the lead brand, where one brand would be given the lead over a certain topic. When this was not the case, this position was held by the holding, which kept the brands on equal footing, therefore closer to balanced decision making, with the holding having a more moderating role. Within HR we were able to observe a few examples of rule-based decision making, and were able to determine the factors and power capabilities behind the creation of the rule. The first factor which strongly influenced which brand would be in the lead was the power of resources. The resource which was particularly important here was experience and knowledge about the topic. Another factor which influenced the choice of lead brand in HR was balance. Indeed, we are in a situation which could be compared to the one in a merger of equals for example, with the idea of making sure that each party gets an equal part, so to speak, is important. Therefore we need to consider that there is also a certain symbolism behind these rules. In R&D we were not able to get details on why a certain brand was chosen to be the lead as these decisions were made very high up in the company, based on strategic group goals. Indeed, when considering the direct consequences of this rule, for HR they can be considered to be minimal, but when looking at R&D these consequences are much more important. We for example came across the example of a department being completely reorganized, which is a non-negligible consequence. This case study has therefore allowed to bring to light certain factors which will influence the creation of the rule, as well as potential consequences, specifically in the case of a holding matrix organization.

Now we would like to develop on our findings related to the contingency theory elaborated upon by Wolf and Egelhoff and how they fit to our empirical findings. To start with, we have found further criteria which could potentially be used to influence the choice for rule-based or balanced decision making. The theoretical criteria of Egelhoff & Wolf are based on the information processing capacity of each form of decision making, however in our case it seems that other criteria also come into play.

To start with, it seems that the status of the relationship had an effect on which kind of decision making was used. Rather than a contingency, in some cases it seemed to be a process. If the relationship is in its infancy, it seems that the balanced form of decision making is used. This allows for the dimensions to build trust and understanding for each other. This decision making then later develops onto rule based decision making, based on the pre-existing relationship. If this stage does not happen there have been reported failures, as the trust and understanding between the parties has not yet been built sufficiently.

A second factor we identified is the level where the decision making is taking place. The lower down in the project structure, the more likely it seemed that the decision making would be balanced. This is an interesting idea, which would deserve to be developed when looking into the question of ambidexterity. Would having these two levels theoretically allow for the best of both worlds from Wolf and Egelhoff's contingency theory? This would allow for novelty and innovativeness, as well as a thorough evaluation of alternatives within the working team where the knowledge is generated, whereas the decision making can be accelerated through escalation, or a decision from the holding. We do not have evidence of this actually working in our case study, however we think that this may be an interesting concept to further look into. What we have found are examples of projects which failed because the people on the lower levels did not communicate enough. They followed the directive from the top, which led to not enough exploration of the issue and the actual technical issue, underlining the importance of the thoroughness of the analysis of alternatives within the working group.

One idea we have also found within our case which we feel could also contribute to further understand the different decision making modes in a matrix organization is the difference made between decision making accountability and actual decision making power. In this case we can see a difference between actually having the power to make the decision and being responsible for coming to a decision. Although there is a rule on who is responsible for the decision, this does not mean that the other dimensions are not included in the decision. This allows us to have the balanced decision making within the working group, yet still having parties responsible for coming to a consensus, therefore moderating and structuring the decision making process, therefore contributing to the point we made in the previous paragraph of the potential value of considering balanced decision making on a lower level, with more rule based decision making on a higher one. We have illustrated this idea in the table below.

Table 14: Decision making accountability versus power (own elaboration)

	Description	Empirical example
Level 1	Decision making power: the governance body which makes the final decision	CHRO
Level 2	Decision accountability: is responsible for bringing a proposal to the governance body	Scania team member
Level 3	Balanced decision: where the decision is created.	All the team members

Finally, we have found another factors which we think could also play a role in the contingency theory companies could use when choosing a decision making style for a certain situation. Indeed, we have found an issue of legitimacy and buy-in related to rule based decision making in the matrix. Indeed it was found that if the brands were not involved as actively within the decision making process, that they could potentially not follow through on decisions or at least be unwilling to do so.

Now that we have given an overview of the theoretical implications of our findings on decision making in the matrix organization, we will describe our findings regarding conflict and how they relate to the existing theoretical knowledge. When we started this research it was clear that we would not be aiming to understand the issue of the quantity of conflict in the matrix organization. Indeed, the idea of comparing the amount of conflict found in elementary structures as compared to matrix organizations was not something we hoped to achieve with our single case study within a matrix organization. However what we have contributed to the topic of conflict and power in the matrix organization is further and deeper understanding of the causes, facilitating factors and power capabilities which are leveraged by the actors in conflict situations.

Our first finding is in line with the view that Galbraith (2009) has of conflict in the matrix organizations, as well as Pondy's (1967) opinion that conflict is a natural consequence of managing. Indeed, in the projects we observed, conflict was part of the decision making process. Each brand would come in with their interests and the goal for the project team was to come to the best solution while taken these interest into consideration. This case study therefore offers and illustration of how the matrix can be used to deal with the three forces found within the literature review, forces for global integration, forces for national differentiation and the need for worldwide innovation (Blazejewski & Becker-Ritterspach, 2011, Bartlett and Ghoshal, 1989). Indeed, each of the brands within our case have their own interest and bringing these together within the matrix organization supports this need for worldwide innovation, as has been found within our section on ambidexterity. This is in line with the literature findings that a matrix organization of some form can be used to deal with these conflicting pressures (Schotter & Beamish, 2011; Bartlett & Ghoshal, 1989).

Furthermore, we have found evidence within our case of the conflict being functional with examples of conflict being precedent setting. However, it must also be noted that there were times when conflict was dysfunctional, in particular if it slowed down decision making too much. We found that this was due to a lack of information sharing in the initial phases of the project. A facilitating factor to dealing with this issue which was mentioned was the importance of building trust. This allows us to identify another role which trust can play within conflict. Indeed, Simons and Peterson (2000) found that trust is essential in order to avoid task conflict turning into relationship conflict. We did not find evidence of this, however, we found that trust plays a role in facilitating information sharing and therefore facilitating the issue. Another facilitating factor which we identified was that the holding has a moderating role in most cases, and sometimes an external person comes in to play this moderation role.

When looking into the sources of conflict, it must be noted that we did not find much evidence of relationship conflict, but that task conflict was the most present. In order to classify the types of task conflict that we found, we have once again based ourselves on the research done by Egelhoff and Wolf, as they have developed a categorization especially for matrix organizations. Using this categorization, we often found the lack of clear goals to be an issue, which potentially led to conflict. Furthermore, the "obvious" matrix conflict stemming from conflicting goals, either between the brands or between the brand goals and Group goals was also illustrated. This is very clearly goal conflict, which we have found can be facilitated through sense-making activities of boundary spanners. Furthermore, we also identified evidence of evaluation conflict, which we have analyzed in this research through the lens of the question of culture and identities in the matrix organization. Indeed, this contributes to the current status of the research on matrix organizations, as it has been found that culture plays a role but it has not yet been elaborated upon how it impacts the matrix organization. Moreover, we found authority conflict to not be prominent within our case study. This is in fact surprising, as the oft cited issue of a matrix is the problem of in-fighting due to questions of who is in charge and who gets to decide. This is potentially due to the nature of this matrix as a holding-company matrix organization, where there is a kind of authority figure to be found in the holding. Furthermore, the people involved all have their own place within their own brand, and the matrix organization as such is an add-on to their current responsibilities.

Finally, when looking at the question of power capabilities deployed by the holding and the subsidiaries within this matrix, we have already elaborated on the figure above in our summary of findings. What is interesting to point out here and where this case study has allowed us to make a real contribution is that in this case the resources (which are usually knowledge and experience) are held by the subsidiaries and not by the Headquarters. This allows us to show how the HQ can still leverage the power of process and meaning, while leveraging the subsidiaries independent to pursue their local goals.

Overall, within our research we have been able to provide empirical evidence of the two modes of decision making used within this holding matrix organization, as well as find further explanation as to why decision making is potentially slower in a matrix. On top of that, we have identified further factors which could be taken into consideration when choosing to use one mode of decision making mode or the other, adding to the existing contingency theory. Furthermore, we have created further understanding as to the sources of conflict as well as the power capabilities leveraged by the headquarters and by the subsidiaries in a conflict situation.

5.1.3   Knowledge Sharing in the Matrix Facilitating Exploration Activities

For obvious reasons, when creating our understanding of the research field, we had a strong focus on the most active researchers on the topic of matric organizations today, Egelhoff and Wolf. They have a theory that a matrix organization could potentially contribute to the ambidexterity of the firm. We therefore choose to integrate this concept, with the hope of empirically contributing to this theoretical framework. This would be value-adding, as innovation has been found to be a key factor for long term success (Jimenéz-Jimenéz et al., 2014). Briefly, the idea developed by Egelhoff and Wolf is that the information processing required for exploitation and exploration correspond to the information processing capacities of rule-based and balanced decision-making, respectively. We have attempted to empirically understand this concept further in our research, as well as simply understand how a matrix can affect the innovative capacities of an MNC. Furthermore, as we have linked innovation to the concept of learning and knowledge, as we found that by gathering and sharing knowledge with their subsidiaries, MNCs were able to innovate (Almeida & Phene, 2004), which also fit to our desire to further understand the changing role of subsidiaries. On top of that, we identified a research gap in the literature, as most research on knowledge transfer tends to focus on the HQ-subsidiary transfer (Minbaeva, 2008) or reverse knowledge transfer, between subsidiaries and headquarters (Rabbiosi, 2011) and we can contribute by further understanding how a matrix can help facilitate knowledge transfer between subsidiaries.

To start with, as found in our desk research, we tried to understand the issues related to knowledge and learning, as antecedents to innovation and the potential impact that the matrix structure had on these two factors. What we found was that the matrix projects themselves where actually made to collect and process knowledge from within the brands. Indeed, when looking into the answers of the interviewees, the first step within each of these projects was knowledge sharing in order to understand the status of each brand and how it could be used within the project. The fact that this is done within the matrix set-up makes it more interesting than in the brands itself, as the knowledge gathered is potentially more varied, allowing for different ideas, alternatives and proposals and therefore potentially more innovation.

On top of that, we found evidence of how a matrix purposefully creates conflict therefore generating knowledge sharing and innovation. In the literature the relationship between innovation and task conflict is known and here we see how the holding organization can create the pre-conditions for it to happen. This is interesting as it is in line with Galbraith's view (2009) on the role of conflict within the matrix, as being a natural and not necessarily negative part of matrix organizations.

Furthermore, in our case it seems that the matrix projects were mostly used for exploration purposes, leaving the exploitation within the brands. However, when looking into the project process, we have found that there tends to be an evolution with balanced decision making in the initial phase and then a potential evolution towards rule based decision making. This is in line with the fact that the options have been thoroughly evaluated, the strategy for action has been defined and then the process or product needs to be developed and rolled-out, therefore it no longer requires the information processing capacities of balanced decision making, as the exploration phase has been completed.

We have found that the matrix organization allows for knowledge sharing which would not naturally have occurred within the MNC. However, certain factors need to be present in order to facilitate this process. Indeed, one of the oft cited issues within matrix projects was the issue of knowledge sharing in the initial phase of the project. Therefore the facilitating factors which we identified, notably the common understanding and trust in order to have open communication, which tend to be built through socialization as well as rules for information sharing, are essential. This led us to identify the importance of boundary spanning for innovation, because it creates the environment for knowledge sharing.

Within this section it must be pointed out that we were not able to observe the concept of the flexible matrix as much as we would have liked. This is due to the fact that we did our research through interviews, therefore if it was not happening we could not trigger it. Furthermore, the nature of the matrix observed is such that it mostly used balanced decision making on the working group level, where the potential for innovation existed.

5.1.4   Organizational Culture and Identity Issues in a Matrix Organization

We decided to add to the existing research on matrix organizations by adding the concept of culture and organizations. Indeed, we found culture to be a key topic of research in MNC literature since the 1980s, and corporate culture plays a key role in organizations, as it serves as guidance for decision making and drives a sense of shared identity (Barmeyer & Davoine, 2006b). This has however yet to be studied when researching matrix organizations. We found that culture can be considered as static, part of the DNA of one group or another, as well as dynamic, created and re-created through interaction (Barmeyer & Davoine, 2019). Furthermore, we also looked into the literature on social-cultural integration in M&As, as we feel that the matrix organization can find some areas of commonality, two dimensions coming into contact can be comparable to the situation in a merger. We have tried to understand how the culture and identity issues affected the success within this matrix organization, as well as understand how a matrix organization can be used as a tool for socio-cultural integration. Finally, we have attempted to find out how the dimensions of the matrix can contribute to dynamics of negotiated culture within the MNC.

This work described the findings which we made regarding the perceived cultural differences between MAN and Scania and the question of identity within our case study. We have contributed to the literature here in multiple ways. To start with, we have empirically found that cultural differences have an impact on a matrix organization. Indeed, as mentioned by Davis and Lawrence (1977), the cultural differences, observed here through different decision making styles and relationship towards hierarchy for example, were a source of conflict for this case. Furthermore, we have also found that the matrix organization can play a symbolic role in the socio-cultural integration between two equals. Indeed, through this holding, each brand is able to preserve their identity, which still being integrated within key areas. This is in line with the concept from Kale et al. (2009) of a partnering M&A rather than an integration. Here the operational autonomy is left intact, while focusing on key synergies. This is interesting as it now only illustrates an idea as of yet only researched in emerging MNCs, but it is also in line with our findings on the changing role of HQ. However, this does mean that the cultural integration that one could observe would then not be visible here. This is normal, considering the matrix set-up and the fact that the goal is not to bring these brands together but rather to facilitate collaboration between them. This was also observed on a cross-brand team level, where the teams and the governance bodies were mixed with members from each brand. This has the same function as in M&A integration, as noted by Barmeyer and Mayrhofer (2002).

We have also been able to observe, within our case, that although the values within the TRATON GROUP have mostly been aligned, these are still "espoused values" (Argyris & Schon, 1978). Indeed, there is however still very much separate and distinct cultures and identities within the brands. An interesting finding that we made during our research which also contributes to the body of knowledge on identities in the MNC. Indeed, we found more identity issues within the R&D function than within HR. We linked this to the fact that the engineers within R&D identified more strongly with the products they had participated in developing. When considering negotiated culture, a key factor in the question of negotiated culture was very much the decision on the lead brand within this case. The dimension with the most resources available, be it knowledge, know-how and time play a role in which dimension is chosen as the lead. However, this is a desire to maintain a form of balance, because of the hard consequences of the choice of lead brand. Knowledge plays the biggest role within HR, the brand with the most experience will be in the lead. This can clearly be seen in HR projects, not so much in R&D. In R&D in the projects observed where this was the case was that one brand only held the knowledge, which led to a customer-supplier relationship. Where they both held the knowledge the decision was made from above, based on political negotiation, not described in this work. The power of processes remains the main source of power for the holding. We were also able to understand how within the cross-brand teams, a working culture was gradually created, through the setting of rules, processes for common work and socialization between the members. This contributes to the further understanding required on how culture is created and recreated (Lee et al., 2015).

Finally when looking at the facilitating factors used to deal with culture and identity issues, we once again identified the importance of boundary spanning activities, which will be addressed in the next section. Furthermore, we found that focusing on external factors helped untangle issues related to cultures, for example focusing the discussion on customer requirements, which helped move away from the identity issues of "my solution" versus "your solution". Furthermore, as noted by Child et al. (2001), HR processes play an important role, especially in the case of cultural differences. Here, we were able to highlight the important role of HR in facilitating the collaborations between brands, and therefore beyond cultural boundaries, in line with the finding of Barmeyer and Mayrhofer (2008). We also noted the difficulties aligning HR processes due to the institutional contexts the brands are embedded in, therefore highlighting the importance of flexibility in HR. This observation can be associated to the M&A situation, where Sarala et al. (2017) also noted the challenge of aligning HR practices.

Overall, we have contributed within this research to further understanding the role of culture and identities within the matrix organization, by empirically observing the impact that cultural differences have on the matrix projects.

5.1.5 Boundary Spanning, Facilitated by and Required in a Matrix Organization

The idea of boundary spanning has of yet to our knowledge not been applied to matrix organizations. However, it seemed to us that boundary spanning would be an excellent literature fit to better understand matrix work, as work bridging across matrix dimensions can be considered as boundary spanning. Indeed, simply by looking at the definition of boundary spanning as a set of communication and coordination activities performed by individuals within an organization and between organizations to integrate activities across multiple cultural, institutional and organizational contexts (Schotter et. al, 2017), we can see that this is what we have observed in the context of our holding matrix organization. We have seen within our case study which boundary spanning activities are performed by the various actors, as well as described how the matrix can influence boundary spanning in the company. Finally, we will described the required skills for effective boundary spanning in a holding company matrix organization.

As we have hinted at throughout this chapter, we have found the question of boundary spanning to be a key facilitating factor within this matrix organization. Due to the fact that the theoretical field of boundary spanning has yet to be applied to the context of matrix organizations, we are able to make many contributions regarding the boundary spanning activities and the boundary spanning skills required to successfully perform these activities. To start with, we were able to provide evidence of how boundary spanners were formalized within the matrix organization, which according to Tushman and Scanlan (1981), facilitates boundary spanning activities. Indeed, much of the current research on boundary spanners looks at particular groups of people such as expatriates who have a kind of formalized boundary spanning role or subsidiary managers who have a boundary spanning function embedded in their formal position (Barmeyer & Davoine, 2019). In our research, we found that the boundary spanning function role was formalized through project participation. This is an interesting point because it also allowed us to observe the virtuous circle related to matrix work, where the boundary spanning actors were able to develop their boundary spanning skills by participating in the matrix projects, and therefore by performing boundary spanning activities. Indeed in our case we found that working in a matrix project offered opportunities for learning and network creating, essential factors to successfully bridge the matrix boundaries. This contributes to the literature on boundary spanning and contributes to the idea that organizations can support people in increasing their boundary spanning skills through increased social capital (Barner-Rasmussen et al., 2010). Furthermore, we have also found evidence that this boundary spanning role is also continued after the project is over or that the skills are used in other projects. This can be compared to the research on the returning expatriates continued boundary spanning activities, and merits further research. On top of that, we have showed how the cultural and geographical boundary in the MNC can be bridged through boundary spanning activities. It requires financial investment, especially at the beginning, as the geographical boundary needs to be physically bridged, through travel. Bridging the geographical boundary supports the bridging the cultural boundary, as the actors gain understanding through socialization. The matrix organization projects create opportunity for socialization, therefore contributing to the supporting the boundary spanning activities. We have also contributed to the very new research regarding the concept of temporal boundary spanning (Stjerne et al., 2019). We have provided evidence within this research of how the issues of different idiosyncratic time within the organizations has affected the success of projects and therefore shown the importance of temporal boundary spanning activities within the contemporary matrix organization. We have found that the decision making processes evolve at different speeds, leading to challenges within these projects, as well as the fact that there is a need to create an understanding within the organization that these matrix projects take time.

It must be pointed out that not everybody is suited to work in this type of matrix organization. We found that there are some elements which can contribute to employee satisfaction within the matrix organization such as the international context, learning and the challenging environment, as found by Au and Fukada (2002). However, it was noted that there could be some dissatisfaction due to heavy workload as well as travelling. This is in line with the point by Cross et al. (2015), that collaboration is time consuming and can lead to over-burdened employees and the fact that boundary spanning activities have been associated with conflict and stress for the boundary spanner (Aldrich & Herker, 1977). Furthermore, as noted by Tushmann (1977), not everybody needs to be a boundary spanner, as this would be inefficient. This brings us to the importance of boundary spanning capabilities required to work in a matrix organization. We have already provided an overview of the practical requirements for team members within the empirical findings, we would like here to provide a more theoretical classification of the skills that we identified and justified, inspired by Arthur et al. (1999).

To start with, we have identified "know-who" as a key capability for boundary spanning in a matrix organization. This is very much aligned with Barner-Rasmussen et al. (2010), who find the possession of social capital, and in particular the interpersonal connections or network, to be an essential resource for boundary spanning. People need to have a strong network within their own dimension, which has already been seen in the literature on boundary spanning. Therefore the choice of people to be part of cross-brand projects is highly strategic. In our case, this is something that is done by the brands as they hold the knowledge on who has the required network and position in the company. However, we have found that the holding can also leverage the power of processes by changing the membership of the teams as well as influencing the membership of the committees within the cross-brand projects. Furthermore we have observed what we call the snowball effect of team membership. Once the people are part of one project, they tend to be invited to be part of the next project. The membership of the cross-brand teams remains quite constant. This could however only be observed in HR projects, the R&D projects are too dispersed and big to be able to observe this phenomenon, within our research. On top of this we have noted the importance of know-how for legitimacy. Indeed, we have found that technical understanding of the issue and the expertize of the actors on the topic is essential. Tushman and Scalan (1981) also stated that the boundary spanners must be perceived as being competent in their work. It is very important to be to be able to legitimize their position within the team as well as bring in the required knowledge and information on the brand-specific conditions regarding the topic. Finally, we have identified a very important factor within our case, which very much contributes to further understanding the required skills and capacities required for successful boundary spanning within the matrix organization. The element we identified is "know-why". Indeed, we found that the actors need to have an understanding of the strategic reasoning behind the project and the decisions made, on three levels. On the first level, within the project: in order to be able to convince the other team members of the value of the project, the team members need to be able to develop meaning in the cross-brand team. Secondly, the boundary spanners need to have an understanding of the added value of the process or product when they bring it back to their brand, in order to be able to sell product to their own dimension. On the third level the actors need to be able to understand why they do things the way they do them within their own brand, in order to defend their position as well as in order to have the capacity for self-reflection when comparing their own product to the one from the other brands. This also contributes to ensuring commitment and buy in, an issue in matrix organizations noted by Sy and Cote (2004).

To conclude this section, we have been able to contribute to the literature on matrix organizations by offering a new theoretical lens through which to observe them, notably boundary spanning. Through this, we have been able to understand how a matrix organization can formalize boundary spanning role, supporting boundary spanning activities. Furthermore, we have also provided further evidence of the potential need for temporal boundary spanning. Finally, we have contributed to the knowledge on boundary spanners and have classified boundary spanning capacities in a new way, namely know-who, know-how and know-why. This contributes further to the exiting knowledge on boundary spanning skills.

5.2 Conclusion

5.2.1   The Research Findings at a Glance

Overall this research has allowed to further empirically understand matrix organizations, contributing to the sparse evidence available regarding matrix structures in the contemporary MNC. We have created a noel framework for the study or matrix organizations, adding to the classic matrix issues, the question of organizational culture and identities and boundary spanning. In this next section we will briefly summarize our findings for each of our main research questions in order to give an overview of this research at a glance.

How can a contemporary holding company matrix facilitate knowledge sharing on a global level while allowing for subsidiary autonomy?

Within our research we found that the holding matrix organization could be used as a form of contemporary HQ, allowing the subsidiaries to keep their autonomy, while identifying and exploiting the key areas for global integration and synergies. The matrix organization provides support for lateral coordination and we identified the importance of HR as a facilitator as well as common IT platforms. Within this matrix organization, the parties are brought together within a project which is essentially a knowledge sharing platform. The output of these projects are then built on the common knowledge gathered from all the subsidiaries and processed thanks to balanced decision making. Furthermore, the matrix organization formalizes boundary spanners within the organization, who will perform essential boundary spanning activities to bring these lateral coordination mechanisms to life. Finally, we identified that in this case, the HQ had to leverage the power of processes and meaning, moving away from the use of the power of resources, which is kept within the subsidiaries.

How are decisions made in a holding matrix organization?

In our study, we identified the clear issue of slow decision making, as had already been mentioned in classic matrix literature. We were able to further contribute to this by extending our knowledge on the reasons behind this slow decision making and how to improve this issue. We identified some factors which strongly influenced decision making in the matrix, in particular the role of top management, and how committees made up of executives could support the legitimization of these matrix projects. On top of that, we also found evidence of the importance of temporal boundary spanning and trust. Furthermore, we found a clear example of balanced decision making being used within our case study and were able to match the benefits found to those already identified in the literature. We also found that in some cases the concept of the "lead brand" was used, which was how rule-based decision making was operationalized in this case. When looking at the contingency theory developed by Wolf and Egelhoff (2017), we found that the in our empirical case the factors for the creation of the rule and how the rule was operationalized were actually different. In particular, we found the level of decision making and the maturity of the relationship to play a role in whether or not the decision making would be rule based.

How is ambidexterity facilitated by a flexible matrix structure?

When we started our research we had the idea to find out how a flexible matrix could facilitate ambidexterity, as was described in the theoretical concept developed by Egelhoff and Wolf (2017). In fact, were not able to observe a flexible matrix as was described in theory but we did find out how a matrix can contribute to innovation, by creating arenas for knowledge sharing and learning as well as intentionally creating conflict so as to find innovative solutions. Furthermore, we did not observe a flexible matrix which changes its decision making to fit the needs of exploration or exploitation, as we mostly had projects evolving around exploration. However, this is also a way a matrix can contribute to the innovative capacities of a firm, as the matrix projects allow for exploration which would not otherwise be permitted with brand resources and knowledge alone.

What role does conflict and the power capabilities deployed by the actors play?

We found within our case study that conflict impacted the matrix projects by slowing them down. But on the other hand we also found this conflict to be precedent setting and potentially a tool to leverage for innovation. Furthermore, we identified the sources of conflict within the matrix as mostly being task conflict and in particular goal and evaluation conflict. In a conflict situation, we found the boundary spanning activities of actors to be an important facilitating factor, and in particular facilitating communication, translating information and building trust to be particularly important. We found that the power capabilities deployed by the holding were generally the power of meaning and power of processes, whereas the power of resources mainly lay within the subsidiaries and that they were also able to deploy the power of meaning, represented by their brand identity.

What is the impact of impact of cultural and identity differences within a matrix organization?

We found culture and identities to be a strong factor within our case study. It was particularly interesting as we did not expect this to be the case both within HR and within R&D. We identified the different cultural differences perceived by the actors and how they affected the matrix projects. In particular, we found within our case study that the differences in leadership style and hierarchy between the two brands strongly affected the matrix projects. Furthermore, we found that there were identity issues within the R&D projects, which were not as present within HR. This was attributed to the attachment of engineers for products they had development, a sentiment perhaps not as strong within HR. Here we once again found more issues at the beginning of the project and found that boundary spanning activities, such as creating a common goal with a focus on the customer for example, helped smooth these issues over.

How is the concept boundary spanning deployed in a matrix organization?

We found boundary spanning to be an essential facilitating factor within a matrix organization, and we were also able to identify and understand the skills required and developed through the matrix projects within our case. We found that all levels of boundary spanning were performed, with a particular importance for trust building as a key boundary spanning activity at the beginning of a project. Furthermore, we were able to describe the key skills for boundary spanning activities within a matrix organization. We called them, know-who, having a network within one's own organization and within the matrix, know-how, having technical and brand specific knowledge and information and know-why, being aware of brand and group goal and being able to sell these goals within the project and towards top management.

5.2.2 Main Contributions

Through this research we have been able to contribute to multiple streams of literature, with a particular focus on the understanding of matrix organizations, of course. Specifically, we have been able to further develop the knowledge on the contemporary matrix organization and how it works, using a framework developed based on existing matrix literature as well as the integration of additional streams of knowledge, namely the research on organizational culture and identities as well as the work done on boundary spanning.

To start with, we have shown an example of how a contemporary HQ could work and its role in promoting lateral co-ordination between subsidiaries. In addition, we could show how to potentially use a matrix organization to deal with the control gap. Here we focused on how these lateral coordination mechanisms were deployed to support not only knowledge transfer from the HQ to the subsidiaries or reverse transfer, but also transfer between the subsidiaries thanks to the use of the holding matrix organization. In our study, we were also able to contribute to the knowledge on decision making and conflict in the matrix, two topics very present in exiting literature on these structures. We provided empirical evidence of the two decision-making approaches used within this holding matrix organization, as well as created more understanding as to why decision-making in a matrix could theoretically be slower. We also defined additional factors that could be taken into account when deciding to use one or the other mode of decision-making, contributing to the existing contingency theory, developed by Egelhoff and Wolf (2017). Regarding ambidexterity, although we have not been able to observe the phenomenon of a flexible matrix as is described in theory, we were able to identify key learning and information sharing issues, as well as point out the importance of boundary spanning and trust for knowledge sharing. On top of that, we have been able to further understand the causes and consequences of conflict in a matrix organization, as well as the power capabilities leveraged both by the holding and by the subsidiaries in these situations. We have also contributed to the literature on culture and identities within the matrix organization. We confirmed that that culture and identity issues do have a role within a matrix organization and how they manifest themselves. We also showed how a holding matrix organization can be used as a mechanism for socio-cultural integration, once again linked to the creating of lateral coordination mechanisms thanks to the matrix structure. We were also able to identify the importance of boundary spanning activities to facilitate cultural issues and we were able to highlight the importance of HR, as found by Barmeyer and Mayrhofer, (2008). Finally, we have been able to contribute to our understanding of matrix organizations by offering a new theoretical lens, namely boundary spanning, through which to analyze such structures. Through this, we were able to demonstrate how a matrix organization can further support lateral coordination by formalizing boundary spanning roles. In addition, we also provided additional evidence of the potential need for temporary boundary spanning and were able to add to this very new field topic of research regarding boundary spanning. We have also classified boundary spanning skills in a new way, with a specific set of boundary spanning skills required for matrix work, namely know-who, know-how and know-why.

Overall, the contributions of this thesis are manifold, both in confirming and empirically demonstrating elements related to existing matrix theory as well as adding new concepts, opening up further opportunities for more research.

5.2.3 Implications for Practice, Limits and Further Research

Within this next section we would like to share the main implications for practice of this research as well as point out the limits of this study and give some potential avenues for further research.

In order to conclude this thesis we would like to point out some of the implications for practice which we have identified within this research. Although, as mentioned previously, the fact that this is a single case study means that we cannot claim a very high level of generalization, (Yin, 2009), we still think that our findings could be of interests for other MNCs, beyond the TRATON GROUP. This thesis uses a practice based approach (Feldman and Orlikowski, 2011) which allows for an analysis of the micro-dynamics of cross-brand projects, understanding how everyday actions and interactions between the actors lead to organizational outcomes. Therefore MNCs can take these results into account when running their own matrix projects, supporting the actors in obtaining successful results. Indeed, the present findings have implications for contemporary MNCs. Overall this research contributes to explaining how a holding company structure can be used to coordinate and control the international activities of MNCs, particularly the role of the governance structure and the boundary spanning activities which facilitate socio-cultural integration. Furthermore, the role HR can play in creating boundary spanners and how developing their skills could be leveraged is described. This understanding could help companies design their integration strategies. When looking at the opinion of our interviewees regarding the matrix organization and when comparing it to the way the VW Group operates, in a more centrally steered way, they agree that having this matrix is an advantage. Indeed, the VW Group functions with a classic headquarter-subsidiary relationship, where a policy will be developed at the headquarters for the whole Group, and then implemented in the brands. The TRATON GROUP however, with the matrix organization, allows the brands to contribute to the policy development, which is more beneficial. There is the sentiment that through this matrix there is a respect and understanding for the brands. Through this, it also potentially makes the implementation of the policies or processes within the brands smoother, as the buy-in and local adaptations have already partially been done. Another important thing to point out is that when the holding was first set up, it was mostly made up of employees from VW and from the brands. This plays a role, as the holding employees therefore also have knowledge of the realities of working within their brand. More specifically, the findings point out the importance of HR in the coordination of a matrix organization, and the significance of developing boundary spanners and their skills. We also noted the importance of technical expertise to legitimize the boundary spanning activities of the cross-brand team members. On top of that it is important that HR create contact points and arenas for people to meet and build trust. MNCs could also use this research and take our recommendation for how to launch a matrix project into account. Based on this thesis, we would recommend starting this kind of matrix project with balanced decision making and create trust between the parties then move towards a certain level of rule based decision making gradually. We would make sure to use face to face meetings and encourage socialization of the actors. Furthermore, we think it would add value to support the matrix actors by formalizing their role, potentially through project participation and legitimization through a matrix governance structure, or in another way. Finally, we have also offered an insight into the skills required for the boundary spanning within the matrix organization. Developing these skills within key actors would therefore be a key take-away from our research.

Even if we attempted to keep our research as sound as possible, as mentioned the methodology section, it must be noted that this case study presents some limitations. To start with, since we have based our research on a single case study, we cannot generalize our results (Yin, 2009), a fact which was already known when we started our research. Indeed, if we had had multiple case studies within multiple companies, we would have been able to have data which allowed for comparability and stronger validity, which would have led to better opportunities for theory building (Yin, 2009). However, by studying multiple projects within two functions with interviewees from different levels, we have attempted to have a broad understanding, even if it is only within this one MNC. Furthermore, certain environmental factors make our case quite unique and therefore difficult to generalize. Indeed, the situation of a newly formed Group, organized as a holding matrix organization in this specific international context, within the automotive industry is rather exceptional. When studying other kinds of matrix organizations, in different industries, we could consider that other studies would find different results. Furthermore, the strategy of this set-up, with a desire to maintain a certain brand independence and focus integration efforts on key synergetic opportunities plays a big role in how the matrix is perceived and on how it functions. Finally, many of the issues and associated facilitating factors which we identified were based on issues of culture and identity, and in particular on a company and brand level. This means that a lot of these issues were specific to our case study and the companies involved. However, one could consider that even if the cultural issues in another case were to be different, it would be pertinent to consider similar facilitating factors, as these are not specific to each individual cultural difference and identity issue itself, but rather a more general facilitating factor, in particular when considering the role of boundary spanning and boundary spanners in the matrix organizations.

Within our research, it was important for us to focus on the how and the why of the question. On top of that, as the research field is still quite open and developing, it was relevant to dig in a qualitative way to gather an understanding of it. However, it would be interesting for further research to focus in a more quantitative way on the questions identified, potentially creating a more accurate bigger on a wider scale. There could be a potential opportunity to take a more longitudinal approach within this case study too, as it would be interesting to see the progress of this organization further down the line. Will it evolve to be more centrally steered? Or will the holding, after having facilitated the initial cooperation work, fade into the background, and have the brands cooperate naturally following this initial push?

Beyond the methodological aspects, we can also see many opportunities for further research on the topic of matrix organizations. We have created a picture of the contemporary matrix organization and the potential role of culture, identities and boundary spanners as key new factors within the matrix, which leads to much potential for development. In particular, do these cultural issues also affect matrix organization which are based around function, product and regional dimensions? To what extent do professional and functional culture affect matrix organization success? When looking into boundary spanning within the matrix, we also see potential for further research, for example further understanding the role of HR and how it can support the development and creation of boundary spanners, and the necessary skills for successful boundary spanning. Overall, the research field on the contemporary matrix organizations still allows for plenty of further research opportunities. We do believe, that in line with the changing role of headquarters, the focus on the importance of the simultaneous use of formal and informal coordination mechanisms, the contemporary matrix organization does offer opportunities in practice too, and therefore potential research fields.

References

ADENFELT, M., and LAGERSTRÖM, K, 2006, "Enabling knowledge creation and sharing in transnational projects", International journal of project management, 24(3), pp. 191-198.

ADLER, N. J., and GUNDERSEN, A., 2007, International dimensions of organizational behavior. Cengage Learning.

ALBERT, S., and WHETTEN, D. A., 1985, "Organizational identity", Research in organizational behavior, 7, pp. 263-295.

ALDRICH, H., and HERKER, D., 1977, "Boundary spanning roles and organization structure", Academy of management review, 2(2), pp. 217-230.

ALMEIDA, P., and PHENE, A., 2004, "Subsidiaries and knowledge creation: The influence of the MNC and host country on innovation", Strategic Management Journal, 25(8-9), pp. 847-864.

ALVESSON, M., 1990, "On the popularity of organizational culture", Acta Sociologica, 33(1), pp. 31-49.

ANDERSON, C.C. and FLEMING, M.M., 1990, "Management control in an engineering matrix organization: a project engineer's perspective", Industrial Management, 32(2), p.8.

ANDERSSON, U., 2003, "Managing the Transfer Of Capabilities Within Multinational Corporations: The Dual Role Of The Subsidiary", Scandinavian Journal Of Management, 19, pp. 425-442.

ANDERSSON, U., FORSGREN, M., and HOLM, U., 2015, "Balancing subsidiary influence in the federative MNC: A business network view". In Knowledge, Networks and Power (pp. 393-420). Palgrave Macmillan, London.

APPELBAUM, S. H., NADEAU, D., and CYR M., 2008, "Performance evaluation in a matrix organization: a case study (part 1, 2 &3) " Industrial and Commercial training, Vol.40, Issue 5, pp. 236–241.

ARGYRIS, C. and SCHON, D.A., 1978, Organisational Learning. Addison-Wesley Longman, Reading, MA.

ARTHUR, M.B., INKSON, D. and PRINGLE, J., 1999, The New Careers: Individual Action and Economic Change, Sage, London.

ASHFORTH, B. and MAEL, F., 1989, "Social identity theory and the organization", Academy of Management Review, Vol. 14, pp. 20-39.

AU, K. Y., and FUKUDA, J., 2002, "Boundary spanning behaviors of expatriates", Journal of World Business, 37(4), pp. 285-296.

AYOKO, O. B., HÄRTEL, C. E., and CALLAN, V. J., 2002, "Resolving the puzzle of productive and destructive conflict in culturally heterogeneous workgroups: A communication accommodation theory approach". International Journal of Conflict Management, 13(2), pp. 165-195.

© Springer Fachmedien Wiesbaden GmbH, part of Springer Nature 2020
J. Shahani, *Limits and Opportunities of a Matrix Organization*, Auto
Uni – Schriftenreihe 149, https://doi.org/10.1007/978-3-658-32261-8

BACHRACH, P., and BARATZ, M. S., 1969, "Power as non-decision-making". Urban Government, pp. 454-464.

BARLEY, S.R., MEYER, G.W. and DASH, D.C., 1988, ``Cultures of culture: academics, practitioners, and the pragmatics of normative control", Administrative Science Quarterly, Vol. 33, pp. 24-60.

BARMEYER, C. and DAVOINE, E., 2006a, "Interkulturelle Zusammenarbeit und Fuhrung in internationalen Teams. Das Beispiel Deutschland-Frankreich", ZfO–Zeitschrift für Führung+ Organisation,, 75(1), 35.

BARMEYER, C. and DAVOINE, E., 2006b, "International corporate cultures: From helpless global convergence to constructive European divergence". In: SCHOLZ, C. AND ZENTES, J., Strategic Management—New Rules for Old Europe (pp. 227-245). Gabler.

BARMEYER, C., and DAVOINE, E., 2008, "Culture et gestion en Allemagne: la 'machine bien huilée'". In: DAVEL, E., DUPUIS, J.-P., CHANLAT J.-F. (eds), Gestion en contexte interculturel: approches, problématiques, pratiques et plongées, Les Presses de l'Université Laval and TÉLUQ/UQAM.

BARMEYER, C., and DAVOINE, E., 2015, "Konstruktive Interkulturalität. Impulse für die Zusammenarbeit in internationalen Organisationen am Fallbeispiel Alleo", ZfO–Zeitschrift für Führung+ Organisation, 84(6), 430-437.

BARMEYER, C., and DAVOINE, E.,2019, "Facilitating intercultural negotiated practices in joint ventures: The case of a French–German railway organization", International Business Review, 28(1), 1-11.

BARMEYER, C., DAVOINE, E., and STOKES, P., 2019, "When the 'well-oiled machine'meets the 'pyramid of people:'Role perceptions and hybrid working practices of middle managers in a binational organization – ARTE"., International Journal of Cross Cultural Management, 19(3), 251-272.

BARMEYER, C., and MAYRHOFER, U., 2008, "The contribution of intercultural management to the success of international mergers and acquisitions: An analysis of the EADS group", International Business Review, 17(1), 28-38.

BARNER-RASMUSSEN, W., EHRNROOTH, M., KOVESHNIKOV, A., and MÄKELÄ, K., 2010, "Functions, resources and types of boundary spanners within the MNC", Academy of Management Proceedings, Vol. 2010, No. 1, pp. 1-6.

BARNER-RASMUSSEN, W., EHRNROOTH, M., KOVESHNIKOV, A., and MÄKELÄ, K., 2014, "Cultural and language skills as resources for boundary spanning within the MNC", Journal of International Business Studies, 45(7), 886-905.

BARTELS, R., 1967, "A Model for Ethics in Marketing", Journal of Marketing 31 (1), pp.20-26.

BARTLETT, C. A., and GHOSHAL, S. 1989, The transnational solution. Boston, Harvard Business School.

BARTLETT, C. A., GHOSHAL, S., 1990, "Matrix management: not a structure, a frame of mind", Harvard Business Review 68, no. 4, July–August, pp. 138–145.

BAZIGOS, M., HARTER, J., 2016, "Revisiting the matrix organization", McKinsey Quarterly.

BERSIN, J., 2016, "Predictions for 2017, everything is becoming digital", Deloitte, available at: https://www2.deloitte.com/content/dam/Deloitte/at/Documents/about-deloitte/predictions-for-2017-final.pdf, published December 6th 2016.

BINGÖL, D., ŞENER, İ., and ÇEVIK, E., 2013, "The effect of organizational culture on organizational image and identity: Evidence from a pharmaceutical company", Procedia-Social and Behavioral Sciences, 99, pp. 222-229.

BIRKINSHAW, J., a LINGBLAD, M., 2005, "Intrafirm competition and charter evolution in the multibusiness firm". Organization science, 16(6), 674-686.

BIRKINSHAW, J., 2002, "The art of Swedish management", Business Strategy Review, 13(2), 11-19.

BLAZEJEWSKI, S., BECKER-RITTERSPACH, F., 2011, "Conflict in headquarters-subsidiary relations: a critical literature review and new directions", Politics and power in the multinational corporation: The role of institutions, interests and identities, pp.139-190.

BODNER, D. A., and ROUSE, W. B., 2007, "Understanding R&D value creation with organizational simulation", Systems Engineering, 10(1), pp. 64-82.

BRANNEN, M. Y., and SALK, J. E., 2000, "Partnering across borders: Negotiating organizational culture in a German-Japanese joint venture" Human relations, 53(4), 451-487.

BROCK, D. M., 2005, "Multinational acquisition integration: the role of national culture in creating synergies", International business review, 14(3), 269-288.

BROWN, J.L. and AGNEW, N.M., 1982, "The balance of power in a matrix structure", Business Horizons, 25(6), pp.51-54.

BURTON R. M., OBEL B., DESANCTIS, G., 2009, Organizational Design: a step by step approach, Cambridge University Press.

BURTON R. M., OBEL B., DØJBAK HÅKONSSON D., 2015, "How to get the matrix organization to work", Journal of Organization Design, Vol. 4, No. 3, 2015, pp. 37-45.

CHILD, J., 1984, Organization: A guide to problems and practice. Sage.

CLEGG, S. R., COURPASSON, D., and PHILLIPS, N., 2006, Power and organizations. Pine Forge Press.

CROSS, R., ERNST, C., ASSIMAKOPOULOS, D., and RANTA, D., 2015, "Investing in boundary-spanning collaboration to drive efficiency and innovation", Organizational Dynamics, 44(3), 204-216.

CROSSAN, M. M., and APAYDIN, M., 2010, "A multi-dimensional framework of organizational innovation: A systematic review of the literature", Journal of management studies, 47(6), pp. 1154-1191.

DAHL, R. A., 1957, "The concept of power", Behavioral science, 2(3), pp.201-215.

DAVIS, S.M. and LAWRENCE, P.R., 1977. Matrix. Reading, Mass.

DAVIS, S.M. and LAWRENCE, P.R., 1978. "Problems of matrix organizations", Harvard Business Review, 56(3), pp.131-142.

DERVEN, M., 2010, "Managing the matrix in the new normal", T+ D, 64(7), pp.42-47.

DEUTSCH, M., 1973, "The resolution of conflict: Constructive and destructive processes". American Behavioral Scientist, 17(2), 248-248.

DONALDSON, L., 2009. "In search of the matrix advantage: A re-examination of the fit of matrix structures to transnational strategy", In Managing, Subsidiary Dynamics: Headquarters Role, Capability Development, and China Strategy (pp. 3-26). Emerald Group Publishing Limited.

DÖRRENBÄCHER, C., and GEPPERT, M. (Eds.), 2011, Politics and power in the multinational corporation: The role of institutions, interests and identities. Cambridge University Press.

DRENNAN, D., 1992, Transforming Company Culture. McGraw-Hill, Maidenhead, UK.

DUTTON, J.E., DUKERICH, J.M. and HARQUAIL, C.V., 1994, "Organizational images and member identification", Administrative Science Quarterly, 39, pp. 239–63.

EGELHOFF, W. G., and WOLF, J. 2017a "The role of headquarters in the contemporary MNC: A contingency model." Multinational corporations and organization theory: Post millennium perspectives. Emerald Publishing Limited, 2017. 71-98.

EGELHOFF, W. G, WOLF, J., 2017b, Understanding matrix structures and their alternatives, the key to designing and managing large complex organizations, Palgrave Macmillan, London.

FELDMAN, M. S., and ORLIKOWSKI, W. J., 2011, "Theorizing practice and practicing theory", Organization science, 22(5), pp. 1240-1253.

FERNER, A., 2000, "The underpinnings of 'bureaucratic' control systems: HRM in European multinationals", Journal of Management Studies, 37(4), pp. 521-540.

FERNER, A., EDWARDS, T., TEMPEL, A., 2012, "Power, institutions and the cross-national transfer of employment practices in multinationals", Human Relations, 65(2), 163-187.

FORBES, 2019, The world's largest public MNCs: https://www.forbes.com/global2000 /list/#tab:overall, accessed on October 25th 2019

FORD, R. C., RANDOLPH W. A., 1992, "Cross-functional structures: a review and integration of matrix organization and project management", Journal of Management, Vol. 18, No. 2, June, pp. 267-294.

GALBRAITH J.R., 2008, Designing matrix organizations that actually work: how IBM, Procter & Gamble and others design for success, Jossey-Bass, San Francisco.

GALBRAITH, J. R., 2014, Designing organizations: Strategy, structure, and process at the business unit and enterprise levels. John Wiley & Sons.

GALBRAITH, J.R., 1971, "Matrix organization designs How to combine functional and project forms", Business horizons, 14(1), pp.29-40.

GALBRAITH, J.R., 2012, "The Future of Organization Design", Journal of Organization Design, 1(1), pp.3-6.

GANDZ, J., and MURRAY, V. V., 1980, "The experience of workplace politics", Academy of Management journal, 23(2), pp. 237-251.

GASSMANN, O., and VON ZEDTWITZ, M., 1998, „Organization of industrial R&D on a global scale. R&D Management", 28(3), pp. 147-161.

GEFEN, D., KARAHANNA, E., STRAUB, D. W., 2003, „Trust and TAM in online shopping: An integrated model", MIS quarterly, 27(1), 51-90.

GIOIA, D. A., SCHULTZ, M., and CORLEY, K. G., 2000, "Organizational identity, image, and adaptive instability". Academy of management Review, 25(1), pp. 63-81.

GOBELI, D. H., LARSON, E. W., 1986, "Matrix management: more than a fad", Engineering management International, Volume 4, Issue 1, October, pp. 71-76.

GOGGIN W. C., 1974, "How the multidimensional structure works at Dow Corning", Harvard Business Review, January–February, pp. 54–65.

GOODMAN, R.A., 1967, "Ambiguous authority definition in project management", Academy of Management Journal, 10(4), pp.395-407.

GOS, K., 2015, "The key advantages and disadvantages of matrix organizational structures", University of Warsaw, Faculty of Management Research Reports, Issue 2, No. 19, 2015, pp. 66-83.

GOTTLIEB M. R., 2007, The matrix organization reloaded: adventures in team and project management, Greenwood Publishing Group, Westport.

GUBA, E. G., and Lincoln, Y. S., 1994, "Competing paradigms in qualitative research", Handbook of qualitative research, 2(163-194), 105.

GUNN, R. A., 2012, "Matrix management lessons from R&D", Strategic Futures, available at: http://www.strategicfutures.com/2012/04/matrix-management-lessons-from-rd/, published April 18th 2012.

HAGGETT, P., 1975, Geography: A Modern Synthesis. Harper & Row, New York, NY.

HARTLEY, J., 2004, "Case study research. Essential guide to qualitative methods", in: organizational research, 1, 323-333.

HATCH, M., and SCHULTZ, M., 1997, "Relations between organizational culture, identity and image", European Journal of marketing, 31(5/6), pp. 356-365.

HEALY, M., and PERRY, C., 2000, "Comprehensive criteria to judge validity and reliability of qualitative research within the realism paradigm", Qualitative market research: An international journal, 3(3), 118-126.

HOBDAY, M., 2000, "The project-based organization: an ideal form for managing complex products and systems?", Research policy, 29(7-8), 871-893.

HOFSTEDE, G., 2015, dimensions data matrix, available at https://geerthofstede.com/research-and-vsm/dimension-data-matrix/, downloaded October 18th 2018.

HOFSTEDE, G., HOFSTEDE, G. J., and MINKOV, M. 2010, "Cultures and organizations: Software of the mind" (3rd ed.). McGraw-Hill.

HOGG, M. A., and TERRY, D. I., 2000, "Social identity and self-categorization processes in organizational contexts", Academy of management review, 25(1), 121-140.

HOUSE, R. J., HANGES, P. J., JAVIDAN, M., DORFMAN, P. W., and GUPTA, V. (Eds.), 2004, Culture, leadership, and organizations: The GLOBE study of 62 societies. Sage publications.

JEHN, K.A., MANNIX, E.A., 2001, "The dynamic nature of conflict: A longitudinal study of intragroup conflict and group performance". Academy of management journal, 44(2), pp.238-251.

JIMENÉZ-JIMENÉZ, D., MARTÍNEZ-COSTA, M., and SANZ-VALLE, R., 2014, "Innovation, organizational learning orientation and reverse knowledge transfer in multinational companies", Electronic Journal of Knowledge Management, 12(1), pp. 47-55.

JOHNSON, L. D., and PAZDERKA, B., 1993, "Firm value and investment in R&D", Managerial and Decision Economics, 14(1), pp. 15-24.

JONES, M.L., 2007, "Hofstede–culturally questionable?", Oxford Bus.Econ.Conf., pp.24–26.

JUNG, T., SCOTT, T., DAVIES, H. T., BOWER, P., WHALLEY, D., MCNALLY, R., and MANNION, R., 2009, "Instruments for exploring organizational culture: A review of the literature", Public administration review, 69(6), pp. 1087-1096.

KALE, P., SINGH, H., RAMAN, A. P., 2009, "Don't integrate your acquisitions, partner with them", Harvard business review, 87 (12), pp. 109-115.

KANTER, M. R., and CORN, I. R., 1994, "Do cultural differences make a business difference? Contextual factors affecting cross-cultural relationship success", Journal of Management Development, 13(2), 5-23.

KATES A., ERICKSON P., 2008, "Virtual collaboration in a matrix organization", in: NEMIRO, J., BEYERLEIN, M.M., BRADLEY, L. AND BEYERLEIN, S. (eds), The handbook of high performance virtual teams: A toolkit for collaborating across boundaries, John Wiley & Sons, San Francisco, pp. 619-651.

KELLER, R. T., and HOLLAND, W. E., 1975, "Boundary-spanning roles in a research and development organization: An empirical investigation", Academy of Management Journal, 18(2), pp. 388-393.

KEMP, S., and DWYER, L., 2001, "An examination of organisational culture—the Regent Hotel, Sydney", International journal of hospitality management, 20(1), pp. 77-93.

KIRKMAN, B. L., LOWE, K. B., and GIBSON, C. B., 2006, "A quarter century of culture's consequences: A review of empirical research incorporating Hofstede's cultural values framework", Journal of international business studies, 37(3), pp. 285-320.

KLIMKEIT, D., 2013, "Organizational context and collaboration on international projects: The case of a professional service firm", International Journal of Project Management, 31(3), pp. 366-377.

KNIGHT, K., 1976, "Matrix organization: a review", The journal of management Studies, Volume 13, Issue 2, May, pp. 111-130.

KOSTOVA, T., and ZAHEER, S., 1999, "Organizational legitimacy under conditions of complexity: The case of the multinational enterprise", Academy of Management review, 24(1), pp. 64-81.

KOTTER, J.P. AND HESKETT, J.L., 1992, Corporate Culture and Performance. Free Press, New York, NY.

KROEBER, A. L. and KLUCKHOHN, C., 1952, "Culture: A critical review of concepts and definitions", Papers Peabody Museum of Archaeology & Ethnology, Harvard University.

KUPRENAS, J.A., 2003, "Implementation and performance of a matrix organization structure", International Journal of Project Management, 21(1), pp.51-62.

LARSON, E.W. and GOBELI, D.H., 1987, "Matrix management: Contradictions and insights", California management review, 29(4), pp.126-138.

LARSSON, R., and LUBATKIN, M., 2001, "Achieving acculturation in mergers and acquisitions: An international case survey", Human relations, 54(12), pp. 1573-1607.

LE NGUYEN, H., LARIMO, J., and ALI, T., 2016, "How do ownership control position and national culture influence conflict resolution strategies in international joint ventures?", International Business Review, 25(2), 559-568.

LEE, S. J., KIM, J., and PARK, B. I., 2015, "Culture clashes in cross-border mergers and acquisitions: A case study of Sweden's Volvo and South Korea's Samsung", International Business Review, 24(4), pp. 580-593.

LEUNG, K., BHAGAT, R. S., BUCHAN, N. R., EREZ, M., and GIBSON, C. B., 2005, "Culture and international business: Recent advances and their implications for future research", Journal of international business studies, 36(4), 357-378.

MAEL, F. and ASHFORTH, B. E., 1992, "Alumni and their alma mater: A partial test of the reformulated model of organizational identification", Journal of Organizational Behavior, 13, pp.103–123

MAN Annual Report, 2018, http://www.volkswagenag.com/presence/investorrelation/ publications/annual-reports/2019/man/MAN_GB_2018_EN.pdf

MARCH, J.G., 1991, "Exploration and exploitation in organizational learning", Organization Science, Vol. 2 No. 1, pp. 71-87

MARRONE, J. A., 2010,"Team boundary spanning: A multilevel review of past research and proposals for the future", Journal of Management, 36(4), 911-940.

Martinez, J. I., and Jarillo, J. C., 1989, "The evolution of research on coordination mechanisms in multinational corporations", Journal of international business studies, 20(3), 489-514.

MEE, J. F., 1964, "Matrix organization", Business Horizons, Volume 7, Issue 2, June, pp. 70-72.

MENDEZ, A., 2003, "The coordination of globalized R&D activities through project teams organization: an exploratory empirical study", Journal of World Business, 38(2), pp 96-109.

MENON, A., BHARADWAJ, S. G., and HOWELL, R., 1996, "The quality and effectiveness of marketing strategy: Effects of functional and dysfunctional conflict in intraorganizational relationships". Journal of the Academy of Marketing Science, 24(4), p 299.

MINBAEVA, D. B., 2008, "HRM practices affecting extrinsic and intrinsic motivation of knowledge receivers and their effect on intra-MNC knowledge transfer", International Business Review, 17(6), pp. 703-713.

MOODLEY, D., SUTHERLAND, M. AND PRETORIUS, P., 2016. "Comparing the power and influence of functional managers with that of project managers in matrix organizations: The challenge in duality of command", South African Journal of Economic and Management Sciences, 19(1), pp.103-117.

MORGAN, G., KRISTENSEN, P. H. and WHITLEY, R., 2001, "The multinational firm: organizing across institutional and national divides", Oxford University Press, USA.

MORGAN, J., 2015, "The 14 Principles Of The Future Organization", Forbes, available at: https://www.forbes.com/sites/jacobmorgan/2015/01/14/the-14-principles-of-the-future-organization/#559adabb3ec2, published: January 14th 2015.

MUDAMBI, R., and PEDERSEN, T., 2007, "Agency theory and resource dependency theory: Complementary explanations for subsidiary power in multinational corporations. Bridging IB theories, constructs, and methods across cultures and social sciences". Basingstoke: Palgrave Macmillan.

NAHAPIET, J., and GHOSHAL, S., 1998, "Social capital, intellectual capital, and the organizational advantage", Academy of management review, 23(2), pp. 242-266.

NOBEL, R., and BIRKINSHAW, J., 1998, "Innovation in multinational corporations: Control and communication patterns in international R&D operations", Strategic Management Journal, 19(5), pp. 479-496.

O'REILLY, C., CHATMAN, J., AND CALDWELL, D., 1991, "People and organizational culture: A Q-sort approach to assessing person-organization fit", Academy of Management Journal, 34, pp. 487-516

PETERS, T., 1979, "Beyond the matrix organization", McKinsey Quarterly, Volume 22, Issue 5, September, pp. 15-27.

PFEFFER, J., 1992, "Understanding power in organizations". California management review, 34(2), 29.

PONDY, L. R., 1967, "Organizational conflict: Concepts and models. Administrative science quarterly, 296-320.

PRAHALAD, C. K., and DOZ, Y. L., 1999, The multinational mission: Balancing local demands and global vision. Simon and Schuster.

PRATT, M. G. and FOREMAN, PETER O., 2000, "Classifying Managerial Responses to Multiple Organizational Identities", The Academy of Management Review.

PRIMECZ, H., ROMANI, L., and SACKMANN, S. (Eds.), 2011, "Cross-cultural management in practice: Culture and negotiated meanings", Edward Elgar Publishing.

QIU, J.X. and DONALDSON, L., 2012, "Stopford and Wells were Right! MNC Matrix Structures do fit a "High-High" Strategy", Management International Review, 52(5), pp.671-689.

RABBIOSI, L., 2011, "Subsidiary roles and reverse knowledge transfer: An investigation of the effects of coordination mechanisms", Journal of International Management, 17(2), pp. 97-113.

RAISCH, S., and BIRKINSHAW, J., 2008, "Organizational ambidexterity: Antecedents, outcomes, and moderators", Journal of management, 34(3), pp. 375-409.

RAVASI, D., and SCHULTZ, M., 2006, "Responding to organizational identity threats: Exploring the role of organizational culture", Academy of management journal, 49(3), pp. 433-458.

RITTI, R.R. AND FUNKHOUSER, G.R., 1982, The Ropes to Skip and the Ropes to Know. John Wiley & Sons, Columbus, OH.

RUIZ-PALOMINO, P., and MARTÍNEZ-CAÑAS, R., 2014, "Ethical culture, ethical intent, and organizational citizenship behavior: The moderating and mediating role of person–organization fit", Journal of business ethics, 120(1), pp. 95-108.

SAPSED, J., and SALTER, A., 2004, "Postcards from the edge: local communities, global programs and boundary objects", Organization studies, 25(9), pp. 1515-1534.

SAYLES, L. R., 1976, "Matrix management: the structure with a future", Organizational Dynamics, Volume 5, Issue 2, September, pp. 2-17.

SCANIA ANNUAL REPORT , 2017 http://www.volkswagenag.com/presence/investor-relation/publications/annual-reports/2019/scania/Scania_Annual_Report_2018.pdf

SCHEIN, E.H., 1991, Organisational Culture and Leadership, 2nd ed. Jossey-Bass, San Francisco, CA.

SCHEIN, E.H., 2004, Organizational culture and leadership. San Francisco, CA: Jossey.

SCHMID, S., and MAURER, J., 2011, "Relationships between MNC subsidiaries–Opening a black box in the international business field". In Internationale Unternehmungen und das Management ausländischer Tochtergesellschaften (pp. 53-83). Gabler.

SCHOTTER, A., and BEAMISH, P. W., 2011a, „Intra-organizational turbulences in multinational corporations". Politics and power in the multinational corporation: The role of institutions, interests and identities, 191-230.

SCHOTTER, A., and BEAMISH, P. W., 2011b. "Performance effects of MNC headquarters–subsidiary conflict and the role of boundary spanners: The case of headquarter initiative rejection". Journal of International Management, 17(3), pp 243-259.

SCHWEIGER, D. M., ATAMER, T., and CALORI, R, 2003, "Transnational project teams and networks: making the multinational organization more effective", Journal of World Business, 38(2), pp 127-140.

SHENKAR, O., 2001, "Cultural distance revisited: Towards a more rigorous conceptualization and measurement of cultural differences", Journal of international business studies, 32(3), pp. 519-535.

SIMONS, T. L., and PETERSON, R. S., 2000, "Task conflict and relationship conflict in top management teams: The pivotal role of intragroup trust", Journal of applied psychology, 85(1), 102.

SMIRCICH, L., 1983, "Organizations as shared meanings". In L. R. PONDY, P. J. FROST, G. MORGAN, and T. DANDRIDGE (Eds.), Organizational symbolism: 55–65. Greenwich, CT: JAI Press.

SOETERS, J., and SCHREUDER, H., 1988, "The interaction between national and organizational cultures in accounting firms", Accounting, Organizations and Society, 13(1), pp. 75-85.

STEENKAMP, J.B., 2017, Global Brand Strategy: World-wise Marketing in the Age of Branding. Springer.

SY, T. and COTE, S., 2004, "Emotional intelligence: A key ability to succeed in the matrix organization", Journal of Management Development, 23(5), pp.437-455.

SY, T., D'ANNUNZIO L.S., 2005, "Challenges and strategies of matrix organizations: top-level and mid-level managers' perspectives", Human Resource Planning, Vol. 28, Issue 1, January, p. 39.

TEMPEL, A., EDWARDS, T., FERNER, A., MULLER-CAMEN, M., and WÄCHTER, H., 2006, "Subsidiary responses to institutional duality: Collective representation practices of US multinationals in Britain and Germany". Human Relations, 59(11), 1543-1570.

THOMAS, K. W., 1992, Conflict and conflict management: Reflections and update. Journal of organizational behavior, 13(3), 265-274.

TIPPINS, M. J., AND SOHI, R. S., 2003, "IT Competency and Firm Performance: Is Organizational Learning a Missing Link?", Strategic Management Journal, 24, pp. 745-761.

TRATON (2019), https://traton.com/en/company/brands.html, accessed April 29th 2019

TUSHMAN, M. L., 1977, "Special boundary roles in the innovation process. Administrative science quarterly", 587-605.

TUSHMAN, M. L., and SCANLAN, T. J., 1981, "Boundary spanning individuals: Their role in information transfer and their antecedents". Academy of management journal, 24(2), 289-305.

UNCTAD WORLD INVESTMENT REPORT, 2009, https://unctad.org/en/Docs/wir2009 overview_en.pdf, accessed October 25th 2019.

UNCTAD WORLD INVESTMENT REPORT, 2019, https://unctad.org/en/Publications Library/wir2019_overview_en.pdf, accessed October 25th 2019.

VAN MAANEN, J., 1976, "Breaking in: socialization to work" in Dubin, R. (Ed.), Handbook of Work, Organization, and Society, Rand McNally, Chicago, IL.

VAN MAANEN, J., 1991, "The smile factory: work at Disneyland", in Frost, P.J., Moore, L., Louis, M., Lundberg, C. and Martin, J. (Eds), Reframing Organisational Culture, Sage Publications, Beverly Hills, CA.

VANCIL, R. F., 1984, "Texas instruments, incorporated: 1983", Harvard Business School Case 9-184-109.

VIEGAS-PIRES, M., 2013, "Multiple levels of culture and post M&A integration: A suggested theoretical framework", Thunderbird International Business Review, 55(4), pp. 357-370.

WHETTEN, D. A., 2006, "Albert and Whetten revisited: Strengthening the concept of organizational identity", Journal of Management Inquiry.

WHITLEY, R., 2001, "How and why are international firms different? The consequences of cross-border managerial coordination for firm characteristics and behavior", in MORGAN, G., KRISTENSEN, P. H. and WHITLEY, R.,The multinational firm: organizing across institutional and national divides (pp 27-68), Oxford University Press, USA.

WILSON, A. M., 2001, "Understanding organisational culture and the implications for corporate marketing", European Journal of Marketing.

WILSON, A.M., 1997, "The nature of corporate culture within a service delivery environment", International Journal of Service Industry Management, 8(1), pp. 87-102.

WITCHALLS, C., 2011, "The Complexity Challenge, How businesses are bearing up", The Economist Intelligence Unit, available at: http://www.eiu.com/report_dl.asp?mode=fi&fi=1367778921.PDF, published: February 2nd 2011.

WOLF, J. and EGELHOFF, W.G., 2012, "Network or matrix? How information-processing theory can help MNCs answer this question", Collaborative communities of firms (pp. 35-57). Springer New York.

WOLF, J. and EGELHOFF, W.G., 2013, "An empirical evaluation of conflict in MNC matrix structure firms", International Business Review, 22(3), pp.591-601.

YAGI, N., and KLEINBERG, J., 2011, "Boundary work: An interpretive ethnographic perspective on negotiating and leveraging cross-cultural identity", Journal of International Business Studies, 42(5), 629-653.

YBEMA, S. B., and BYUN, H. H. 2011, "Unequal power relations, identity discourse, and cultural distinction drawing in MNCs". In C. Dörrenbächer, and M. Geppert (Eds.), Politics and power in the multinational corporation: The role of institutions, interests and identities (pp. 315-345). Cambridge: Cambridge University Press.

YIN, R.K., 2009, Case study research. Design and methods. Thousand Oaks: Sage.

ZAHEER, S., SCHOMAKER, M., and GENC, M., 2003, "Identity versus culture in mergers of equals", European Management Journal, 21(2), pp. 185-191.

Annexes

© Springer Fachmedien Wiesbaden GmbH, part of Springer Nature 2020
J. Shahani, *Limits and Opportunities of a Matrix Organization*, Auto
Uni – Schriftenreihe 149, https://doi.org/10.1007/978-3-658-32261-8

A.1 Research Questions and Sub-Questions

1. **How can a contemporary holding company matrix facilitate knowledge sharing on a global level while allowing for subsidiary autonomy?**
   1.1. How are the mechanisms of control and coordination in a matrix organization deployed?
   1.2. How does the holding influence decision making through these mechanisms?

2. **How are decisions made in a holding matrix organization?**
   2.1. What are the antecedents for the use of rule based or balanced decision making?
   2.2. What are the consequences for the use of rule-based or balanced decision making?

3. **How is ambidexterity facilitated by a flexible matrix structure?**
   3.1. How is knowledge sharing and innovation affected by a matrix organizational structure?

4. **What role does conflict and the power capabilities deployed by the actors play?**
   4.1. How does conflict manifest itself in a matrix?
   4.2. What are the sources of conflict?
   4.3. What power capabilities are deployed by the subsidiaries in a conflict situation?
   4.4. What power capabilities are deployed by the holding in a conflict situation?

5. **What is the impact of impact of cultural and identity differences within a matrix organization?**
   5.1. How do the cultural and identity differences between the matrix dimensions manifest themselves?
   5.2. How can the matrix organization be used as a coordination modus for cultural integration?
   5.3. What power capabilities are leveraged to influence negotiated culture?

6. **How is the concept boundary spanning deployed in a matrix organization?**
   6.1. What is the role of boundary spanning and boundary spanners in the matrix organizations?
   6.2. What impact does the matrix organizational structure have on boundary spanning?
   6.3. How can boundary spanners facilitate the matrix? What skills are required?

A.2 Interview Template

Introduction

Hello and thank you for being here, your input will really be very valuable to my research and help me understand matrix organizations empirically. In order to have a fully standardized interview and to not influence the results in any way, I will be reading a set introduction to you, as I will do for all the interviewees.

Present myself
My name is Jasmine Shahani. I am a PhD Candidate within VWTB in cooperation with the University of Fribourg in Switzerland. To start off this interview I will give you a quick idea of my research as well as explain data protection issues and other practicalities of this interview.

Present Project
As you may know the VWTB group was set-up as a matrix. By matrix, I mean that the VWTB holding was created to link together MAN, MAN LA, Scania, RIO and to a certain extent VWN. The goal of this matrix is to drive synergies between the brands in order to create a successful Truck & Bus group.

Through your input on your experience working within this set-up I hope to gain a better understanding of what "working in a matrix" means, what is positive and what is negative in the hopes of building a set of best practices for future reference.

Data
In order to make the most of this interview, and with your consent, I will record it. I will then transcribe the interview but your personal information will be redacted so that it will be impossible to tell where and who this information came from. This personal data will only be used in the case of generalized statements such as "50% of engineers found that..."

Do you agree with this?

Interview modalities
This interview will last between 45minutes and an hour, so don't hesitate to elaborate on your thoughts.
I will start by asking you relatively open questions and we will dive deeper into the topic as we go along.

So, if it's fine with you, let's get started!

Learning about interviewee
1. Please introduce yourself, your current position and briefly explain your experience within your company and beforehand.
1.1 How long have you been working at *brand*?
1.2 What are your daily tasks and goals?
1.3 How often do you work across brands
1.4 Who do you report to?
1.5 Do you have subordinates – how many?
1.6 To you belong to any committees or cross-brand teams?

How do employees perceive and understand the VWTB matrix?
2. How would you describe the Volkswagen Truck and Bus Group matrix?
3. Can you draw the Volkswagen Truck and Bus matrix for me?
4. What are the (differentiating) characteristics of this matrix?
5. Where does your team fit in this matrix? Can you illustrate it?
6. In your opinion what has changed since the matrix has been implemented?
6.1 How do you expect things to change further in the future?
7. How has your daily work life been affected by the matrix?
8. What are the advantages and disadvantages of this matrix?
8.1 How does it affect you personally?
8.2 What about your team and department?
8.3 And for the group as a whole?
9. What would you change within this matrix? Please give concrete examples.

Getting things done in a matrix
We are now going to go into more detail. Please think of a project that you worked on recently in a matrix situation. Please make sure this project is relevant, meaning it had some kind of impact, for your department or for the organization. I will give you a couple of minutes to think of one and then ask you some questions about it. Please let me know when you have a project in mind.
10. Please give me an overview of the project.
10.1 How was the project launched, where did the drive come from?
10.2 What were the objectives of this project? Did these objectives evolve over time?
10.3 What were the obligations and constraints for this project?
10.4 What is the value of this project, what does it bring to the organization?
10.5 How many people were involved in this project?
10.6 Who did you have to work with outside the project team? To what extent?
10.7 What was your role in this project? What work did you do as part of this project?
10.8 How did you communicate within this project and how often?
10.9 What were the benefits of this project for your company?
10.10 What were the benefits of this project for you personally?
10.11 Did you enjoy working on this project?
11. How were decisions made during this project?
11.1 Who had the final say when a decision needed to be made?

11.2 Was the decision making mode always the same or was it sometimes different?
11.3 In what cases was it different?
11.4 Which way of making decisions seemed to work the best?
12. Would you describe this project as innovative? To what extent?
13. What were challenges you faced? Please give concrete examples.
13.1 How did you solve the issues?
13.2 Which issues do you feel could have been solved better?
13.3 Can you think of a project where these issues did not occur? Why is that?
14. Were there conflicts during this project?
14.1 How often were there conflicts within this project?
14.2 What were the conflicts about?
14.3 How did they impact the performance of the project?
14.4 How were these conflicts solved?
14.5 Would there have been less conflict in a non matrix-situation?
14.6 Can you think of a project where there were fewer conflicts? (more if none beforehand)
14.7 Which factors influenced the fact that there were fewer conflicts?
14.8 How could you apply this to other projects in the future?
15. Overall, would you say this project was successful?
15.1 Where the objectives of the project met? To what extent?
15.2 How would you say the matrix influenced the success of this project?
16.Please think of a project that went significantly better or worse than this one
16.1 Why did this project go better / worse?
16.2 Would it be possible to apply this/avoid this for projects in the future?
17. How has working in a matrix impact you personally?
17.1 Has working in a matrix situation impacted the way you work? To what extent?
17.2 Has working in the matrix brought more understanding of the organization? To what extent?
17.2 What do you think could help you personally to get things done within this matrix context?
18. Do you have another project you would like to talk about where the issues were different? (*If yes, repeat questions 10 through 17*)
19. Do you have anything else you would like to mention? (*Keep asking this question until answer is "no"*).
Conclusion
Thank you very much for taking the time to answer my questions. With the results of the interview I will attempt to create a global picture of our Volkswagen Truck & Bus matrix and potentially identify areas where we could improve the way it functions.
20. Are you interested in the results of this research? What specifically interests you?
21. Do you have any feedback you would like to give me about this interview?
So that concludes our interview, I will now turn off the recording device. Thank you again for participating.

A.3 Declaration of Consent

Declaration of consent for the collection and processing of personal interview data

Research project: Limits and opportunities of a matrix organization

Entity carrying out the research: TRATON AG

Project owner: Jasmine Shahani   **Contact:** jasmine.shahani@traton.com

Responsible manager: Dr. Martin Hofmann   **Contact:** martin.hofmann@traton.com

Data protection officer: Dr. Karl Heinz Müller   **Contact:** karl-heinz.mueller@man.eu

Interview type: ☐ Face-to-face ☐ Telephone Interview ☐ Skype / Lync Interview

Interviewer: Jasmine Shahani

Interview date:

General Information

This interview in the context of a PhD research project is done in order to gather data or opinions from individual employees. This method is used in order to take into account the views and experience of employees. If, for any reason, you are unsatisfied with this process, you may lodge a complaint with the supervisor (contact above).

Recording and transcription

The interviews will be recorded with a recording device. In order to analyze the data, a written transcript will be made of the recording. All information which could lead to the identification of the interviewee will be modified or removed from the transcript. You have the right to request a copy of your interview transcripts.

Data storage

Personal contact details will be stored separately from interview data. Upon completion of the research project, and at the latest on September 1st 2019 the recordings containing personal information will be permanently deleted. All data collected will be kept strictly confidential and will only be used for the agreed purpose.

Participation

Participation in the interview is voluntary and the names of people who did not wish to participate will be deleted. At any time, the interviewee may stop an interview, refuse further interviews and withdraw consent to the recording and transcription of the interview. You also have the right to request the erasure of personal data at any time.

Consent	Signature
1. ☐I agree to participate in an interview as part of this research project. *2.* ☐I do not agree to participate in an interview as part of this research project.	Name: Date: Signature:

A.4 Initial Coding Grid

Codes	Sub-Codes
Issues	Decision making time
	Complexity
	Need for clear goals
	Resistance
	Other issues
Communication	Language
	IT
	Face to face contact
Boundary spanning	Skills
	Activities
	Challenges
	Impact on employee
Holding	HR Role
	Negotiated culture
	Benchmark opportunities
	Lead brand
	Holding role
	Added internal value
Structure	Decision implementation
	Escalation
	Structure
	Authority

A.5 Example of an Adapted Coding Grid

Codes and sub-codes	Descriptions and examples (when relevant)
Task conflict - Goal - Authority - Evaluation	Goal: goals or interests of party A differ from those of Party B Authority: Party A and party B have different views regarding their authority Evaluation: Party A and party B assesses a solution differently (Wolf & Egelhoff, 2013)
Relationship conflict	Relationship conflict: interpersonal incompatibilities, includes tension, annoyance animosity (Jehn, 1995)
Conflict resolution - Escalation processes	N.B: Escalation, best when it is precedent setting policy issues (will not need to escalate next time). (Galbraith, 2008)
Conflict resolution style - Cooperative - Confirming - Competitive - Avoiding	Cooperative: mutual goal, joint benefit, incorporation of several positions, Confirming: acceptance of others position, avoids insults and blaming Competitive: win lose struggle, forceful and coercion Avoiding : smoothing, maintaining harmony (Barker et al, 1988)
Interpersonal-trust building - Social interaction ties - Common goals and values - Calculativeness - Institutional structures	Social interaction ties: strength of relationship, amount of time spent, communication frequency (Hsu & Chang, 2014) Common goals and values: also include shared knowledge-sharing vision. (Hsu & Chang, 2014)
System Trust Dispositional trust	System trust: perceived reliability of system or institution (Hsu & Chang, 2014) Dispositional trust: the extent to which one displays a tendency to trust others (Hsu & Chang, 2014)
Rule – based decision making	Rule-based decision making: Formal or informal rules pre-assign decision-making to one dimension of the matrix

- Rule: Permanent or Temporary? - Rule: formally stated or commonly understood? Balanced decision making	Balanced decision making: both dimensions of the matrix have relatively equal power and influence in the decision making
Power capabilities - Resources - Processes - Meaning	Resources: power derived from the control of scarce resources (hiring, firing, rewards and sanctions, expertise) Processes: procedures and political routines/ can prevent people from participating in the decision or add groups into the decision making Meaning: management of meaning and deployment of symbolic actions, brings hidden taken-for-granted processes to light (Ferner et al, 2012).
Boundary spanning activities - Information exchanging - Linking - Facilitating - Intervening	Exchanging: Gathering or delivering Linking: create links between disconnected actors or groups Facilitating: assist in cross-border interaction of others (act as channel, interpretation, explaining behaviors…) Intervening: resolving misunderstandings, managing conflict, building inter-group trust (Barner-Rasmussen et al, 2014).

A.6 Number of Interviewees per Project

HUMAN RESOURCES	
Project	**Number of interviewees**
MAIN PROJECTS	
Development programs	6
Pluralism & Inclusion	6
Job Grading	3
Management Dialogue	3
Global Assignment toolbox	4
SECONDARY PROJECTS	
Common health project	1
RIO employee move	1
New Compensation logic at TRATON AB	1
Executive group compensation (Bonus)	1 + 1 (mentioned)
Stimmungsbarometer (StiBa)	2
RESEARCH & DEVELOPMENT	
Project	**Number of interviewees**
MAIN PROJECTS	
CHAMP	7
Engine	3
Axle	4
Gearbox	4
SECONDARY PROJECTS	
Battery monitoring device	1
Common autonomous driving system	1
Entertainment system	1
Fasteners	1
Waste heat recovery	1
Perseus	1

The manufacturer's authorised representative in the EU is Springer
Nature Customer Service Centre GmbH, Europaplatz 3, 69115 Heidelberg,
Germany. If you have any concerns regarding our products, please
contact ProductSafety@springernature.com

Printed and bound by CPI Group (UK) Ltd, Croydon, CR0 4YY

24/04/2026

02096340-0002